Writing Reimagined

Writing Reimagined

Bridging Critical Theories and Pedagogical Practices in Elementary Classrooms

**Edited by
Grace Y. Kang
Sonia M. Kline**

BLOOMSBURY ACADEMIC
NEW YORK • LONDON • OXFORD • NEW DELHI • SYDNEY

BLOOMSBURY ACADEMIC
Bloomsbury Publishing Inc, 1359 Broadway, New York, NY 10018, USA
Bloomsbury Publishing Plc, 50 Bedford Square, London, WC1B 3DP, UK
Bloomsbury Publishing Ireland, 29 Earlsfort Terrace, Dublin 2, D02 AY28, Ireland

BLOOMSBURY, BLOOMSBURY ACADEMIC and the Diana logo are
trademarks of Bloomsbury Publishing Plc

First published in the United States of America 2026

Copyright © Bloomsbury Publishing, 2026

Cover design by Kathi Ha
Cover images © iStock.com/ivetavaicule and spxChrome

All rights reserved. No part of this publication may be: i) reproduced or transmitted in any form, electronic or mechanical, including photocopying, recording or by means of any information storage or retrieval system without prior permission in writing from the publishers; or ii) used or reproduced in any way for the training, development or operation of artificial intelligence (AI) technologies, including generative AI technologies. The rights holders expressly reserve this publication from the text and data mining exception as per Article 4(3) of the Digital Single Market Directive (EU) 2019/790.

Bloomsbury Publishing Inc does not have any control over, or responsibility for, any third-party websites referred to or in this book. All internet addresses given in this book were correct at the time of going to press. The author and publisher regret any inconvenience caused if addresses have changed or sites have ceased to exist, but can accept no responsibility for any such changes.

Library of Congress Cataloging-in-Publication Data is available

ISBN: HB: 979-8-8818-0366-7
PB: 979-8-8818-0367-4
ePDF: 979-8-8818-6792-8
eBook: 979-8-8818-0368-1

Typeset by Integra Software Services Pvt. Ltd.
Printed and bound in the United States of America

For product safety related questions contact productsafety@bloomsbury.com.

To find out more about our authors and books visit www.bloomsbury.com
and sign up for our newsletters.

*For our past, present, and future students—
And for all the teachers who embody criticality,
humanity, and joy!
In memory of Crystal Chen Lee (1987–2025),
who truly lived out these qualities, and whose
legacy of brilliance, love, and advocacy will
continue to inspire future generations.*

CONTENTS

Foreword by Cornelius Minor ix
Preface: Together by Grace Y. Kang and Sonia M. Kline xi

Introduction 1
What Is Critical Humanizing Writing Pedagogy? *by Grace Y. Kang and Sonia M. Kline* 1

1 Identity 25
At the Core: Student Identities and Writing Instruction in the Elementary Classroom *by Katie B. Peachey and Crystal Chen Lee* 25

2 Translanguaging 51
Translanguaging Writing Pedagogy to Leverage Multilingual Writers' Funds of Knowledge and Identity *by Margarita Gómez and Joanna W. Wong* 51

3 Raciolinguistics 77
Centering Cultural Language as Resistance, Belonging, and Affirmation *by Roberta Price Gardner and Sanjuana C. Rodriguez* 77

4 Trauma 103
"We go through a story together": Considering Trauma in Critical, Humanizing Writing Classrooms *by Elizabeth Dutro* 103

5 Multimodality 125

The Power and Promise of Multimodal Composition for Enacting Critical Humanizing Writing Pedagogies *by Shawna Coppola* 125

6 Pop Culture 147

Powerful "X-people" and Rhythmic "Teen-age-ers": Popular Culture in Childhood Composing *by Anne Haas Dyson* 147

7 Play 167

Storying Identity as Curricular Practice: The Multimodal Resonances of Play and Writing *by Haeny Yoon* 167

8 Activism 195

Environmental Artivism as a Critical Multimodal Writing Pedagogy *by Rebecca Woodard and Kristine Schutz* 195

9 Resistance 219

Writing as Resistance: Poetic Inquiry as a Liberatory Practice in the Classroom *by Darius Phelps* 219

10 Love 243

Revolutionary Love: A Critical Approach for Teaching Young Writers *by Michele Myers* 243

Closing Thoughts by Grace Y. Kang and Sonia M. Kline 263
Index 265
About the Editors 272
About the Authors 274

Foreword

Everything exists in a specific context. Understanding the environment that produced a thing is critical to the understanding of that thing.

So, it is important to note that this book arrives at a time when American educators are still grappling with what the anxiety of a pandemic has done to our culture in general, and to school culture specifically ...

While human life is being extinguished by militants and death is sanctioned by governments who mistake vengeance for justice ...

While there are migrant children whose parents have been told that they are not welcome here—despite the promises made to them in 1776 and etched on statues in New York Harbor ...

While the earth itself responds to our collective failure to be good stewards of the environment with wildfire and superstorms and lead in the water of our most vulnerable children ...

While the world watches American democracy stumble over its own hubris. Facts only matter if they are clickable. Histories only matter if they are convenient, and reality is shaped by algorithms into digestible 21-second danceable videos.

Educators, writers, friends; we are lovers of thought and of language.

We are also lovers of action.

We are committed to raising communities of children that are thoughtful, perceptive, and literate brokers of language. So they see all of this. And they question us, because they are children—born truth seekers.

And some adults have met young people's quest for truth with mythology disguised as history or by burying heads in the sand altogether.

Enlightenment thinking suggests that it is what we do in these difficult moments that will define us.

Conversely, the Black folk wisdom of my parents and ancestors sees plainly and presents a more observational truth. This historical moment has already defined us. The United States of America is a nation characterized by a few small bullies and the scores of bystanders whose inaction enables them.

We see injustice. We clutch pearls. We post to social media. And then we sip coffee while CNN and Fox compete for the opportunity to tell us what to do next. This is a failure of literacy. And of empathy. And, potentially, of humanity.

I am not okay with this. Neither are the educators collected here.

Neither are you.

You are reading this because your commitment to learning, to thinking, and to powerful expression match your commitment to children. Our shared circumstances compel us to do something. This is why we teach.

Honestly, this is why we teach writing.

In the face of all the things that can feel dark, this book is illumination, because it explores what it means to use writing in school as a way to deepen thinking, sharpen vision, and grow connections. In the hands of children, these are powerful practices. This kind of creativity does not just make beautiful things. It changes whole realities.

Children who are writers—not just assignment completers—are empowered to live more of their humanity in ways that are truly free. This is the promise of education, and this collection is such an important part of realizing that promise.

As we seek to educate our way into powerful futures for all children, the chapters assembled here are necessary guidance. They are sound theory and practical wisdom. Beyond this, the practices described here are evidence that as people who are ill at ease with the way things are, we are not alone in our desire for the life-giving pedagogies, inclusive methodologies, and accessible experiences that will ensure powerful futures for all of our children.

If we truly believe that education exists for a better tomorrow, then the ideas presented here are the dawn of that bright new day. These thinkers and practitioners show us the way by giving us a clear map.

But a good cartographer alone does not get us to the destination. The road is ours to travel, and the path will be as challenging as it is beautiful. I am honored to be on the journey with you.

Cornelius Minor
Brooklyn, New York
Autumn 2025

Preface: Together

We are both elementary educators at heart. This identity shaped us long before we became professors, researchers, or writers—and it continues to ground everything we do. Though we began our teaching on opposite sides of the Atlantic—Grace in Champaign, Illinois, in the United States, and Sonia in Canterbury, Kent, in the United Kingdom—we share surprisingly similar experiences when it came to our initial elementary educator preparation: writing was largely neglected, and critical theories were almost entirely absent.

Grace

It never seemed problematic to me that the books I read up to middle school had primarily white characters written by white authors. When I read Amy Tan's *Joy Luck Club* in high school, it was the first time I read a book written by an Asian author with Asian characters discussing Asian norms. This revolutionized my enjoyment of reading and my perspective on making connections with the characters' experiences and the author's themes.

In the same vein, in writing classes, I was not encouraged to draw from my own experiences, interests, or backgrounds. Then, when I started teaching, I did not have any courses on the teaching of writing, so I devoured writing workshop texts and attended all the professional development sessions. I enacted these practices and established a strong writing workshop structure and writing community in my fifth-grade classroom. However, something was missing.

As a child of immigrants, my family lacked various forms of capital—Dominant American English, language practices, social class, and social norms. I was encouraged to leave my cultural, racial, and linguistic identities and histories at the door. Not only did I feel uncomfortable sharing honestly and vulnerably about myself and my family, but I was also embarrassed and nervous to be labeled as different. This book advocates for all students' full selves to be welcomed, regardless whether they adhere to society's white dominant norms and all the more to ensure students don't need to follow the status quo. When I reflect on my experiences with writing both as a child and as a teacher, this critical piece of valuing, honoring, and uplifting students' identities and histories is of supreme importance and often is missing.

Sonia

As a child, I was painfully shy and never imagined that writing could become a way to find my voice. In school, writing felt like a test I was destined to fail—focused more on rules and red ink than on expression and meaning. Later, as a teacher, I repeated many of those same patterns: assigning writing, correcting it, and moving on. Some students impressed me with their words, but for most, writing was a painful rather than empowering experience. It wasn't until years later that I began to reflect more deeply and to recognize how my well-intentioned teaching mirrored broader systems of power that silence, rather than support, many young writers.

My growing awareness of these dynamics became more personal after I moved to the United States. My British accent and spelling were met with curiosity and admiration—an experience that revealed how certain forms of English, often associated with whiteness, class privilege, and colonial legacies, are positioned as more legitimate or intelligent, while other forms—especially those tied to racially and linguistically marginalized communities—are too often devalued or erased.

My understanding deepened further through my daughter, Emma, who has limited speech but is a powerful multimodal communicator. Her expressive brilliance reminds me daily that communication is not just about correctness or convention—it's about meaning-making, agency, and connection. This evolving understanding continues to shape how I teach writing: as an expansive practice that honors my students' identities and communities and empowers them to express themselves with confidence and purpose.

Together

We first met in graduate school, as doctoral students at the University of Illinois at Urbana-Champaign. Since then, our professional lives—and our friendship—have grown in tandem. At Illinois State, we've become work sisters: going up for tenure together, co-designing more courses and research projects than we can count, and now celebrating our promotions to Full Professor as we complete this book.

As this book advocates for humanizing perspectives, we've attempted to live this out in our partnership. Our relationship has been a space for critical growth and care. Grace has experienced the tragic loss of her brother and tried to support her father as he has battled Parkinson's for over fifteen years. Sonia has navigated a divorce and the ongoing challenges of caring for a child—now a young adult—with complex medical, communication, mobility, and educational needs. We've shown up for one another through births, deaths, heartaches, joys, and celebrations.

Through it all, we've continued to push each other's thinking and deepen our commitment to advocacy, justice, and resistance. We've come to realize the necessity of being disruptors—of causing good trouble—and doing so alongside people who love, challenge, and walk beside you. We are profoundly grateful for the kind of partnership that allows us to be both critical and humanizing in our teaching, research, and daily lives. We cannot stress enough the importance of finding your people—collaborators who sustain you, inspire you, and show up to do the hard stuff with you.

Beyond all we have learned through our life experiences, our thinking has also been shaped by many other people and places—graduate seminars where we were challenged to think outside our norms while holding true to our values; the National Writing Project summer institute where we developed our own writerly identities; and our classrooms where our students have taught us more than they'll ever know.

Classrooms are not silos—they are shaped by the values, beliefs, and experiences of the people within them. Over the years, we've returned to the idea that all educators operate within theories, whether we name them or not. Much of our professional lives have been spent grappling with how to bridge theory and practice, especially when it comes to bringing critical theories to life in elementary writing classrooms. We don't have all the answers. But in this book, we've thoughtfully curated ten critical topics, each illuminated by brilliant authors who help us reimagine writing instruction—rooted in humanity, justice, and possibility.

This is the book our younger selves wished we'd had. We hope it helps you make space for your students' full selves—and honors the work you already do in showing up, again and again, with care and courage. We know that powerful writing instruction cannot be scripted or standardized. It relies on the local knowledge, creativity, and insight of educators like you.

Thank you for all you do.
With gratitude,
Grace Kang and Sonia Kline

Introduction: What Is Critical Humanizing Writing Pedagogy?

This book is filled with powerful ideas for enacting meaningful and engaging writing instruction that affirms the brilliance of both elementary children and their teachers. But it is much more than a collection of teaching strategies—it is a framework, a constellation of generative pathways, and a call to action. Together, these elements honor teachers' autonomy and local knowledge while inviting educators to examine assumptions, deepen understanding, and reimagine writing instruction in ways that are both *critical* and *humanizing*.

At the heart of this work is a foundational understanding that literacy theory and practice are not separate spheres, but deeply interconnected (Handsfield, 2016). Too often, researchers and educators are siloed—disconnected by systems that undervalue classroom teachers' lived experiences and professional knowledge, and limit their access to all but a narrow range of theories and research. *Writing Reimagined* seeks to bridge this divide by centering both the transformative possibilities of critical theories and the pragmatic wisdom of educators.

To do this, our book draws on a range of critical theories that help us understand power dynamics, name injustices, and reimagine liberatory and humanizing possibilities. We believe that theory can inform and transform classroom practice, and that, in turn, classroom practitioners should challenge, refine, and extend theory. Importantly, critical theories should not remain abstract or disconnected from everyday realities in schools, but instead should guide instruction that is anti-racist, culturally sustaining, and rooted in care, joy, and justice.

Despite their transformative potential, critical and humanizing approaches are still rarely included in professional texts for elementary educators—and, as a result, are too often missing from elementary classrooms. This book responds to an urgent call for approaches to literacy instruction that are critical, culturally sustaining, and deeply humanizing (Bomer, 2017).

We value the foundational work of the writing process and workshop advocates, such as Atwell (1987), Calkins (1994), Fletcher & Portalupi (2001), Graves (1983), Murray (1982), and Ray (1999) who have championed student voice, choice, and extended time for authentic writing. However, these texts often do not fully center students' racial, cultural, and linguistic identities—an essential shift if writing instruction is to be truly equitable and affirming (Kang & Kline, 2020). Alongside contemporary scholars and educators committed to joyful and justice-orientated instruction (e.g., Baker-Bell, 2020; Christensen, 2009; Flint, 2022; Genishi & Dyson, 2009; Heffernan, 2004; Johnson & Sullivan, 2020; Lewison, Leland, & Harste, 2007; C. Minor, 2018; K. Minor, 2023; Muhammad, 2023; Tatum, 2021; Vasquez, 2014; Winn & Johnson, 2011), we argue for a reimagining of elementary writing classrooms as spaces where all students' histories, languages, and ways of knowing are not only welcomed, but honored and placed at the heart of instruction.

This introductory chapter provides an overview of the core concepts explored throughout the book and is designed to help you navigate the text with purpose. It lays out the why, what, and how of the book, organized around these guiding questions:

- Why does it matter how we teach writing?
- What is Critical Humanizing Writing Pedagogy?
- How is this book organized?
- How might you use this book to reimagine your writing instruction?

This book is a labor of love—not just ours, but that of many educators, activists, scholars, and students whose work fills these pages. They challenge, inspire, and deepen our collective understanding of how to teach writing.

Why Does It Matter *How* We Teach Writing?

Writing is power—the power to name, to resist, to dream, and to be heard. It determines whose knowledge is recognized, whose stories are told, and whose voices are amplified—or silenced. What's at stake is nothing less than the power of writing to affirm identities, challenge injustices, and expand possibilities for all learners.

Teaching writing is never just about pedagogy. It is always about power. Politics, identity, and access are inseparable from our instructional choices. How we teach writing shapes not just student outcomes; it shapes their sense of self, agency, and belonging. To truly understand why it matters how we teach writing, we must also confront the historical and systemic forces that have shaped—and continue to shape—access to literacy.

Literacy, Power, and Politics: A Historical Overview

Throughout history, those in power have understood that controlling literacy—especially writing—means controlling knowledge, identity, and resistance (Muhammad, 2020; 2023). Reading has often been restricted for fear of exposing people to new ideas, but writing is even more subversive. Writing allows individuals to generate and share their own ideas, compose their own narratives—and counternarratives—and challenge dominant power structures. Reading allows consumption; writing enables authorship.

Across time and context, literacy has never been neutral; it has always functioned as both a tool for resistance and a mechanism of control (Freire & Macedo, 1987). Because of its power, access to literacy has never been granted equally. Instead, it has been systematically policed, denied, and restricted. The following are just a few of many examples that show how various communities have been deliberately excluded, erased, and silenced—denied the full power and promise of literacy.

- **Enslaved people** in the United States were brutally denied the right to read and write—stripped of access to literacy because those in power feared the liberating force of words. Writing offered the power to resist, to advocate for freedom, and to reclaim stolen humanity (Gates, 2020).

- **Indigenous children** were torn from their families and forced into boarding schools to erase their languages, literacies, and cultural identities. These schools inflicted profound harm, severing children from their communities and silencing generations of knowledge (Lomawaima & McCarty, 2006).
- **Racialized bilingual students** have long faced systemic barriers to literacy, as schools enforce monolingual policies that silence bilingualism and erase linguistic diversity, where students are shamed for speaking their home languages or dialects and pressured to conform to narrow standards of "correctness" that devalue their voices, cultures, and ways of knowing (Flores & Rosa, 2015).
- **Black students in segregated schools** were systematically denied equal resources and opportunities, a stark reflection of deep-rooted racism. Even after legal desegregation, these injustices have endured, depriving generations of Black and Brown students of rich, affirming, and empowering literacy experiences (Ladson-Billings, 2006).
- *Brown v. Board of Education* (1954) legally ended segregation, yet it led to the forced displacement of thousands of Black teachers and administrators—educators who not only shared cultural ties with their students but also honored and nurtured them. Their removal stripped Black students of critical role models, advocates, and teachers who affirmed their potential and brilliance (Tillman, 2004).
- **Black Language**—rich, complex, and rooted in history—has been relentlessly denied legitimacy and dismissed as slang, rather than recognized as a powerful, rule-governed language, attempting to silence Black voices and perpetuating deep harm to identity and self-expression. Efforts to affirm Black Language, such as the 1996 Ebonics Resolution, were met with national backlash, reinforcing linguistic racism in schools (Alim & Smitherman, 2012).
- **Individuals with disabilities** have long been excluded from meaningful literacy access—segregated in schools, denied essential accessibility tools, and subjected to dehumanizing, ableist beliefs about who is "capable" of reading and writing.

These injustices have silenced voices, denied agency, and limited the full participation and potential of individuals in literacy and life (Baglieri & Knopf, 2004).

These forces are not relics of the past—they continue to shape classrooms today, influencing who is empowered through writing and who is constrained, not because of ability but because of systems that fail to honor their full humanity.

The Politics of Teaching in Our Time

Today, these dehumanizing policies and practices persist in both familiar and evolving forms. Book bans and curriculum restrictions limit students' ability to engage with, respond to, and compose narratives about race, gender, and social justice—reinforcing whose lives and stories are deemed acceptable and whose are erased (Hicks et al., 2022; NCTE, 2017; PEN America, 2022). At the same time, standardized assessments and mandated curricula impose rigid linguistic and cultural norms that privilege White, middle-class, patriarchal ways of knowing and doing, while silencing diverse voices and restricting self-expression and criticality (Baker-Bell, 2020; Dyson, 2016; Yoon, 2013; Yoon & Templeton, 2022).

Within this context, an overemphasis on the Science of Reading has led to narrow phonics and skills-based instruction, stripping literacy education of meaning-making, inquiry, and creativity (McCarthey, 2008; Paugh, Handsfield, & MacPhee, 2025; Paugh & MacPhee, 2023). To be clear, phonics, phonemic awareness, and skills are essential, but not enough. All students deserve access to literacy instruction that fosters critical thinking and social, cultural, and political engagement (Aukerman, 2022). Yet too often, students from historically marginalized communities are subjected to reductive, compliance-driven instruction that prioritizes control over curiosity, and conformity over creativity—deepening inequities in access to rich, humanizing literacy experiences (Dyson, 2021; Genishi & Dyson, 2009).

Compounding these harms, inequities, and injustices are reinforced by broader political forces. State and federal policies, including legislative attacks on Critical Race Theory and so-called "divisive concepts" laws, have sought to ban discussions of systemic racism, colonialism, and historical oppression in classrooms (Love, 2019). These laws seek to limit educators' ability to teach truthfully about history and inequity, further constraining the potential of literacy and writing as a tool for justice, critical inquiry, and change (Price-Dennis & Sealey-Ruiz, 2021).

Similarly, legislative attacks on the LGBTQ+ communities—including restrictions on the use of chosen names and pronouns, bans on discussions of gender identities, censorship of LGBTQ+ authors and narratives, and anti-trans laws with far-reaching effects in healthcare, employment, education, and public life—reinforce narrow norms about whose identities and experiences are deemed acceptable in schools and society (McQuillan, Lebovitz, & Harbin, 2024).

These are not neutral decisions—they strip students of their humanity, denying them the right to see themselves in the curriculum, to speak in their own voices, and to use writing as a tool for reflection, resistance, and liberation.

Amid these escalating attacks, the rapid rise of generative artificial intelligence has added another layer of complexity—and concern (Higgs & Stornaiuolo, 2024; Stornaiuolo et al., 2023). While GenAI may hold the potential to expand opportunities for writing and multimodal communication, it is also deployed for surveilling and policing language. Many GenAI tools—trained on predominantly White, middle-class, patriarchal datasets—flag students' racial, political, and culturally rooted linguistic choices as incorrect or undesirable, reinforcing harmful biases and further perpetuating dominant language practices that privilege certain forms of communication while marginalizing others.

The second term of the Trump presidency has ushered in an all-out war on Diversity, Equity, Inclusion, and Access, reversing progress, spreading hate, and leaving many fighting for their existence and fearing for their lives. This political climate seeks to suppress truth and reassert dominant power across every level of society, including our classrooms. Within this context, individual educators—like you and us—hold immense power, even when systems try to convince us otherwise. We can choose to uphold injustice or to disrupt it. We have the power to harm, and the power to heal.

How we teach writing matters. Neutrality in the face of injustice is not passive—it is complicity. We propose Critical Humanizing Writing Pedagogy for educators who resist conformity, confront inequity, and teach for joy, justice, and transformation.

What Is Critical Humanizing Writing Pedagogy?

Critical Humanizing Writing Pedagogy (CHWP) is more than an instructional approach—it is a theoretical framework that challenges dominant ideologies about writing and literacy, a lens that shapes how we see writers and writing, and a practice that transforms how we teach writing. It is a way of being, a way of seeing, and a way of doing.

CHWP as a Theoretical Framework, Lens, and Practice

As a **theoretical framework**, CHWP is rooted in the belief that literacy education should liberate rather than oppress and that writing is a tool for social, cultural, and political transformation. It recognizes writing as a source of joy, creativity, and expression, affirming that all writers bring valuable cultural, linguistic, and experiential resources to their composing.

As a **lens,** CHWP orients how we see writers and writing, challenging narrow definitions of "good writing" and whose voices are valued. It reveals writing as an expansive, playful, and messy act—multimodal, multilingual, and deeply connected to identity, agency, and the power to shape and share ideas with purpose.

As a **practice**, CHWP transforms writing instruction by centering student agency, identities, interests, and lived experiences. It calls on educators to create spaces where students can write with passion, curiosity, and joy, composing and sharing work that matters to them and their communities.

Why "Critical" and "Humanizing"?

Together, these dimensions—theoretical framework, lens, and practice—shape an approach to writing that is both critical and humanizing. But do we really need to name both "critical" and "humanizing"?

To explain why we do, we first acknowledge the rich body of scholarship that informs and inspires this work, including Critical pedagogy

(Bartolomé, 1994; Freire, 1970; Giroux, 1998; hooks, 1994), Multicultural Education (Banks, 1989; Nieto, 1992), Culturally Responsive Pedagogy (Gay, 2018), Culturally Relevant Pedagogy (Haddix, 2015; Ladson-Billings, 1994; 2014), Culturally Sustaining Pedagogies (Flint, 2022; Kinloch, Burkhard, & Penn, 2019; Paris & Alim, 2017; Winn & Johnson, 2011), Culturally and Historical Responsive Literacy (Muhammad, 2020, 2023), Raciolinguists (Baker-Bell, 2020; Flores & Rosa, 2015), and Abolitionist Teaching (Love, 2019). These scholars have long emphasized that education is inherently political, and that interrogating systems of power and oppression is central to any pedagogy committed to equity and justice.

While the work of these scholars often overlaps, each brings distinct insights that shape how we view writing as a tool for liberation, affirmation, and transformation. Together, they provide the foundation for how we define "critical" and "humanizing" within CHWP.

What Do We Mean by "Critical"?

- Interrogating systems of privilege, power, and oppression
- Centering justice in teaching and learning
- Empowering individuals and communities as agents of change
- Attending to intersectionality and positionality
- Inviting critique, resistance, and action

What Do We Mean by "Humanizing"?

- Centering students' full humanity—identities, emotions, and lived experiences
- Honoring languages, cultures, and ways of knowing
- Creating spaces of belonging, affirmation, care, and joy
- Recognizing the co-construction of knowledge
- Fostering creativity, healing, and well-being

We believe that if pedagogy is truly humanizing, it must also be critical—and if it is truly critical, it must also be humanizing. Yet, we choose to name both because each term carries a distinct emphasis, and words and our related actions matter.

Being critical without being humanizing can turn writing pedagogy into a joyless critique of oppression, one that fails to affirm students' identities, creativity, and agency. Conversely, being humanizing without being critical can lead to celebrating identity and diversity without addressing systems of power, leaving students ill-equipped to challenge injustice.

CHWP demands both: critique and care, liberation and affirmation, the disruption of injustice, and the space for joy, healing, and transformation.

Revisiting Fundamental Questions About Writing

Our commitment to both criticality and humanization challenges us to revisit the most fundamental questions about writing—questions that may seem self-evident, but are often shaped by unexamined assumptions rooted in dominant cultural norms: Who is a writer? What is writing? How, when, and where do we write? Why do we write? (Tondreau et al., 2025). From a critical and humanizing perspective, these questions take on new depth and urgency. Reimagining them brings us closer to the core challenge of this book: reimagining how we teach writing in both critical and humanizing ways.

Before viewing the chart below, we invite you to pause and reflect on how you would currently answer these questions. Surfacing your own beliefs and experiences can illuminate where your current practice aligns with—or is constrained by—dominant narratives. This reflection lays the groundwork for making intentional shifts in practice. The chart (see Table I.1) that follows highlights how these questions are understood through a critical humanizing lens, offering an expanded vision of who writers are—and what writing can be—in our classrooms and beyond. We imagine that much of what you read here will feel deeply familiar and affirming. These are ideas that many of us carry in our hearts and try to embody in our teaching. At the same time, we hope parts of the chart spark new questions, fresh insights, or gentle nudges to reflect and rethink.

Table I.1 Reimagining Writers and Writing: A Critical Humanizing Perspective

Reimagining Writers and Writing: A Critical Humanizing Perspective	
WRITING IDENTITIES Who is a Writer?	A writer is someone who ... • Draws on multiple identities, languages, and lived experiences • Writes for personally meaningful social, cultural, and political purposes • Makes intentional decisions about topic, language, audience, and context • Embraces writing as messy, complex, and challenging • Engages in reflection, revision, and reimagining • Finds joy, fulfillment, and connection through creating meaningful texts • Uses writing to express self, build community, and advocate for justice • Resists constraints, injustice, and oppressive systems of power • Develops voice and confidence across contexts and over a lifespan
WRITING PRODUCTS What is writing?	Writing is ... • Rooted in the writer's identities, cultures, experiences, and purposes • Multilingual, multimodal, and takes unlimited forms • Shaped by social, cultural, historical, and political contexts • Collaborative, relational, and often created in community • An act of meaning-making that allows for creativity, exploration, and play • A tool for connection, expression, healing, liberation, and transformation • Resistant to narrow standards and dominant definitions of "good writing"
WRITING PROCESSES How, when, and where do we write?	Writing involves ... • Embodiment, emotion, and affect as central to the process • Flexibility, non-linearity, and unfolding uniquely for each writer • Discovery, spontaneity, and creative flow—not just planning and structure • Honoring individual rhythms, needs, and creative environments • Conversation, collaboration, and community in development and feedback • Using diverse tools and technologies • Development over time and across space • Power, identity, and positionality—shaped by access, culture, and context

Reimagining Writers and Writing: A Critical Humanizing Perspective	
WRITING PURPOSES Why do we write?	**We write to ...** • Reflect, explore, and express identity, memory, and lived experience • Process emotions, experiences, and trauma • Experience joy, connection, healing, and creative fulfillment • Document experiences and bear witness to injustice, resilience, and change • Celebrate language, culture, and ways of knowing • Communicate needs, boundaries, and intentions • Build community, dialogue, and collective knowledge • Entertain, delight, and engage others through storytelling and self-expression • Inquire, investigate, and deepen understanding • Advocate, resist, and work for justice and liberation • Think critically and make meaning • Organize thoughts, solve problems, and plan action • Imagine new futures and inspire personal, social, and political change

Commitments and Practices of Critical Humanizing Writing Teachers

Reimagining writers and writing through a critical humanizing lens is essential—but this vision must translate into practice. What does this mean for us as educators in writing classrooms, especially amid the constraints we face?

CHWP is not a specific method—such as direct instruction, writing workshop, genre, or project-based writing—nor is it limited to a particular set of strategies like minilessons, mentor texts, or conferencing. Instead, it is a flexible and responsive framework that centers students' humanity, integrates skills with identity and creativity, and opens space for critical consciousness, joy, and transformation.

The following commitments provide an overview of the role of critical humanizing writing teachers.

1. Co-construct collaborative classroom communities that affirm and celebrate students' full identities
2. Center relationships, care, and brave vulnerability
3. Honor students' multiple languages and sustain practices of linguistic justice

4. Share your own writing life and showcase the legacies of writers who write for joy and justice
5. Position students as capable and curious researchers and writers with agency
6. Expand what "counts" as writing in schools
7. Illuminate the embodied, heterogeneous, and messy nature of writing
8. Integrate technology with intention, supporting authentic multimodal expression and meaningful connection
9. Cultivate critical consciousness and social imagination through writing
10. Engage students in writing as a form of social action and democratic participation

These commitments are not a checklist or prescription—they are an invitation. An invitation to reflect, adapt, and imagine what is possible when writing instruction centers students' full humanity. As you move through this book, we encourage you to return to these commitments often. Consider which ones feel familiar, which ones stretch your thinking, and which ones might offer new possibilities in your context. In the chapters that follow, you'll find real examples of these commitments in action.

How Is This Book Organized?

This book includes ten chapters written by equity-centered writing educators and scholars—both established and emerging voices—who bring critical perspectives and powerful classroom insights to the work of writing instruction. We are immensely grateful to these authors for their generosity in sharing their expertise and experience. Each chapter centers around a different concept vital to CHWP: (1) identity, (2) translanguaging, (3) raciolinguistics, (4) trauma, (5) multimodality, (6) pop culture, (7) play, (8) activism, (9) resistance, and (10) love. While each chapter offers a unique lens, they share a similar structure designed to support both deep reflection and practical application.

- **Introduction:** Establishes the concept and explains why it matters.
- **Background:** Grounds the concept in theory and research.

- **Pedagogical Implications:** Outlines three to five big takeaways for teaching.
- **Pedagogical Practices:** Shows examples of the critical concept in action.
- **Closing & Reflective Questions:** Promotes inquiry and discussion about the concept and encourages educators to generate ideas of how they might bring it to life in their own classrooms.

In addition, this book is supported by a companion website (www.writingreimagined.org) designed to extend and deepen your engagement with CHWP. The site includes additional resources for each chapter, reading lists, interviews with contributing authors, and practical suggestions for using the book in courses, professional learning communities, and individual reflection. Whether you are looking for discussion guides, adaptable handouts, or multimedia examples of pedagogy in action, the website offers resources to support you in bringing these ideas to life in your own context.

Overview of the Chapters

Chapter 1, At the Core: Student Identities and Writing Instruction in the Elementary Classroom

This chapter opens the book by centering identity as foundational to CHWP. Katie Peachey and Crystal Chen Lee remind us that identity isn't a fixed label, but something dynamic, multifaceted, and always evolving. When children show up in classrooms, they should be welcomed fully—and empowered to draw on their whole selves as writers. Peachey and Chen also name what's at stake: "The exclusion of students' identities from the classroom can lead to a disconnection between school and home, student disengagement, and disproportionate opportunities for students, especially for students of color" (p. 25). This chapter offers powerful practical ways to affirm students' identities through writing. Their message is clear: when we center identity in our writing instruction, we create classrooms where every student feels seen, valued, and inspired to write—not just for school, but in ways that honor who they are and the broader communities they belong to.

Building on the foundational importance of identity, the next two chapters turn to language as one of its most visible and politicized expressions. Through the lenses of translanguaging and raciolinguistics, these chapters explore how students' linguistic practices are deeply connected to who they are, and how honoring those practices is essential to critical, humanizing writing instruction.

Chapter 2, Translanguaging Writing Pedagogy to Leverage Multilingual Writers' Funds of Knowledge and Identity

In this chapter, Margarita Gómez and Joanna W. Wong invite us to reimagine writing instruction through a translanguaging lens—one that honors students' full linguistic repertoires and recognizes language as central to identity and humanity. Drawing from their work with multilingual learners, they present translanguaging writing pedagogy as an expansive, strengths-based approach that challenges deficit and narrow views. They also explore how teachers can develop language awareness through self-reflexive inquiry to critique and counter oppressive language ideologies that often go unquestioned in schools. The authors articulate three big ideas that guide this stance and share practical ways to ensure multilingual learners' full linguistic repertoires are embodied in writing classrooms. As Gómez and Wong powerfully remind us, "to recognize students' full humanity one must adopt a translanguaging stance, or the ideology that a person's humanity includes their self-expression using their full linguistic repertoire" (p. 55).

Chapter 3, Centering Cultural Language as Resistance, Belonging, and Affirmation

In this chapter, Roberta Price Gardner and Sanjuana Rodriguez explore the role of diverse children's literature in fostering critical cultural language experiences within K-6 writing classrooms. Grounded in the theoretical frameworks of raciolinguistics and revolutionary love, they examine how culturally distinct and racially conscious language practices in literature challenge dominant social hierarchies and offer students opportunities to explore their experiences and identities through writing. Strategies include using mentor texts, integrating multilingual and dialectical language, and incorporating visual symbolism that enriches narrative and fosters cultural pride. Through vivid classroom examples, the chapter demonstrates how educators can use critical diverse children's literature to expand students' linguistic repertoires and empower them to use writing as a tool for resistance and identity affirmation. As Gardner and Rodriguez poignantly write, "Providing exposure to critical cultural language experiences across multiple genres can help students locate their cultural experiences and the associative language to support their emerging identities and resist racist structures" (p. 98).

Just as honoring students' languages is essential to affirming their identities, so too is making space for their full emotions and lived experiences. The next chapter turns our attention to trauma—recognizing it not as something to avoid or erase, but as part of the knowledge students carry with them into the classroom and onto the page.

Chapter 4, "We go through a story together": Considering Trauma in Critical, Humanizing Writing Classrooms

Trauma lives in every classroom. Elizabeth Dutro, author of *The Vulnerable Heart of Literacy: Centering Trauma as Powerful Pedagogy*, helps us understand how we can meet it—not with silence and avoidance, but with compassion, curiosity, and care. Drawing from both research and classroom experience, Dutro presents trauma as multifaceted and systemic—not just personal hardship, but the result of structural inequities. She shares a powerful framework for Trauma-Informed Writing Pedagogy rooted in testimony and critical witness, offering examples of how children have taken up invitations to write about difficult experiences in their school writing. As Dutro poetically reminds us, "this is always both heartwork steeped in human connection *and* fiercely critical and analytical work, brewed in the deepest commitments to folding children into loving classrooms and pursuing action and advocacy for their right to be seen, represented, and exist" (p. 120).

While honoring students' difficult experiences is essential to a humanizing approach, so too is nurturing their joy, imagination, and agency. Too often, writing in schools is narrowly defined. The next three chapters invite us to continue to think expansively—exploring multimodality, pop culture, and play.

Chapter 5, The Power and Promise of Multimodal Composition for Enacting Critical Humanizing Writing Pedagogies

This chapter, written by Shawna Coppola—author of *Writing, Redefined* and *Literacy for All: A Framework for Anti-Oppressive Teaching*—explores the historical and contemporary significance of multimodal composing and its potential for enacting critical humanizing pedagogies. Coppola thoughtfully highlights how multimodal forms have long been used to craft counternarratives, challenge dominant norms, and honor diverse ways of knowing. She critiques the ideological hierarchy that privileges print-based texts—often at the expense of the home and community literacies rooted in non-Western traditions—and calls on educators to rethink what "counts" as writing. The chapter concludes by offering concrete ways for educators to enact critical humanizing pedagogies through student engagement in multimodal composing. As Coppola states, "In some cases, the end goal is not to craft an 'audience-ready' *product*, but rather to spend some time in a supportive, playful, and low-risk environment moving through a *process* that, regardless of the outcome, helps further their development as writers of multimodal and/or digital texts" (p. 142).

Chapter 6, Powerful "X-people" and Rhythmic "Teen-age-ers": Popular Culture in Childhood Composing

In this chapter, Anne Haas Dyson, renowned writing researcher and author of books such as *Writing Superheroes* and *The Brothers and Sisters Learn to Write*, explores the vital role of pop culture in children's lives and its pedagogical implications for writing instruction. Dyson sheds light on how we can embody CHWP by tailoring instruction to children's interests, cultures, and identities, especially those connected to pop culture. This is not an add-on, but an embodiment. Dyson writes, "in any classroom, children come with a myriad of diverse resources, imaginations, and expressive desires. And the way they weave themselves into a community of writers, guided by their responsive teacher, is a joy available to all who teach" (p. 162). She masterfully weaves together vignettes from children's classrooms, illustrating how students engage in dialogue and play around identities through composing. Intermingled in their composing are their playful drawing, talking, and writing about popular culture—such as superhero media and "teen-age-er" music—which serve as rich texts for exploration and expression. Dyson's critical questions are thought-provoking and can be considered alongside students' engagement with pop culture and the ways in which we challenge scripted curricula to be infused with children's interests, passions, and backgrounds.

Chapter 7, Storying Identity as Curricular Practice: The Multimodal Resonances of Play and Writing

Play is a powerful space for children to negotiate communication, meaning-making, and social relationships. This chapter illuminates how play is inextricably linked to children's multilayered identities, and offers educators pathways for building writing communities where children can explore play in nuanced, fun, and critical ways. Haeny Yoon, author of *Rethinking Early Literacies: Reading and Rewriting Worlds* and host of the *Pop & Play* podcast, draws from student work and "play stories" in a kindergarten classroom in New York City to highlight children's meaning-making processes and their deep social connections. For children, writing and play are embodied experiences in which their interests and voices come alive. Don't miss "play stories" like *Cowabunga Dudes*, *The Food Exposion*, and *Car Math* that reveal what truly matters to them. Yoon thoughtfully reminds us:

> While teachers juggle countless roles and decisions, one of their most crucial responsibilities is deeply understanding their students—developing the skills to study and analyze young people's work. No premade curriculum can fully address the unique characteristics and needs of individual classrooms (p. 183).

The next two chapters explore writing as a form of activism and resistance—highlighting how children can use writing not only to reflect who they are, but also to question, challenge, advocate, and reimagine.

Chapter 8, Environmental Artivism as a Critical Multimodal Writing Pedagogy

This chapter is framed by the concept of *urgent literacy pedagogies* that promote learning about timely topics that matter through reading, composition, interdisciplinary inquiry, and collaboration, with an emphasis on activism. Rebecca Woodard and Kristine Schutz, authors of *Teaching Climate Change to Children: Literacy Pedagogy that Cultivates Sustainable Futures*, focus on art for activism, or "artivism", as a form of critical multimodal composition that supports meaning-making, communication, and disruption/criticality through multiple modes. They seamlessly merge theory and practice by walking us through three artforms—sculpture, collaborative poetry with mixed-media, and disintegration-style art—that can be created in our own classrooms that represent urgent social issues through artivism. They offer us a challenge: "Combining literacy learning about urgent, social issues with opportunities to engage as multimodal composers through artivism allows learners of all ages to explore, make sense of, and communicate, critique, and advocate about pressing, meaningful issues" (p. 213).

Chapter 9, Writing as Resistance: Poetic Inquiry as a Liberatory Practice in the Classroom

Darius Phelps, a poet, writer, professor, and former elementary classroom teacher, shares the ways his students used poetry to connect their personal experiences to the world around them, connecting their identities and emotions to injustices. This chapter reveals how poetic inquiry not only allows students to express themselves, it offers them a space to disrupt traditional academic norms and amplify voices that are often silenced. He notes, "Poetic inquiry is not just a method of writing; it is a transformative act that helps students resist dominant narratives, reclaim their stories, and envision a more just world" (p. 239). Phelps offers strategies for integrating poetic inquiry in elementary classrooms, including fostering emotional literacy, building community through poetry circles, and linking creative writing to advocacy. Phelps beautifully offers insight into how poetic inquiry can be used as a tool for empowerment and resistance, showing how children can write to protest oppressive systems and be a part of a movement toward justice.

While writing can be a form of resistance, it is also an expression of care, connection, and possibility. The final chapter centers revolutionary love—not as sentiment, but as a critical and intentional practice that affirms students' full humanity and challenges systems of oppression.

Chapter 10, Revolutionary Love: A Critical Approach for Teaching Young Writers

Michele Myers, one of the authors of *Revolutionary Love: Creating a Culturally Inclusive Classroom*, explores revolutionary love as a critical orientation. She writes, "Revolutionary Love is enacted through the intentional and critical pedagogical moves that educators perform to fight against racist and oppressive systems while honoring and affirming the humanity, intelligence, ethnic and racial identities, and linguistic practices of the young writers they teach" (p. 246). Myers eloquently shares about a unit, *The Stories of Our Lives*, which was designed to support teacher candidates to center stories reflecting lived experiences when teaching writing. Children have brilliant stories to tell, and writing teachers have the opportunity to affirm their rich, cultural, and linguistic identities. Myers details the Believe-Know-Do Framework to showcase the pedagogical implications that educators perform when they act, teach, and care for children in revolutionary ways. She guides educators through pedagogical practices to emphasize justice, humanity, and social transformation by empowering writers to center their voices and lived experiences while at the same time critiquing traditional power dynamics in educational settings.

Collectively, these chapters illuminate pathways toward more just and joyful writing classrooms. Teaching, and in particular teaching writing, requires deep reflection, room for growth, and constant revision—we hope these chapters provide such opportunities for you.

How Might You Use this Book to Reimagine Writing Instruction?

This book is for pre-service teachers, classroom teachers, and teacher educators. Whether you're just beginning to explore how to support young writers or have been nurturing their voices for years, we hope this text offers ideas and inspiration. We envision it supporting transformative teaching and professional growth in a variety of spaces. Here are just a few ways it might be used:

Teacher Education Courses

- Use as a core text in undergraduate or graduate literacy courses.
- Assign chapters flexibly—either as stand-alone modules or as a cohesive course of study.
- Start with the foundational questions in the introduction, then use the end-of-chapter questions to spark meaningful dialogue and inquiry.
- Draw on the pedagogical practices sections to inform course assignments and classroom applications.

PLCs, Inquiry Groups, or Grade Level Teams

- Read and discuss chapters collaboratively.
- Try out classroom practices, then reconvene to reflect, share, and adapt.
- Support school writing instruction inquiry.
- Connect chapter themes to local classroom or schoolwide goals to make learning relevant and actionable.

Professional Development for New and Experienced Teachers

- Provide practical entry points for teaching writing.
- Use examples and resources (in the book and on the companion website) to inspire action and adaptation.
- Support teachers in designing lessons, units, and communities rooted in a framework of CHWP.
- Use the book to spark conversation about writing instruction that challenges assumptions.

Ultimately, *Writing Reimagined* empowers educators to create communities where young students write with purpose—for justice, for joy, and for themselves. We hope this book sparks new ideas, raises meaningful questions, and opens new possibilities. Above all, we hope this book inspires ongoing reflection, experimentation, and transformation in your writing classroom.

References

Alim, H. S., & Smitherman, G. (2012). *Articulate while Black: Barack Obama, language, and race in the US*. Oxford University Press.

Atwell, N. (1987). *In the middle: Writing, reading, and learning with adolescents*. Heinemann.

Aukerman, M. (2022). The science of reading and the media: Is reporting biased? *Literacy Research Association*. https://literacyresearchassociation.org/stories/the-science-of-reading-and-the-media-is-reporting-biased/

Baglieri, S., & Knopf, J. H. (2004). Normalizing difference in inclusive teaching. *Journal of Learning Disabilities*, 37(6), 525–529.

Baker-Bell, A. (2020). *Linguistic justice: Black language, literacy, identity, and pedagogy*. Routledge.

Banks, J. A. (1989). *An introduction to multicultural education*. Allyn & Bacon.

Bartolomé, L. I. (1994). Beyond the methods fetish: Toward a humanizing pedagogy. *Harvard Educational Review*, 64(2), 173–194.

Bomer, R. (2017). Leading the call: What would it mean for English language arts to become more culturally responsive and sustaining? *Voices from the Middle*, 24(3), 11–15.

Calkins, L. M. (1994). *The art of teaching writing* (2nd ed.). Heinemann.

Christensen, L. (2009). *Teaching for joy and justice: Re-imagining the language arts classroom*. Rethinking Schools.

Dyson, A. H. (2016). *Negotiating a permeable curriculum: On literacy, diversity, and the interplay of children's and teacher's worlds*. Garn Press.

Dyson, A. H. (2021). *Writing the school house blues: Literacy, equity, and belonging in a child's early schooling*. Teachers College Press.

Flint, A. S. (2022). "See, that's me. I'm proud": Manifestations of a humanizing and culturally sustaining writing pedagogy for young writers. *Language Arts*, 100(2), 83–95.

Flint, A. S., Laman, T. T., & Jackson, T. O. (2022). Culturally sustaining pedagogies in education. *Theory Into Practice*, 61(3), 234–243.

Fletcher, R., & Portalupi, J. (2001). *Writing workshop: The essential guide.* Heinemann.

Flores, N., & Rosa, J. (2015). Undoing appropriateness: Raciolinguistic ideologies and language diversity in education. *Harvard Educational Review*, 85(2), 149–171.

Freire, P. (1970). *Pedagogy of the oppressed.* Continuum.

Freire, P., & Macedo, D. (1987). *Literacy: Reading the word and the world.* Bergin & Garvey.

Gates Jr, H. L. (2020). *Stony the road: Reconstruction, white supremacy, and the rise of Jim Crow.* Penguin.

Gay, G. (2018). *Culturally responsive teaching: Theory, research, and practice.* Teachers College Press.

Genishi, C., & Dyson, A. H. (2009). *Children, language and literacy: Diverse learners in diverse times.* Teachers College Press.

Giroux, H. A. (1998). *Teachers as intellectuals: Toward a critical pedagogy of learning.* Bergin & Garvey.

Graves, D. H. (1983). *Writing: Teachers and children at work.* Heinemann.

Haddix, M. (2015). Culturally relevant pedagogy 2.0: A.k.a. the remix. *Harvard Educational Review*, 85(1), 74–84.

Handsfield, L. J. (2016). *Literacy theory as practice: Connecting critical literacy and language learning in the classroom.* Teachers College Press.

Heffernan, L. (2004). *Critical literacy and writer's workshop: Bringing purpose and passion to student writing.* International Reading Association.

Hicks, T., Gabrion, L., Lester, K., & Schoenborn, A. (2022). Standing up and pushing back: Resources from a conversation around book bans and censorship. *Michigan Reading Journal*, 54(3), 61–73.

Higgs, J. M., & Stornaiuolo, A. (2024). Being human in the age of generative AI: Young people's ethical concerns about writing and living with machines. *Reading Research Quarterly*, 59(4), 632–650.

hooks, b. (1994). *Teaching to transgress: Education as the practice of freedom.* Routledge.

Johnson, L. P., & Sullivan, H. (2020). Revealing the human and the writer: The promise of a humanizing writing pedagogy for Black students. *Research in the Teaching of English*, 54(4), 418–438.

Kang, G. Y., & Kline, S. (2020). Critical literacy as a tool for social change: Negotiating tensions in a pre-service teacher education writing course. *Journal of Language and Literacy Education*, 16(2), 1–16.

Kinloch, V., Burkhard, T., & Penn, C. M. (Eds.). (2019). *Race, justice, and activism in literacy instruction.* Teachers College Press.

Ladson-Billings, G. (1994). *The dreamkeepers: Successful teachers of African American children*. Jossey-Bass.

Ladson-Billings, G. (2006). From the achievement gap to the education debt: Understanding achievement in U.S. schools. *Educational Researcher*, 35(7), 3–12.

Ladson-Billings, G. (2014). Culturally relevant pedagogy 2.0: A.k.a. the remix. *Harvard Educational Review*, 84(1), 74–84.

Lewison, M., Leland, C., & Harste, J. C. (2007). *Creating critical classrooms: K–8 reading and writing with an edge*. Lawrence Erlbaum Associates.

Lomawaima, K. T., & McCarty, T. L. (2006). *"To remain an Indian": Lessons in democracy from a century of Native American education*. Teachers College Press.

Love, B. L. (2019). *We want to do more than survive: Abolitionist teaching and the pursuit of educational freedom*. Beacon Press.

MacPhee, D., & Paugh, P. (2023). *Learning to be literate: More than a single story*. W.W. Norton & Company.

McCarthey, S. J. (2008). The impact of No Child Left Behind on teachers' writing instruction. *Written Communication*, 25(4), 462–505.

McQuillan, M. T., Lebovitz, B. A., & Harbin, L. (2024). The disruptive power of policy erasure: How state legislators and school boards fail to take up trans-affirming policies while leaning into anti-LGBTQ+ policies. *Educational Policy*, 38(3), 642–699.

Minor, C. (2018). *We got this: Equity, access, and the quest to be who our students need us to be*. Heinemann.

Minor, K. (2023). *Teaching fiercely: Spreading joy and justice in our schools*. Jossey-Bass.

Muhammad, G. (2020). *Cultivating genius: An equity framework for culturally and historically responsive literacy*. Scholastic.

Muhammad, G. (2023). *Unearthing joy: A guide to culturally and historically responsive curriculum and instruction*. Scholastic.

Murray, D. M. (1982). *Learning by teaching: Selected articles on writing and teaching*. Heinemann.

National Council of Teachers of English. (2017). *Statement on classroom libraries*. https://ncte.org/statement/classroom-libraries/

Nieto, S. (1992). *Affirming diversity: The sociopolitical context of multicultural education*. Longman.

Paris, D., & Alim, H. S. (Eds.). (2017). *Culturally sustaining pedagogies: Teaching and learning for justice in a changing world*. Teachers College Press.

Paugh, P., Handsfield, L. J., & MacPhee, D. (2025). Religious metaphor in media reporting on the "science of reading." *Journal of Literacy Research*, 57(2), 163–191.

PEN America. (2022). *Banned in the USA: Rising school book bans threaten free expression and students' First Amendment rights*. https://pen.org/banned-in-the-usa/

Price-Dennis, D., & Sealey-Ruiz, Y. (2021). *Advancing racial literacies in teacher education: Activism for equity in digital spaces*. Teachers College Press.

Ray, K. W. (1999). *Wondrous words: Writers and writing in the elementary classroom*. National Council of Teachers of English.

Stornaiuolo, A., Higgs, J., Nichols, T. P., Leblanc, R. J., & de Roock, R. S. (2023). The platformization of writing instruction: Considering educational equity in new learning ecologies. *Review of Research in Education*, 47(1), 311–359.

Tatum, A. W. (2021). *Teaching Black boys in the elementary grades: Advanced disciplinary reading and writing to secure their futures*. Teachers College Press.

Tillman, L. C. (2004). (Un)intended consequences? The impact of the *Brown v. Board of Education* decision on the employment status of Black educators. *Education and Urban Society*, 36(3), 280–303.

Tondreau, A., Kline, S., Kang, G., Yang, S., Wall, A., Chen, X., Ikpeze, C., Kaosayapandhu, M., Tracy, K., Smetana, L., & Scales, R. (2025, in press). Illuminating discourses of disruption: Teacher candidates' personal writing experiences as potentially subversive. *English Education*.

Vasquez, V. M. (2014). *Negotiating Critical Literacies with Young Children* (10th Anniversary Edition). Routledge.

Winn, M. T., & Johnson, L. P. (2011). *Writing instruction in the culturally relevant classroom*. National Council of Teachers of English.

Yoon, H. S. (2013). Rewriting the curricular script: Teachers and children translating writing practices in a kindergarten classroom. *Research in the Teaching of English*, 48(2), 148–174.

Yoon, H. S., & Templeton, T. N. (2022). Reflecting, representing, and expanding the narrative(s) in early childhood curriculum. *Urban Education*, 59(8), 2269–2299.

1

Identity

At the Core: Student Identities and Writing Instruction in the Elementary Classroom

Katie B. Peachey and Crystal Chen Lee

The desks are arranged, bulletin boards decorated, folders and schedules printed, name tags placed, lessons prepared, and family letters sent out. It is the first day of school. As you look out at the little humans that now fill your once quiet classroom, you realize that the most important part of your job begins now: getting to know each child. Whether you are a first-year or veteran teacher, this intricate task begins each year anew. What makes this challenging and yet rewarding is the unique complexity of each student's identities. Every learner brings with them a rich constellation of identities related to their race, gender, religion, abilities, social and economic experiences, personalities, interests, and family and cultural wealth, to name a few. These identities intersect in important ways and impact how students experience and engage in school and build relationships with others.

Too often, students, especially those from nondominant communities, are asked to leave their identities at the classroom door. The exclusion of students' identities from the classroom can lead to a disconnection between school and home, student disengagement, and disproportionate opportunities for students, especially for students of color. The act of welcoming students' identities into the classroom is a critical step in this humanizing work. In this current sociopolitical context that has been riddled with violence against Black and Brown bodies, policing of gender and transgender rights, and censorship of social justice topics in schools, it is even more vital that we as teachers continuously reflect on the role of students' identities and welcome their complex selves into the classroom. The writing curriculum holds particular potential for centering and exploring students' identities.

To begin this important work, it is imperative that we first reflect on the rich theoretical and pedagogical history of critical and humanizing educators and researchers who have come before us. In this chapter, we will share a brief history and background on identity and important framings for this work. Then, we provide key pedagogical implications and ideas for implementing writing instruction centered around students' identities. Finally, we leave you with some concluding thoughts and reflective questions to take with you into your own classroom.

Identity Matters: A Brief Overview

In the introduction to this book, Kang and Kline define Critical Humanizing Writing Pedagogy (CHWP) and outline its core commitments. Among these, they highlight as foundational the call for educators to **co-construct collaborative classroom communities that affirm and celebrate students' full identities.**

It is clear why this comes first. Honoring and valuing students' multiple identities—and acting in ways that make this commitment visible—is at the heart of a critical and humanizing approach to writing instruction. Identity matters. We need to know our students and create space for them to show up fully, as their whole selves.

But what do we mean by *identity*, and why is it so central to writing instruction? In this section, we provide a brief overview and introduce the thinking of scholars and educators whose work has shaped our understanding and whose insights show us how writing and identity are inextricably connected.

Defining Identity and Intersectionality

We draw on Norton's (2013) definition that identity is "the way a person understands his or her [their] relationship to the world, how that relationship is constructed across time and space, and how the person understands possibilities for the future" (Norton, 2013, p. 4). This definition emphasizes that identity is inherently subjective and relational, shaped by lived experience, history, and context. Crucially, identity is not fixed or singular but continually constructed and reconstructed across time and space.

Other scholars have conceptualized identity in multiple and overlapping ways. Moje and Luke (2009), for example, describe five metaphors for identity: as difference, as sense of self/subjectivity, as mind or consciousness, as narrative, and as position. These metaphors illustrate how identities are fluid, contextual, and always in the process of becoming. Moje and Luke remind us that "implications for identity or identifying are always depending on the context in which identities are made, represented, or enacted" (p. 433). How students see themselves—and how they are perceived by others—depends not only on their internal self, but also on the specific social, cultural, and institutional settings in which their identities take shape.

Alongside these perspectives on identity, Crenshaw's (1989) concept of intersectionality offers a vital framework for understanding how individuals' multiple identities—such as race, gender, class, and ability—interact to shape their lived experiences. Intersectionality moves beyond viewing identities in isolation; instead, it draws attention to the ways systems of oppression—like racism, sexism, classism, and ablism—interconnect and intensify one another.

For educators, using the lenses of identity and intersectionality helps us recognize how school policies, curriculum, and everyday classroom interactions can either affirm or marginalize students. Understanding identity in this multidimensional way allows us to better see our students, not as one-dimensional learners, but as complex, evolving individuals navigating complex systems of power.

Writing and Identity Exploration

Identity is defined, constructed, and tied to writing from multiple perspectives (Fine, 2018; Flores, 2021; Moje & Luke, 2009). A humanizing approach to writing instruction opens up powerful possibilities for students to explore, negotiate, and express their identities. Writers do not simply bring their identities to the page; they actively construct and reconstruct them through writing. Humanizing pedagogy that centers students' lived experiences and identities results in students making personal and critical connections to the world (Flint, 2022). This approach positions identity work as essential—not incidental—to the writing classroom.

Writing about the self especially empowers students who have been underserved due to systemic racial, ethnic, and social inequities. Students whose experiences run counter to white, middle-class normative assumptions are often silenced in traditional schooling (Mann & Lee, 2022). Through self-reflective writing, students can challenge dominant assumptions and affirm and transform themselves. Rooted in identity exploration, this kind of reflection is essential to critical consciousness and action (Freire, 1970).

Self-reflective writing is also part of a broader process of becoming—how students wrestle with and actively shape their identities over time. Through writing, students examine who they are and how they fit into the world. As students write, they examine, reimagine, and reconstruct their self-concept, developing empathy and perspective-taking. These practices align with the four dimensions of critical literacy—disrupting the commonplace, considering multiple viewpoints, focusing on the sociopolitical, and taking action to promote social justice (Lee, Picart, & Mann, 2024a; Lewison, Flint, & Sluys, 2002).

Literacy-and-identity studies further reinforce this view, pushing back against reductive notions of academic writing as merely skill- or rule-based and positioning student voice as central (Flint, 2022; Johnson, 2017; Land, 2020). Voice emerges as students use writing to navigate their social realities, articulate their perspectives, and claim authorship in spaces where they may have been excluded. From this perspective, writing is not just a means of expression, but a powerful act of becoming—one that affirms students' humanity, cultivates voice, and fosters critical engagement.

Students' Agency and Linguistic and Cultural Identities

Because language and culture are closely tied to identity, centering them is essential for humanizing writing instruction (Flores, 2021; Kline &

Kang, 2022; Kwon, 2022; Lee, Jacobs, & Mann, 2024b). Whether through essays, short stories, poetry, social media posts, or multimodal creations, students, especially those from linguistically and culturally nondominant communities, benefit from opportunities to use writing to push back on the ways that literacy norms have silenced them in traditional educational settings. When students choose their audiences, express themselves in multiple languages and dialects, and connect their writing to issues they care about, they claim agency and power as writers.

By equipping students to "identify, critique, and transform oppressive power structures in the world around them" (Fine, 2018, p. 120), students can develop critical thinking to engage in "the realities of their lives, past, present, and future" (Flores, 2021, p. 72). This restorative practice of critiquing the world is important for humanizing writing instruction because it acknowledges the oppression that students and their communities experience while also empowering them to change it (Johnson, 2017, p. 13).

Agency is not just a byproduct of writing—it is central to how students experience it. As Flint (2022) emphasizes, "students embody agentive stances in their writing when they have the freedom to create and control what semiotic resources are used and what is produced" (p. 90). When students are trusted to make meaningful choices about content, form, language, and writing tools, they are positioned as powerful meaning-makers—authors whose voices and decisions matter.

These agentive stances offer students opportunities to confront, deconstruct, and reconstruct identities of self (Fine et al., 2000). In their research, Lee et al. (2022) found this especially powerful for girls of diverse backgrounds, noting that naming and resisting injustice created space for authenticity and belonging within the classroom. Writing can provide a pathway to deeper belonging and engagement within the classroom community (Lee et al., 2022).

Pedagogical Implications

Identity and intersectionality offer key insights for CHWP, including providing space for counternarratives, centering students' agency and voice, honoring students' multiple identities, and highlighting context and community. These key ideas assist in centering students' experiences, contextually situating instruction, and disrupting the traditional banking model of education, in which students are viewed as empty vessels to be filled rather than active meaning-makers (Freire, 1970/2018).

Providing Space for Counternarratives

Many students, especially those from marginalized communities, are not given meaningful opportunities to share their stories and experiences. Traditional writing instruction often centers dominant narratives, leaving little room for students to voice their truths or challenge the status quo. CHWP creates space for disruption, inviting students to speak out against oppressive structures and share their lived experience (Comber, 2014).

Writing about the self becomes a platform for change through counternarratives (Lee, Jacobs, & Mann, 2024b). Solórzano and Yosso (2002) define counternarrative as "a method of telling the stories of those people whose experiences are not often told. The counterstory is also a tool for exposing, analyzing, and challenging the majoritarian stories of racial privilege" (p. 32). Counternarratives may take many forms—poems, personal narratives, and multimodal compositions—serving both personal and political purposes (Cappello, Wiseman, & Taylor, 2019).

In reflecting on your teaching, ask yourself: *Do I invite students to share stories from their own lives, cultures, and communities? Do I encourage students to challenge "single stories" or stereotypes they encounter? In what ways do I help students recognize and question dominant narratives in the stories we read and write? How do I honor multiple ways of telling stories (e.g., oral storytelling, art, music, multiple languages, and modalities)?*

Counternarratives empower students to reclaim authorship of their stories and reaffirm their dignity and humanity (Lee, Jacobs, & Mann, 2024b).

Centering Students' Agency and Voice

As we considered the potential power of counternarratives in affirming students' humanity and empowering them to enact change, we asked ourselves: What do students need to help them craft these stories? They need teachers to position them as experts and give space for their agency and voice (Land, 2020; Linares, 2018). Agency is a core part of the Reflect, Reimagine, and Revisit Framework for centering critical writing pedagogy

(Kline & Kang, 2022), which informs this text. Through an agentive process, students become intentional writers and storytellers (Flores, 2021; Muhammad, 2015; Woodard, Vaughan, & Coppola, 2020).

Agency in writing instruction creates opportunities for us to learn about our students and what matters most to them, an important element of humanizing pedagogy (Behizadeh, 2019). Agency is pivotal for centering students' identities and opens up space for our students to be vulnerable, authentic, and intentional in their writing. It shifts writing from rule-following to a practice of expression and exploration, raising questions like: *Who am I? What do I want to share with the world? How will my words impact the world?*

In our classrooms, agency across the writing process can take many forms, from supporting student-led processes to fostering collaborative writing. You might begin this work by asking yourself: *What topics do my students care about? How might I support student-led writing processes? How might I increase opportunities for cooperative and collaborative writing and response? How can I dialogue with my students more about their writing and writing process?*

Agency in the writing classroom doesn't negate the importance of modeling, structured support, or rigorous writing standards. Instead, it is an intentional teaching stance that privileges students' existing knowledge and experiences in ways that promote writer identity formation and positions our students as writers with intelligence, personalities, and stories worth telling (Muhammad, 2015). An essential part of this process for us as teachers is to help our students understand what makes their voices unique and empower them to make choices in their writing accordingly. Ultimately, when students are able to make choices about their language use, audience, genre, topic, and style, they can see themselves as writers.

Honoring Students' Multiple Identities

Related to agency, how we speak and communicate in the world is directly connected to our intersecting identities. Honoring students' multiple identities is central to reimagining writing instruction. One way we can approach this in our classrooms is to invite students to share the unique experiences and funds of knowledge they bring—the everyday knowledge, skills, and wisdom rooted in their homes, cultures, and communities (Moll et al., 1992). Through these invitations, students can become co-constructors of knowledge with us as we acknowledge their rich linguistic repertoires (Otheguy, García, & Reid, 2015). Humanizing writing embraces students' identities by viewing students' language(s) as assets to the writing classroom (de los Ríos & Seltzer, 2017; Linares, 2018; Stewart & Hansen-Thomas, 2016). Making space for students' languages also invites their full identities into the writing classroom.

Translanguaging—the intentional integration of students' full linguistic repertoires—offers one powerful way to honor identities. While translanguaging will be further explored in a subsequent chapter, it is vital to note its importance and connection to students' identities. Translanguaging can "mobilize students' racial, ethnic, and linguistic social worlds towards the center of their writing" (Zoch et al., 2021, p. 69). Through this mobilization, students can see that their intersectional identities have a place in school writing.

We honor students' identities by offering choice throughout the writing process, sharing texts with diverse and representative authors, and reflecting on the role that feedback may play. In reflecting on the ways you honor students' multiple identities, you might ask yourself: *How do my classroom materials and mentor texts reflect the diverse identities and experiences of my students? How do I create space for students to draw from their home languages and community knowledge as they write? How might my feedback on student writing affirm, rather than erase, students' linguistic and cultural identities? What steps can I take to ensure that every student feels their identities are welcomed, valued, and celebrated in our writing community?*

Honoring students' multiple identities is not just about inclusion—it is about affirmation, celebration, and transformation. When we invite students to bring their full selves into the writing classroom, we create spaces where every story matters, every language is an asset, and every child's way of knowing is seen as powerful.

Highlighting Context and Communities

In addition to honoring students' individual identities, humanizing writing instruction also highlights the context in which students live, learn, and grow. One way is to design authentic writing tasks that connect students' school writing to their lives. Authenticity in writing can be understood as "students' perception that a writing task connects to their life, that the task is meaningful to them and connects to their experiences, culture, interests, and goals" (Behizadeh, 2019, pp. 411–412). Research on authentic writing emphasizes the value of expanding students' audiences beyond the classroom to include peers, families, and communities. Authentic audiences and topics help students to see that their writing holds meaning beyond the classroom (David, Consalvo, & Vetter, 2019; Lee et al., 2022; Petrone et al., 2022).

Research points to the benefits of these collective writing experiences (Flores, 2021; Sperling & Woodlief, 1997). As you consider ways to highlight your school context and students' communities, you might begin by asking yourself: *What are the values and cultural practices of my students' communities? What roles do my students play in those communities? How can I draw connections between my writing instruction and the broader community context? What connections can help bridge school and community?*

Understanding students' roles in their families and communities is vital to consider and incorporate into our writing spaces. Through this practice of freedom (hooks, 1994), students develop and foster their own writer identities while engaging in their local communities. Highlighting context helps students see that their writing expertise has value that extends beyond our classrooms (Land, 2020).

Pedagogical Practices

This next section explores specific pedagogical practices for engaging with identity work in the writing classroom, including the use of critical mentor text sets, place-based writing, journaling, and writing communities.

Pedagogical Practice #1: Critical Mentor Text Sets

To humanize writing instruction and center students' identities, an essential step is to expose students to texts written by authors from nondominant backgrounds and identities. One way to do this is by incorporating critical mentor text sets. Critical mentor text sets are "a group of texts written by diverse authors across multiple modes that facilitate understanding of a writing genre, and develop students' writer identities, skills, intellectualism, criticality, and joy" (Muhammad, 2020; Nelson & Opatz, 2023, p. 76).

These mentor texts are vital tools because they allow students to see how diverse and talented writers integrate important aspects of their own identities and how they enact change through crafting counternarratives. Critical mentor texts can be integrated across the writing process from brainstorming to revising, and can be seen as an iterative tool (see Textbox 1.1 for an example of how to build a critical mentor text).

As you begin to build your text sets, you will want to consider the intersectional identities of the students in your classroom, selecting texts that serve multiple purposes. Some texts should act as *mirrors*, reflecting students' own cultures, experiences, and identities back to them; others should serve as *windows*, offering insights into lives and experiences different from their own; and some should function as *sliding glass doors*, inviting students to step into, experience, and build empathy with worlds beyond their own (Bishop, 1990).

In addition, critical mentor text sets should also disrupt dominant narratives and challenge the status quo, offering diverse perspectives and inviting critical conversations. Mentor texts are not limited to traditional books; multimodal texts—such as videos, podcasts, art, music, and digital compositions—can and should be incorporated.

When creating a critical mentor text set, you will want to consider your specific goals and objectives for the writing as well as student interests, the local context, and issues facing your communities. Table 1.1 provides an example of a critical mentor text set focused on inclusion in sports. This set could be utilized during a narrative writing unit or an informational text unit. In their writing, students could write about a related topic of inclusion or consider ways that their own stories relate to or connect to the athletes featured in these texts.

These texts can serve as dynamic models, offering students examples to draw from as they brainstorm, draft, and revise their own counternarratives or other types of writing. To introduce students to these text sets, think about modeling how to interact with and speak back to the texts in ways that help students to think and respond like writers (Marchetti & O'Dell, 2015). For example, as you interact with the texts, you might ask: *How did the author/writer/artist stand up for what they believed in? How did this medium or genre help the author/writer/artist to get their point across? What do you notice about how the author/writer used their unique voice to*

Textbox 1.1 Building and Using a Critical Mentor Text Set

1. **Step #1: Big Idea**
   a. Determine a relevant and important topic or theme that can center on identity, social justice, environmental concerns, family, and community (e.g., food deserts, climate change, bullying, family traditions, celebrating differences)
2. **Step #2: Text Selection**
   a. Begin selecting texts (consider including voices that represent different viewpoints, perspectives, and backgrounds)
   b. Find text across different genres, styles, and modalities (e.g., picture books, informational articles, social media posts, images, etc.)
3. **Step #3: Craft Questions**
   a. Craft some guiding questions based on your guiding theme to consider as they read through the text.
   b. These questions should be critical in nature and encourage students to analyze the author's word choices, style, voice, and purpose. (e.g., How does the author utilize their own unique voice to reveal their argument?)
4. **Step #4: Student Engagement**
   a. After modeling how to talk back to the texts, have students engage with the text set with the guiding question.
5. **Step #5: Student Writing**
   a. After discussing their findings with the class, have students begin writing their own pieces based on aspects of the mentor texts that stood out to them.
6. **Step #6: Student Revision and Sharing**
   a. Using the mentor texts as a guide, help students to revise their writing.
   b. If students feel comfortable, have them share their writing with the class or in small groups.

Table 1.1 Critical Mentor Text Set Example

Athletes Who Inspire: Sports Stories of Inclusion, Innovation, and Strength

Potential Use	Genre	Text
Introduction	Informational Video	Special Olympics North Carolina "Come Join Us"
Main Mentor Text	Nonfiction	*Tenacious: Fifteen Adventures Alongside Disabled Athletes* by: Patty Cisneros Prevo and Dion MBD
Complementary Text	Picture Book	*The Girl Who Figured it Out* by Minda Dentler and Stephanie Dehennin
Textured Text	Online Interactive Art Exhibit	"Gold Medal Prosthetics: Discover the Engineering Feat of Jonnie Peacock's Blade" by Museum of Engineering Innovation

advocate for an issue they care about? What words/illustrations/features did the author/writer/artist use to share their message? What did I learn about their identities from their piece?

Critical mentor text sets offer students more than just writing models—they invite students to engage their identities, challenge dominant narratives, and write toward authenticity and change. By thoughtfully curating mentor text sets and modeling how to interact with them, we create a foundation for deeper identity work within the writing classroom.

Pedagogical Practice #2: Place-Based Writing

Identities are intricately connected to place and context (Esposito, 2012), making place-based writing a valuable practice. Place-based writing invites students to write meaningfully about the important places and environments that they inhabit, focusing on a specific issue in their community. Through this process, students connect with authentic audiences, tap into a clear and meaningful purpose, and contribute to the betterment of their specific communities (Petrone et al., 2022). For example, students might write letters to community members or politicians, craft blog posts, or social media posts for a wider audience, or perform poetry in local venues.

Textbox 1.2 Show-and-Tell Writing Graphic Organizer

Physical Details	Personal Connections
What does this item look like? What does it feel like? What does it sound like? Are there any other sensory details that are connected to this item?	What does this item make you think about? Are there memories or experiences you think about when you look at this item? What does this item tell other people about you? Why is this item important to you?

One example of place-based writing is show-and-tell writing, which invites students to share an object of significance connected to a specific place. Much like the popular classroom activity, this approach encourages reflection, sensory details, identity expression, and connection to place. After sharing about their item with a partner or a small group, students are asked to think about all the physical details of their item. You could have students complete a brainstorming activity like a graphic organizer (see Textbox 1.2 for an example). Next, you can encourage them to think about the memories or feelings they connect to this item. After this brainstorming process, students are invited to write about their items. Some potential genres for show-and-tell writing include poetry, narratives, or multimodal pieces. If some students need additional scaffolded support, you could provide them with a template or sentence stems to help them begin their writing.

Textbox 1.3 features a student example about a special necklace given to her by her grandmother. This middle school student was a part of a writing program at a local community organization. However, this type of writing can be adapted across grade levels and contexts. The original

Textbox 1.3 Show and Tell Poem Example

Un Collar Mágico	**A Magic Necklace**
Cuando lo veo, veo una sonrisa en tu rostro.	When I see it, I see a smile on your face.
Cuando le escucho, escucho que me dices te quiero.	When I listen to you, I hear you tell me "I love you."
Cuando lo siento, siento cuando me dabas dulces y que no la dijera a mi mama.	When I'm sad, I feel when you give me candy and don't tell my mom.
Cuando pienso en ti, recuerdo cómo me salvas de mi mama enojada.	When I think of you, I remember how you saved me from my angry mom.
Cuando te imagino, imagino tú y yo juntas para siempre	When I imagine you, I imagine you and me together forever.
Cuando otras personas te ven, ven un collar cualquiera	When others see you, they see whatever necklace.
Cuando te veo, veo mi mundo.	When I see you, I see my world.
Cuando me siento mal, yo recuerdo cuando tú me dices te quiero mucho.	When I feel bad, I remember when you tell me you love me.
Cuando otras personas me dicen eres horrible, tú dices que soy hermosa.	When other people tell me "You're horrible," you say I'm beautiful

poem was written in Spanish and then translated into English. For this student, thinking and writing about her necklace gave her an opportunity to explore important memories of spending time with her grandmother and allowed her to express aspects of her cultural and linguistic identities. While this student chose to write a free-verse poem, other forms may be more accessible and appropriate for some students. Writing your own show-and-tell poem alongside your students can also be a great way for them to get to know you more and further build a classroom community of trust and sharing.

This type of writing has the potential to disrupt the status quo and honor students' multiple identities by creating space for students to write about meaningful parts of their own lives, and challenge stereotypes and limiting beliefs through sharing parts of their identities. Through place-based writing, we can honor the ways identity is rooted in place and community, while empowering students to use writing as a way to preserve, share, and celebrate stories.

Pedagogical Practice #3: Journaling

Journaling is another powerful pedagogical practice that can connect writing to students' identities and place. This form of free-writing encourages self-reflection, connects to students' identities, and may reduce fears or anxiety toward writing. One approach to developing students' writing voices is through reflective practices such as dialogue journals, described as "an encounter in which two or more individuals are united and engaged in a mutual and collaborative effort to understand and reflect on what is shared" (Linares, 2018, p. 522). Dialogue journals create a space for ongoing, identity-affirming, and authentic exchange between and among students and teachers. These written conversations invite meaningful reflection and communication, while also providing opportunities for teachers to offer humanizing feedback.

Building a Journaling Practice

To begin a journal practice, we often invite students to choose from a series of invitations, such as: *Who am I? What do I care about? Who do I love? What makes me me? What do I want others to know about me? What do I hope to do in the future? How do I care for the people in my life?* Students are also given the option to write freely about a topic of their choice. Textbox 1.4 provides an example of a graphic organizer that can be used to begin journaling time with your students. However, there are many ways you can incorporate journaling into your class routine, so feel free to experiment and see what works best for your students. The primary goal of this first stage of journaling is to get students to write and reflect on an important topic that connects to their identities. Journaling can then be extended to meaningfully and critically connect back to students' identities and provide them with opportunities to construct counterstories. Textbox 1.4 also provides counterstorying prompts that can be paired with the original journal prompt.

Textbox 1.4 Example Journal Prompt

Option 1: What does community mean to you? What are important elements of a community? Describe a community or group you've been a part of that was important to you. Why was this community important to you?

Option 2: Choose to write about a different topic or idea. This free writing can be any genre/form (poetry, sketching, journaling, etc.) and be about any topic or idea.

Counterstorying Prompts: What false beliefs or stereotypes do other people have in relation to your community? How are these beliefs incorrect? How do they make you feel? What would you want people to know about your community instead? What stories would you want to share about your community with the world?

After creating initial drafts, students can create more formal pieces or participate in meaningful discussions with their peers about their journaling.

Transparent Journaling

One powerful way to make journaling more visible, multimodal, and engaging is to utilize transparent journaling. This practice begins with students writing about a specific topic. Then, using art supplies like colored pencils or watercolor paints, students add a transparent layer onto their page. They are encouraged to include images, designs, or symbols that connect to their writing or identities. An important thing to note is that they can choose to cover up parts of their journal entry or leave parts of their writing visible.

This activity opens up opportunities to explore meaningful questions with students, such as: *What parts of my writing or story do I want to share with others? What parts of my writing are just for me? What might people learn from my writing? How does art help me to reflect my thoughts or ideas with the world?* By allowing students to make choices about what to share and what to keep private, transparent journaling powerfully centers students' agency and voice.

While Figure 1.1 features examples from secondary multilingual learners from refugee backgrounds who participated in an after-school writing program, the same practice can be thoughtfully adapted for elementary students. When working with younger writers, teachers might offer more structured writing invitations, provide simple sentence starters, or model transparent journaling themselves.

Transparent journaling can also be framed as counterstorying through intentional prompts and discussions. It can serve as a bridge to more formal writing tasks, connect thematically to reading units, or stand alone as a creative exploration of identity and voice.

Journaling offers multiple pathways for centering students' agency and voice by giving them space to explore topics and issues that matter to them. This practice can also empower students to disrupt the status quo and engage critically with the world around them. At the same time, journaling can offer teachers authentic windows into their students' lives, providing opportunities to tailor instruction in ways that connect meaningfully to students' multiple identities, contexts, and individual voices.

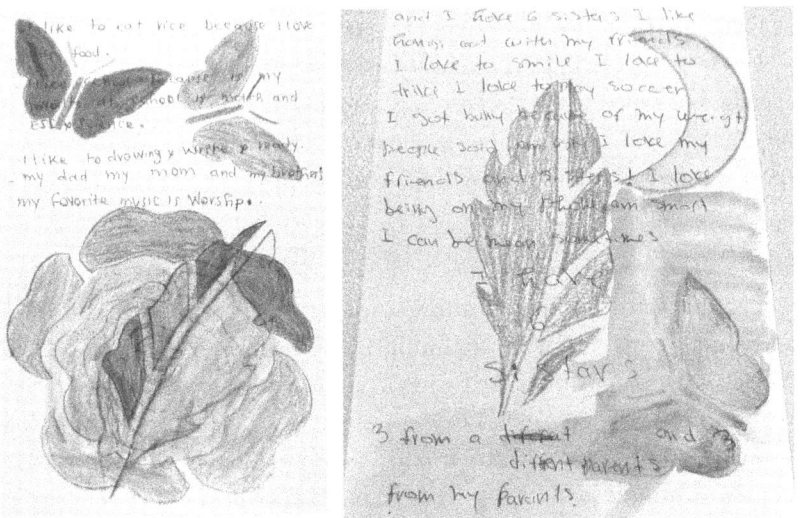

Figure 1.1 Student examples: Transparent journaling.
By Amani and Yasin.

Pedagogical Practice #4: Creating Communities of Writers

Writing thrives in community. Before students can take creative and critical risks with their words, they need a classroom environment that fosters brave work and feels supportive and collaborative. Creating a community of writers involves intentionally establishing shared norms, engaging in collective writing activities, and creating opportunities for meaningful peer sharing and feedback.

Establishing Community Norms

For students to share vulnerable stories about their identities and experiences, a foundation of trust and accountability is essential. One way to build this foundation is by co-creating a writing community creed or agreement (Muhammad, 2015). While these agreements can take many forms, their central purpose is to encourage students to think about how they want their writing community to support each member. Table 1.2 provides guiding questions to help students craft their writing creeds. Showing examples from other classrooms can further inspire their thinking.

Writing agreements can be revisited throughout the writing process and serve as a valuable resource when conflicts, misunderstandings, or challenges arise.

Co-creating writing community norms places value on students' agency and voice while decentering teachers as the sole authority, and inviting student advocacy and leadership—critical moves for disrupting the status quo of traditional writing instruction.

Collective Writing Activities

Collective writing activities allow students to learn from one another and build trust in their communities. One powerful approach to collective writing, which can be incorporated into a poetry or narrative writing unit, is Tapestry Poetry, coined by creative writers Avril Meallem and Shernaz Wadia in 2013. The premise of this innovative poetry technique is that each writer constructs a nine-line poem about a co-selected topic, often one that reflects aspects of their identities. To support younger writers in selecting meaningful topics, you might

Table 1.2 Writing Agreement Guiding Topics and Questions

Topics	Example Questions
Purposes and Hopes	What do we hope to get out of our writing community? What do we hope to add to it?
Safety and Trust	How can our writing community help you feel confident and brave in sharing your ideas? How can we show that every voice and story matters in our community?
Care and Responsibility	How do we want to treat each other's words and ideas? What should we do when someone shares something challenging or vulnerable?
Repair and Inclusion	What should we do if someone's words hurt someone else, even by accident? How will we show respect for diverse ideas and different voices?
Feedback and Celebration	What does good feedback sound like and feel like in our writing community? How will we celebrate each other's ideas, efforts, and growth as writers?

begin by offering a few guiding questions, such as: *What is something we both care about or have experienced? What are we both excited to write about? What topics might we explore? Examples: A place that feels safe, a time I felt brave, something important about my family, a dream I have for the future, a place that matters to me, a tradition I celebrate, an animal I love.*

After completing their individual lines, partners work together to weave their poems into an 18-line collective piece, choosing either to alternate lines or rearrange them creatively.

Tapestry poems provide an opportunity to connect their personal stories to those of others, while still maintaining space to express what matters most to them. Figure 1.2 shows a tapestry poem created by two youth writers in a holistic educational support program. The structure of the activity can be easily adapted: the number of lines can be shortened depending on grade level or writing experience, and students are encouraged to incorporate their home languages, cultures, and unique styles.

Beyond fostering connection, collective writing practices like Tapestry Poetry invite students to explore critical themes such as social justice,

Cats
Author #1

I love cats
Cats are so cuddly and soft
They always give me hope
Tabs and Peaches
Are the cats at my school
They remind me of spring!
They are so adventurous

Cats
Author #2

Running—up and down
Across and parallel
Yarn falls from the scratching post,
Yells–
I don't take well—
They sleep non-stop
They like to play with the shiny dot.

Cats
Collective Piece

Running–up and down
Across and parallel
They are so adventurous
Cats are so cuddly and soft.
Yarn falls from the scratching post–
Yells, I don't take well–
Tabs and Peaches are cats at school
They sleep non-stop
and play with the shiny dot.
They remind me of spring!
They always give me hope.
We love cats.

Figure 1.2 Tapestry poetry example.
By Mía and Peyton.

identity, and community concerns, strengthening both their writing skills and their awareness of the world around them.

Building Community Through Sharing and Celebration

An important component of incorporating writing communities is to provide students with opportunities to share and celebrate their writing with their peers, the school community, and an outside audience. Writing communities become powerful spaces where "storytelling and the arts can be vehicles to forge coalition across difference toward a vision of educational equity and immigrant rights" (Ghiso et al., 2019). From

Table 1.3 Incorporating Community Sharing

Example	Description
Partnership with a local non-profit organization	The class community can partner with a local non-profit organization to produce writing/art that supports the organization's cause.
Reading at a local library or bookstore	Teachers and students can work with a local library or bookstore to host a community reading and/or Q&A with the student writers, enabling them to share topics they care about with their community.
Digital Gallery	Students can help to create a digital gallery on a school website or another secure website. This digital gallery can be shared with families and community members to reach a broader audience.
Family Literacy Night	Teachers and students can plan and implement a family literacy night that displays or presents students' writing. This event can also be an excellent opportunity to invite families to write alongside or co-author with their students, further expanding the writing community.

this perspective, storytelling and sharing function to affirm individual stories as unique and important in their own right and forge connections across differences in ways that are not homogenizing. Community sharing can take many forms, so feel free to reflect on your own school/community context for potential ways to integrate this. See Table 1.3 for examples of ways teachers can incorporate community sharing into their writing instruction.

Community sharing is ultimately an act of celebration. It honors students' hard work, creativity, and growth, while also building connections across classroom, family, and community spaces. When we create authentic opportunities for students to share their voices, we affirm their identities and remind them that their stories matter.

Conclusion

The writing classroom can be reimagined when students' identities and whole selves are centered. When students see themselves—and others—reflected in writing practices and products, they are better able to make personal, critical, and transformative connections to learning. As demonstrated through our examples (critical mentor texts, place-based writing, journaling, and collective writing), writing is a shared practice that is a dialogue with past writers, current writers, and future writers. Young writers model those who came before them and contribute their own writing for those still to come. In this light, writing is not a static product, but a living act with the power to shape self and society.

CHWP centers students' sociocultural realities and affirms their racial, cultural, and linguistic identities (Bartolomé, 1994; Kline & Kang, 2022). Children enter classrooms with a wealth of cultural and linguistic knowledge (Moll et al., 1992), yet traditional writing instruction often disregards these assets (Land, 2020; Machado et al., 2019) and forces students to erase their native languages and cultures to find success in educational spaces (Salazar, 2010). In contrast, when students write themselves and their experiences into their pieces, they become creative meaning-makers (Linares, 2018) and designers of their own narratives (Land, 2020). This is even more powerful when we create space for students to explore how writing impacts all aspects of their identities and beings, including their physical bodies (Woodard, Vaughan, & Coppola, 2020). Further, when we center students' linguistic choices in the writing classroom, we help students see that language is "layered with others' discourses, histories, and ideologies" (Flint, 2022, p. 86).

A humanizing posture toward writing acknowledges past, current, and future selves as students develop their writing identities through engaging with their past, wrestling with their present, and dreaming their futures. When students participate in these activities alongside other young writers, they build relationships and even embolden one another to take risks in writing. Sharing writing creates a space of collective vulnerability and courage (Lee et al., 2022). When students' full identities are seen, centered, and amplified, classrooms become more than learning spaces—they become communities rooted in one another's life stories, histories, and future possibilities.

Reflective Questions

1. In what ways do my current writing curriculum and pedagogical practices invite or exclude my students' complex identities?
2. What do I already know about my students' identities? How can I reimagine my writing curriculum in ways that allow me to learn more about and honor my students' identities?

3. More broadly, how can I advocate for and take steps to center students' identities across educational spaces?

References

Bartolomé, L. (1994). Beyond the methods fetish: Toward a humanizing pedagogy. *Harvard Educational Review, 64*, 173–195.

Behizadeh, N. (2019). Aiming for authenticity: Successes and struggles of an attempt to increase authenticity in writing. *Journal of Adolescent and Adult Literacy, 62*(4), pp. 411–419. https://doi.org/10.1002/jaal.911

Bishop, R. S. (1990). Mirrors, windows, and sliding glass doors. *Perspectives, 6*(3), ix–xi.

Cappello, M., Wiseman, A. M., & Turner, J. D. (2019). Framing equitable classroom practices: Potentials of critical multimodal literacy research. *Literacy Research: Theory, Method, and Practice, 68*(1), 205–225. https://doi.org/10.1177/2381336919870274

Comber, B. (2014). Critical literacy and social justice. *Journal of Adolescent and Adult Literacy, 58*(5), 358–363.

Crenshaw, K. (1989). Demarginalizing the intersection of race and sex: A Black feminist critique of antidiscrimination doctrine, feminist theory and antiracist politics. *University of Chicago Legal Forum, 139*. https://scholarship.law.columbia.edu/faculty_scholarship/3007/?utm_s

David, A. D., Consalvo, A., & Vetter, A. (2019). Crafting communities of writers: Advice from teens. *English Journal, 109*(1), 67–73. https://doi.org/10.58680/ej201930276

de Los Ríos, C. V., & Seltzer, K. (2017). Translanguaging, coloniality, and English classrooms: An exploration of two bicoastal urban classrooms. *Research in the Teaching of English, 52*(1), 55–76. https://doi.org/10.58680/rte201729200

Esposito, L. (2012). Where to begin? Using place-based writing to connect students with their local communities. *The English Journal, 101*(4), 70–76. https://doi.org/10.58680/ej201218751

Flint, A. S. (2022). "See, that's me. I'm proud": Manifestations of a humanizing and culturally sustaining writing pedagogy for young writers. *Language Arts, 100*(2), 83–95. https://doi.org/10.58680/la202232136

Fine, S. M. (2018). Teaching in the restorative window: Authenticity, conviction, and critical-restorative pedagogy in the work of one teacher-leader. *Harvard Educational Review, 88*(1), 103–125. http://dx.doi.org/10.17763/1943-5045-88.1.103

Fine, M., Weis, L., Centrie, C., & Roberts, R. (2000). Educating beyond the borders of schooling. *Anthropology & Education Quarterly*, 31(2), 131–151. https://doi.org/10.1525/aeq.2000.31.2.131

Flores, T. T. (2021). Fighting to be heard: Latina adolescent girls writing toward change. *Journal of Adolescent & Adult Literacy*, 65(1), 65–73. https://doi.org/10.1002/jaal.1177

Freire, P. (1970/2018). *Pedagogy of the oppressed*. Bloomsbury Publishing USA.

Ghiso, M., Campano, G. Player, G., Krishanwongo, B., & Gultom, F. (2019). Braiding stories toward a common cause: Coalitional inquiry as activism. In Valerie Kinloch, Tanja Burkhard, & Carlotta Penn (Eds.), *Race, justice, and activism in literacy instruction* (pp. 181–200). Teachers College Press.

hooks, b. (1994). *Teaching to transgress: Education as the practice of freedom*. Routledge.

Johnson, L. P. (2017). Writing the self: Black queer youth challenge heteronormative ways of being in an after-school writing club. *Research in the Teaching of English*, 52(1), 13–33. https://doi.org/10.58680/rte201729198

Kline, S., & Kang, G. (2022). Reflect, reimagine, revisit: A framework for centering critical writing pedagogy. *Language Arts*, 99(5), 300–311. https://doi.org/10.58680/la202231790

Kwon, J. (2022). *Understanding the transnational lives and literacies of immigrant children*. Teachers College Press.

Land, C. L. (2020). Recentering purpose and audience as part of a critical, humanizing approach to writing instruction. *Reading Research Quarterly*, 57(1), 37–58. https://doi.org/10.1002/rrq.371

Lee, C. C., Dufrense, K. V., Jacobs, L., Donovan, C., & Mann, J. C. (2022). Voicing vulnerability: Narratives of healing among culturally diverse adolescent girls in a community-based organization. In Barbara Guzzetti (Ed.), *Genders, cultures and literacies: Understanding intersecting identities* (pp. 93–106). Routledge.

Lee, C. C., Picart, J., & Mann, J. C. (2024a). *Amplifying Youth Voices through Critical Literacy and Positive Youth Development: The Potential of University-Community Partnerships*. Taylor & Francis. https://doi.org/10.4324/9781003320135

Lee, C. C., Jacobs, L., & Mann, J. C. (2024b). Writing with dignity among youth in urban communities: Using mentor texts as a reflective tool for transformation. *Urban Education*, 59(5), 1365–1395. https://doi.org/10.1177/00420859221081765

Lewison, M., Flint, A. S., & Sluys, K. V. (2002). Taking on critical literacy: The journey of newcomers and novices. *Language Arts*, 79(5), 382–392. https://doi.org/10.58680/la2002255

Linares, R.E. (2018). Meaningful writing opportunities: Write-alouds and dialogue journaling with newcomer and English learner high schoolers. *Journal of Adolescent & Adult Literacy*, 62(5), 521–530. https://doi.org/10.1002/jaal.932

Machado, E., & Flores, T. T. (2021). Picturebook creators as translingual writing mentors. *Language Arts*, 98(5), 235–245. https://doi.org/10.58680/la202131211

Machado, E., Woodard, R., Coppola, R., & Vaughan, A. (2019). Student voices: Cultivating opportunities for young adolescents to use multilingual and multicultural resources in school writing. *Voices from the Middle*, 26, 35–40.

Mann, J. C., & Lee, C. C. (2022). "They just go by making their own hate story": Interrogating stereotypes with refugee students in community-based spaces. *Language Arts*, 99(6), 417–420. https://doi.org/10.58680/la202231965

Marchetti, A., & O'Dell, R. (2015). *Writing with mentors: How to reach every writer in the room using current, engaging mentor texts*. Heinemann.

Moje, E. B., & Luke, A. (2009). Literacy and identity: Examining the metaphors in history and contemporary research. *Reading Research Quarterly*, 44(4), 415–437. https://doi.org/10.1598/rrq.44.4.7

Moll, L. C., Amanti, C., Neff, D., & Gonzalez, N. (1992). Funds of knowledge for teaching: Using a qualitative approach to connect homes and classrooms. *Theory into Practice*, 31(2), 132–141. https://doi.org/10.1080/00405849209543534

Muhammad, G. E. (2015). Searching for full vision: Writing representations of African American adolescent girls. *Research in the Teaching of English*, 49(3), 224–247. https://doi.org/10.58680/rte201526868

Muhammad, G. E. (2020). *Cultivating genius: An equity framework for culturally and historically responsive literacy*. Scholastic.

Nelson, E. T., & Opatz, M. O. (2023). Mirrors, windows, and mentors: Developing critical mentor text sets to cultivate students' writer identities. *English Journal*, 113(1), 75–83. https://doi.org/10.58680/ej202332633

Norton, B. (2013). *Identity and language learning: Extending the conversation*. Multilingual Matters.

Otheguy, R., García, O., & Reid, W. (2015). Clarifying translanguaging and deconstructing named languages: A perspective from linguistics. *Applied Linguistics Review*, 6(3), 281–307. https://doi.org/10.1515/applirev-2015-0014

Petrone, R., Mirra, N., Goodman, S., & Garcia, A. (2022). Youth civic participation and activism (youth participatory action research). In J. Z. Pandya, R. A. Mora, J. H. Alford, N. A. Golden, & R. Santiago de Roock (Eds.), *The handbook of critical literacies* (pp. 50–60). Routledge.

Salazar, M. C. (2010). Pedagogical stances of high school ESL teachers: Huelgas in high school ESL classrooms. *Bilingual Research Journal*, 33(1), 111–124.

Salazar, M. (2013). A humanizing pedagogy: Reinventing the principles and practice of education as a journey toward liberation. *Review of Research in Education*, 37(1), 121–148. https://doi.org/10.3102/0091732X12464032

Solórzano, D. G., & Yosso, T. J. (2002). Critical race methodology: Counter-storytelling as an analytical framework for education research. *Qualitative Inquiry*, 8(1), 23–44. https://doi.org/10.1177/107780040200800103

Sperling, M., & Woodlief, L. (1997). Two classrooms, two writing communities: Urban and suburban tenth-graders learning to write. *Research in the Teaching of English*, 31(2), 205–239. http://dx.doi.org/10.58680/rte19973881

Stewart, M.A., & Hansen-Thomas, H. (2016). Sanctioning a space for translanguaging in the secondary English classroom: A case of a transnational youth. *Research in the Teaching of English*, 50(4), 450–472. www.jstor.org/stable/24889944

Woodard, R., Vaughan, A., & Coppola, R. (2020). Writing beyond "the four corners": Adolescent girls writing by, in, from, and for bodies in school. *Journal of Literacy Research*, 52(1), 6–31. https://doi.org/10.1177/1086296x19896496

Zoch, M., Marhatta, P., Vetter, A., Faircloth, B., & McDaniel, D. (2021). "Let your voice lead you": Critical community-building to support the writing of recently resettled youth. *Multicultural Perspectives*, 23(4), 241–247. https://doi.org/10.1080/15210960.2021.1979404

2

Translanguaging

Translanguaging Writing Pedagogy to Leverage Multilingual Writers' Funds of Knowledge and Identity

Margarita Gómez and Joanna W. Wong

On a fall afternoon, Ms. Egan shares the English language arts lesson objective to prepare sixth-grade students for writing (All names are pseudonyms). The class has been reading Names/Nombres by Julia Alvarez (1985). Ms. Egan explains, "Today's objective is to determine the theme of Names/Nombres." She continues, "First, let's define this term. Can someone tell me what theme means?"

A student raises her hand and offers, "I want to tell you the answer—theme is the lesson of the story." Another student says, "Necesito copiar," to which Ms. Egan responds, "You can do that from the binder," and continues the lesson.

"In Names/Nombres, Julia Alvarez suggests writing a list of your different identities," Ms Egan says. "For example, I'm a teacher, sister, daughter, dog-owner, and friend. Now, I'd like you to write a list of your different identities."

Next, Ms. Egan asks students to share their identities with their partners. The volume in the room rises as students begin to talk, switching fluidly between Spanish and English. Ms. Egan interjects, "So my next question is:

When do you identify with one identity and when with another? Do you act differently in those identities? Turn and talk to your neighbors."

I [Margarita, first author] listen in and overhear two girls discussing their national and cultural identities. One says, "Mi familia somos de El Salvador, habló Español en mi casa con mi familia y escuchamos la musica de mi pais y de los jovenes." Her partner agrees in Spanish and adds, "Yeah, I don't like American culture, me gusta más la cultura Latina."

Ms. Egan, having heard the girls' conversation, responds, "Perhaps it's not just the culture, but the age group." She then brings the class back to the lesson objective: "So, theme is the main idea of a written work."

Next, Ms. Egan asks students to consider the theme of Names/Nombres. "Write what you think the theme of Names/Nombres is and support your opinion with text. Explain why you think what you think." Students continue their conversations, drawing on both named languages—Spanish and English—before turning to their writing.

This classroom vignette is an example of translanguaging pedagogy in action, as enacted by Ms. Egan—a participant in a two-year professional learning project facilitated by Margarita, first author. The project brought together teachers at a Spanish-English dual language K-8 school to collaboratively explore writing instruction through a multilingual lens.

Prior to the project, most participating teachers had implemented dual language pedagogy involving explicit separation of named languages during instruction. However, as we observed children writing, we noticed how students were naturally drawing on their full linguistic repertoires—both in discussions and in their writing—even when this practice was not explicitly encouraged. This sparked curiosity about multilingual writing and prompted further inquiry.

Together, we delved into Escamilla et al.'s (2014) work on the Literacy Squared project and Beeman and Urow's (2012) *Teaching for Biliteracy*. These texts offered new perspectives for seeing children and their multilingual practices—not as parallel, compartmentalized processes, but as part of a holistic approach to meaning-making. Through ongoing dialogue, reflection, and shared classroom inquiry, teachers began to shift how they understood and valued students' multilingual languaging—their use of language as a verb, or the active use of their full linguistic repertoire.

Teachers noticed students fluidly drawing on their linguistic repertoires for various purposes. For instance, a first grader wrote "barras de monos" rather than monkey bars, translating directly from her oral language experience. In other cases, students created inventive approximations—like *ansemra* for encima—(on top of) based on how the word sounded in conversation (Gómez Zisselsberger & González, 2019). Most often, however, students engaged in translingual writing simply because it was just what came naturally.

As teachers began to look and listen "more deeply" to their students, many began to see that parallel monolingual rubrics (Spanish-only and English-only rubrics) could not capture the richness of the languaging that occurred. As the vignette demonstrates, Ms. Egan normalized multilingual students' use of their full linguistic repertoire. There was no interruption to instruction when the girls used translanguaging, and no request for direct translations. In sum, teachers learned to expand their views of multilingual writing. Many teachers saw that multilingual and multimodal (drawings, pictures, etc.) resources contributed to students' development of their linguistic repertoires and their unique writing trajectories.

Our work, as literacy researchers and teacher educators, focuses on expansive pedagogy for multilingual learners (MLs) with the goals of achieving racial and linguistic justice. We are situated in the U.S., a multilingual and multicultural home for many children, where there is an urgency to better prepare teachers to serve racialized MLs. During 2018–2022, 32% of children (ages 0–8) lived in multilingual households (Migrant Policy Institute). In 2021, 21.3% (11,698) of school-aged children (ages 5–17) spoke a language other than English at home (Federal Interagency Forum on Child and Family Statistics). The four most commonly spoken languages by emergent bilingual (EB) children were: Spanish (76.4%), Arabic (2.5%), Chinese (1.8%), and Vietnamese (1.4%) (National Center for Education Statistics, 2024). We use the term *emergent bilinguals* to affirm and value multilingual students' dynamic languaging practices and problematize the deficit label of *English learners*, which positions students only according to their use of English (García, 2009).

In this chapter, we address how taking a translanguaging stance, "a teacher's belief that a bilingual student has one holistic language repertoire" (García et al., 2017, pp. 49–50), toward writing instruction is a humanizing pedagogy that leverages MLs' cultural backgrounds and linguistic repertoires for effective expression. We begin by providing a background on translanguaging pedagogy and writing instruction, then we present three big ideas for translanguaging writing pedagogy, followed by recommendations for putting these ideas into practice. Finally, we end this chapter with questions for educators to consider as they take up translanguaging writing pedagogy.

Translanguaging Writing Pedagogy: Leveraging Students' Multilingualism and Funds of Knowledge

We advocate for translanguaging writing pedagogy because it actively counters the linguistic discrimination racialized MLs face in schools and mainstream society. Too often, MLs are stigmatized for their multilingualism, expected to replace their primary language with English. This devaluing of linguistic diversity, coupled with a pervasive deficit orientation toward racialized MLs (Flores & Rosa, 2015), often leads to basic skills-focused writing instruction, limiting opportunities for MLs to fully participate in learning and advance as writers (Fu, 2009; McCarthey, 2008; Menken, 2006; Wong, 2016; Wright & Choi, 2006). These harmful perceptions of multilingualism for racialized students expose the deep inequity of a system that simultaneously celebrates and rewards the same practices when exhibited by white students.

Teaching for equity requires pedagogy and policies that normalize multilingualism enacted through the employment of intellectually challenging, culturally sustaining curriculum (Paris, 2012). A multilingual, culturally sustaining framework works actively to shift monolingual ideologies that perpetuate English-only policies, linguistic discrimination, and myths of a "standard" language (Lippi-Green, 2011). To enact such pedagogy, teachers must learn about, affirm, and integrate their MLs' *funds of knowledge*—the cultural and linguistic practices in students' homes and communities (Moll et al., 1992). Such a shift requires educators to engage in critical self-reflection, examining their own beliefs about language and multilingual students (Athanases et al., 2019). Educators must also commit to enacting Culturally Sustaining Writing Pedagogy (CSWP) that leverages students' full linguistic repertoires (Espinosa & Ascenzi-Moreno, 2021; Fu, 2009; Gómez & Collins, 2021; Wong, Athanases, & Banes, 2020). Teachers who welcome MLs' complex identities and invite students to employ their languaging practices in fluid and dynamic ways for meaning-making and expression enact *translanguaging pedagogy* (García et al., 2017).

Translanguaging as a Critical Humanizing Approach to Writing

In the past decade, research on translanguaging as a pedagogical practice has shown positive results for working with MLs. Some literature on translanguaging emphasizes how it may be employed to scaffold MLs' writing practices (Salmerón, 2022). However, viewing translanguaging as a scaffold toward English development still limits the MLs' full potential when their full linguistic repertoires are not completely valued, which includes students' identities and lived experiences. Critical humanizing translanguaging approaches center both the external and internal language practices that a person uses as valid, normalizing the use of their full linguistic repertoires—defined as a person's complete set of communicative resources, including their use of vocabulary, grammatical structures, rhetorical organization, multimodal thinking, identity, and lived experiences (García et al., 2017). Thus, to recognize students' full humanity, one must adopt a translanguaging stance— an ideological commitment to honoring a person's right to express themselves through their full linguistic repertoire. García, Johnson, and Seltzer (2017) emphasize the importance of this stance as foundational for enacting translanguaging pedagogy. From this more expansive, critical perspective, teachers can design lessons with more flexibility and intention, responding to students in humanizing and culturally sustaining ways (García et al., 2017; García-Mateus et al., 2022; Land, 2022; Tian & Lau, 2022; Zisselsberger, 2016).

When we employ Critical Humanizing Writing Pedagogy (CHWP), we actively reject deficit teaching that limits both the student and teacher (Freire, 2005). Our goal is to recognize, honor, and sustain students' funds of knowledge and resources. When we take a humanizing approach to writing instruction, we disrupt traditional practices and co-construct knowledge with students. We work with students to examine power relations and student agency, addressing issues that are important to learners. For example, Ms. B., a fifth-grade teacher, integrated her students' voices into the writing curriculum as part of CHWP (Zisselsberger, 2016). She created space for students to draw on their full linguistic repertoires to make sense of how they were learning to write in English. While using mentor texts to introduce target genres, she invited students to lead translingual discussions and incorporate their cultural and linguistic identities into their writing. In their persuasive writing, students actively addressed topics important to them. Ms. B. trusted students to use tools for exploring genre structures and listened to students' ideas and concerns. As a consequence, students felt comfortable translanguaging, such as code-meshing across languages and dialects, including Spanish, English, and Black Language (Baker-Bell, 2020).

Another example of CHWP comes from a fourth-grade teacher who used design thinking—a flexible, feedback-driven process for addressing issues and solving problems—to explore purpose and audience with her students. She provided them with choices that encouraged flexible thinking and helped them to focus on the message they wanted to communicate to their envisioned audience (Land, 2022). The teacher and student worked toward mutual humanization through agentive and liberating practices that highlighted how students wanted to change their worlds. The practices that brought about agentive writing were to allow students to generate topics of interest that were either fun or had social justice lenses, versus writing to respond to literature or standardized prompts. Students were then agentive in generating topics such as having healthy drinking water or taking a stance against the production of weapons, such as bombs. The teacher and students were able to think about their audience to leverage their message (Land, 2022). Another practice the teacher took up was to focus on discussing language choices as related to the audience's needs, and this provided more creativity in the revision process, rather than focusing on correctness in language/grammar, and form. As they shared their writing with peers in other grades or other target audiences, they came up with plans for addressing questions asked by the desired audience and used that to develop empathy with the reader, moving away from a decontextualized checklist. These examples pave the way for teachers to develop humanizing translanguaging pedagogy that honors the critical thoughts, voices, cultures, and languages of students.

The Expansive Affordances of Multilingual, Multicultural, and Multimodal Practice in Critical Humanizing Writing Pedagogy

When we integrate a translanguaging framework with a critical humanizing approach to writing, we expand possibilities for student and teacher expression. Features of a translanguaging stance include multilingual, multicultural, and multimodal aspects of languaging, which require innovative and student-centered teaching (Nuñez, 2019; Tian & Lau, 2022). The key to student-centered teaching that values students' funds of knowledge is inviting families and their approaches to the classroom. Often, multilingual families are not included in the instructional planning of their children's language and literacy development in schools. When we collaborate with families to include their approaches and funds of knowledge, we are enacting CHWP (Nuñez, 2019).

Teachers may leverage families' home literacy practices by building on students' everyday use of digital tools such as tablets and phones to integrate MLs' full repertoires. One example of this humanizing approach can be found in Idalia Nuñez's work with three Mexican mothers to support their children's bilingualism and biliteracy development (2019). The mothers used a myriad of complex transmodal events. For instance, one mother asked her children to respond in Spanish to text messages from family members; these children used oral and written modes to convey the mother's message. Another mother showed movies in English with Spanish captions on a tablet to support her children's bilingualism. To extend their children's learning through play, this mother purchased toys associated with the movies. Children's play included movement, visual, auditory modes, and using the English they learned from the movies. Nuñez recommends that teachers invite families to document the various ways they use multimodal tools for language and literacy development. Teachers can also bring families together for storytelling and offer resources for families to develop collaborative partnerships in support of multiliteracy.

In translanguaging classrooms, we may find that all students have more opportunities to participate in meaning-making through multilingual, multimodal writing. Teaching writing with a translanguaging stance requires us to use a variety of tools to engage students to process word meanings through drawing, discussion, written definitions, and meaningful uses of vocabulary. For example, Chinese-English bilingual third graders' engaged in complex integration of languages and expressive modes, using visual compositions alongside oral narratives—part of a language current that often goes unseen, but is always present. This combination of multimodal meaning-making and processing led to increased Chinese-English bilingual student engagement and use of Pinyin and Chinese for writing (Tian & Lau, 2022).

In the context of multilingual learners, "corriente" (Spanish for "current" or "flow")—a concept central to translanguaging—refers to the dynamic, underlying, ever-present language current—whether at the surface or just below it—that MLs draw on to learn, engage with content, and make sense of the world (García et al., 2017). Accordingly, multiple languages should not be viewed as threats but recognized as powerful tools for deeper understanding and meaning-making. Tapping into students' corriente involves engaging their physical, mental, and emotional knowledge—what is often referred to as embodied knowledge. Drawing on the corriente contributes to students' deep engagement with language expression, both oral and written. Classroom discussions, drawings, and collaborations can contribute to analyzing and challenging arbitrary policies around language and implicit principles contained in beliefs about language and language learning. A huge takeaway is the importance of understanding students' languaging as a complex set of interrelated features that are not limited to words, but include the embodied, multimodal, multicultural, and multilingual processes involved in language use and writing (Tian & Lau, 2022).

When we integrate critical translanguaging humanizing pedagogies into our writing instruction, we hold an expansive view of multilingual writing instruction. We are able to transform and challenge dominant language ideologies and structures that perpetuate deficit views of MLs and their languaging practices. Critical translanguaging approaches to the teaching and assessment of writing are not only liberatory for the student but also for us as teachers. Teaching writing in these ways cultivates student voice and agency and supports students' writing goals. Additionally, we intentionally create safe spaces for our students so they are excited to bring their full, authentic selves to their writing and to identify meaningful writing goals.

Pedagogical Implications

Many educators are ready to embrace translanguaging in writing instruction but wonder how to begin. In this section, we present three interrelated concepts that we identify as foundational to enacting translanguaging writing pedagogy: (1) creating a positive and welcoming multilingual learning environment that expands learning opportunities for all learners and removes curricular and linguistic barriers; (2) integrating MLs' funds of knowledge and sustaining multilingualism as a cultural and linguistic resource for writing that honors MLs' identities and voices; and (3) employing strength-based writing assessment practices that recognize MLs' use of their linguistic repertoire and potential.

Big Idea 1: Create a Positive and Welcoming Multilingual Learning Environment

Student engagement and motivation are critical for student learning, risk-taking, and writing development. As teachers of MLs, it is important for us to consider how our classroom environment, interactions with MLs, and the curriculum reflect diverse perspectives and languaging practices.

One way to ensure our classroom environment values multilingualism and supports translingual writing practices is to have classroom labels, environmental print, and word walls in students' home languages. As we learn about students' backgrounds, we may invite MLs to contribute to these labels with words in their home languages. This models for all students on how to be welcoming language learners who affirm all students' linguistic backgrounds.

Our classroom libraries should be vibrant with diverse texts that include topics of student interests, along with multilingual characters and protagonists. When we create classroom libraries with culturally and linguistically sustaining texts, students may be more encouraged to read and explore new worlds and ideas through texts. Students' reading habits influence their writing development. As students read more widely, they gain increased exposure to diverse sentence structures, vocabulary, and ideas for writing. When MLs read texts by culturally diverse authors, they may come to see how their voices contribute to collective knowledge in the classroom and beyond, and identify as being authors themselves.

Moreover, inviting MLs to write in both their primary languages and English allows them to demonstrate their thinking while developing increasingly complex writing skills and content knowledge. Requiring multilingual writers to only express themselves in English limits their participation, thinking, and expression while increasing students' frustration (Fu, 2009). Intentionally leveraging MLs' dynamic linguistic repertoires so they are fully and meaningfully engaged in all writing opportunities is one positive benefit of adopting a translanguaging writing pedagogy. In fact, decades of research document how MLs (Edelsky, 1986; Fu, 2009; Hudelson, 1984; Reyes, 1991; Samway, 2006) are able to begin expressing their thoughts using what they know of English much earlier than imagined, particularly when they are supported to use translingual practices. When we encourage students' full linguistic repertoires, we recognize MLs are capable members of the classroom community.

Big Idea 2: Valuing Dynamic Multilingual and Multicultural Identities and Voices

Our commitment to developing knowledge of students is a sign of trust and care. Teaching from a translanguaging stance requires us to invest in learning about students' lives, communities, and languaging practices with the goal of integrating this knowledge into the curriculum and classroom (e.g., interest inventories, multilingual texts, family and community members as expert guest speakers). By centering students' lives in the curriculum, we cultivate a positive, multilingual learning context that values our dynamic MLs (Espinosa & Ascenzi-Moreno, 2021; Laman, 2013; Zapata & Laman, 2016). Our use of translanguaging writing pedagogy demonstrates trust in our MLs. We show MLs that we believe in their communicative competence and recognize their full humanity. We trust that elementary multilingual writers "know the best language form to use to appropriately present their ideas and feelings" (Fu, 2009, p. 75). Consequently, multilingual writers who employ translanguaging develop increasingly sophisticated metalinguistic awareness, informing their linguistic decisions in relation to the writing task, purpose, and audience. MLs employ "code-switching" as a problem-solving strategy when faced with a challenging linguistic activity (Fu, 2009). Trusting MLs is essential to believing in their capacity.

We honor MLs' cultural heritages, experiences, intersectional identities, and voices by teaching writing with a translanguaging framework. These practices position multilingualism as a resource for writing and stand in stark contrast to traditional literacy curricula and the Common Core State Standards, which fail to center multilingual students' lives and languages. We can begin this work by valuing dynamic multilingual voices and multicultural identities through close analysis of students' writing, documentation of their languaging practices, and listening to MLs' corriente. The translanguaging corriente (García et al., 2017), with its dynamic and fluid enactment of MLs' "funds of knowledge" (Moll et al., 1992) and the "funds of identity" (Esteban Guitart & Moll, 2014) is nuanced and complex. Thus, teachers seeking to integrate MLs' corriente require a nuanced understanding of each ML's unique language system— their *idiolect*, defined as "a person's own unique, personal language, the person's mental grammar that emerges in interaction with other speakers and enables the person's use of language" (Otheguy et al., 2015, p. 289). For example, when a student decides to fluidly use their full linguistic repertoires to respond to a writing prompt about a friend and they write, "Un dia [mi amiga] y yo fue a la maestra Ms. A. clase. Dispues when nosotros got there, nosotros got our tabletas" (see Figure 2.1), the student is using their idiolect, making linguistic choices based upon a variety of personal and contextual information, including the student's linguistic repertoire, enrollment in a dual language school, and knowledge of the multilingual audience. This enables MLs to make meaning in ways that reflect their unique linguistic and grammatical system and their voice.

If we think of a person's idiolect as a deconstructed cake, it is the underlying invisible ingredients that make up each uniquely flavored cake, as each person has their own unique flavor profile or ingredient combinations that, when bound together, make up the cake (Leider & Proctor, 2024). A cake might share some ingredients, like vanilla, with another cake, but the amounts might be different, leading to differences in how the flavor profile shows up in each finished cake. Each unique voice is expressed through speech and writing, reflecting the identity (or flavor profile) of the speaker/writer (cake). When we open up spaces for MLs to reflect their idiolects, we make space for their humanity in our classrooms and break away from arbitrary boundaries. Valuing MLs' corriente, that fluid use of repertoire, requires that the listener work juntos—together—alongside MLs to understand how the idiolects are expressions of MLs' strategic choices and identities (or layers of flavor profiles in their own specific cake).

Students and teachers have opportunities to see and hear the world with a wider perspective when teachers tap into students' funds of knowledge and funds of identity to shape writing instruction. Students' process and products of their compositions offer novel windows and mirrors (Bishop, 1990) for their audience. Students may recognize their own linguistic practices and experiences in their peers' writing, finding affirmation through this mirror. All students have windows of opportunity to learn new languaging practices and ways of knowing as peers and teachers share their translingual writing. Translanguaging writing pedagogy may cultivate students' curiosity about new languages and cultural practices. Additionally, this approach to writing instruction inherently fosters creative and complex expression because translingual writing practices cannot be reduced to skills or be scripted.

When we commit to sustaining multilingualism and multicultural identities through employing translanguaging writing pedagogy, we advance critical consciousness. We work with our students to actively disrupt linguistic discrimination and counter authoritative English-dominant policies and practices in their everyday writing practices. Through these conscious acts to affirm linguistic diversity, students may be more able to recognize social injustice and act for positive change.

Big Idea 3: Strengths-Based Writing Assessment Practices

Strengths-based writing assessment practices are a critical component of translanguaging humanizing pedagogy, essential for noticing how students bring their full linguistic repertoires to their multilingual, multicultural, and often multimodal written communication. When teachers employ assessment practices without recognizing students' strengths and identities, they fail to support and sustain students' full range of competencies. Opportunities for students to enact their full linguistic selves and draw on the translanguaging *corriente*—the natural flow of their linguistic and cultural lived experiences and identities expressed through writing—must be accompanied by assessment practices that are flexible and nuanced enough to capture students' essence and genius (Muhammad, 2022).

We enact strengths-based writing assessment practices by showing students that all forms of communication and ideas, whether oral or written, are valid to normalize multilingualism (Zapata & Laman, 2016). We can do this by engaging students in purposeful writing assessment practices through joint negotiation and mutual understanding of the human experience (Kinloch, 2018). From this more liberated humanizing stance, we can look more closely at multilinguals' writing to see what it reveals. Strengths-based approaches to analyzing student writing development begin with a close analysis of student work (Athanases, Wahleithner, & Bennett, 2013; Wong, Athanases, & Houk, 2024). Our close looking is guided by a decolonized framework, so we begin by valuing what students have accomplished. The close analysis should involve deep knowledge of students and their use of their idiolects (Otheguy et al., 2015)—their personal, unique mental grammar—to ensure that multilinguals' full, authentic selves are included in what is observed. These analytical practices can lead to socially just assessments that document students' achievements—especially in relation to MLs' purpose, audience, and intended outcomes for their writing.

Pedagogical Practices

Understanding Linguistic Power and Privilege: Critical Self-Reflection on Language Ideologies

In our work as literacy-focused teacher educators, we have found that enactments of translanguaging and CSWP require educators to develop language awareness (Athanases, Banes, & Wong, 2015; Athanases et al., 2019). This awareness is essential for understanding how language ideologies—beliefs and values that individuals and groups hold about linguistic practices (Kroskrity, 2004; Schieffelin, Woolard, & Kroskrity,

1998)—impact instructional decision-making and literacy assessment practices (Gómez & Collins, 2021; Wong, 2023). To begin this important work of interrogating language ideologies, we must first recognize the privileged status of the English language. This includes questioning and critiquing the power and privileges afforded to certain forms and speakers of English—both in the U.S. and globally—across political, educational, and economic spheres, and examining how these power structures uphold white supremacy culture.

At the same time, we examine our beliefs about multilinguals and multilingualism. We consider how MLs of color and their linguistic practices are racialized and oppressed within traditional schooling practices. Flores and Rosa (2015) provide a helpful lens for understanding raciolinguistic ideologies—how race and language are conflated in ways that grant power and privilege to white speakers while perpetuating linguistic discrimination toward people of color. For example, when a Black student writes, "We ready for y'all" in an assignment for school, some educators might mark this as deficient or an error. However, when the National Football League uses "We ready" in a television commercial promoting the 2018–2019 playoffs, it is viewed as an acceptable tool for entertainment and profits (Gómez & Collins, 2021). Equipped with these critical lenses, we are able to examine how language ideologies are reflected in writing pedagogy, and shift towards strengths-based orientations of our MLs. We argue this shift is necessary for employing critical and humanizing translanguaging pedagogy in our writing instruction.

We recommend that educators engage in critical self-reflexive inquiry into language use as a necessary step toward developing language awareness and adopting a translanguaging stance. This practice helps us examine how and why we use diverse languaging practices across contexts, and how language ideologies shape how we position ourselves and others. Joanna, the second author, collaborated on a four-year program of research on critical self-reflexive inquiry into language and culture in an upper-division undergraduate course for future teachers and students pursuing education minors and other majors (see Athanases, Banes, & Wong, 2015; Athanases, Wong, & Banes, 2016; Athanases et al., 2019; Banes et al., 2016; Wong, Athanases, & Banes, 2020). To cultivate language awareness, students read and discussed Amy Tan's essay, "Mother Tongue" (1999), in which she reflects on the different Englishes she and her mother use, as well as their experiences with linguistic discrimination in the U.S. This text along with other readings focused on linguistic diversity—such as Nieto and Bode's (2012) *Affirming Diversity: The Sociopolitical Context of Education*—grounded students' self-reflexive inquiry as they situated themselves as language users within the U.S. sociopolitical context.

Critical self-reflexive inquiry can begin with a "Personal Language Inventory" (see Banes et al., 2016). First, read Tan's "Mother Tongue" essay and pay attention to themes of language use tied to intimacy, privilege, and discrimination. Then, begin your Personal Language Inventory by documenting ways in which you use varieties of language(s) in different contexts within one week (e.g., home, classroom, colleagues, friends, etc.), and consider the experiences/themes raised by Tan. Next, engage in critical reflection on your experiences as a language user. Consider the implications of your diverse languaging practices in different contexts, how you perceive others, and how others perceive you. Have you ever felt judged as inferior based on your language use? Finally, consider how your beliefs and experiences with language impact your teaching and students' learning in your classroom.

From our experience working with teachers committed to CSWP, we've found that educators require safe spaces to openly and honestly unpack their own languaging and writing experiences—including what was valued, what was not, by whom, and why (Wong, 2023). We understand that equity-focused teachers may struggle with shifting away from notions of "Standard English" and what counts as writing. In a professional learning project led by Joanna, teacher participants embraced the idea of translanguaging pedagogy and how it would serve their MLs, but at the same time, they worried about how translingual writing would be perceived by others. Participants needed time, critical discussion, reflective opportunities, engagement with literature and examples, and compassionate guidance to begin unlearning oppressive raciolinguistic ideologies internalized through socialization in schools, homes, and communities. Over an academic year, teachers were able to develop more expansive language ideologies to integrate and value MLs' languaging practices along with their own (Wong, 2023).

Learning from and with Multilingual Student Writers

As teachers developed their expansive language ideologies and integrated MLs' languaging practices, they provided spaces to acknowledge students' full humanity. In the writing project conducted by Margarita, teachers' expansive ideologies led them to see how translanguaging and students' idiolects were part of their everyday meaning-making practices. This enabled teachers to be more open to recognizing students' diverse language repertoires and to going with the students' language flow, their corriente. For example, a sixth-grade Spanish language arts teacher provided an open-ended writing prompt inviting students to use their language(s) to write about a friend. Students responded using their idiolects: some wrote entirely in Spanish, others in English, and some used a combination of both languages. We share two samples to illustrate how MLs draw on their full linguistic repertoires.

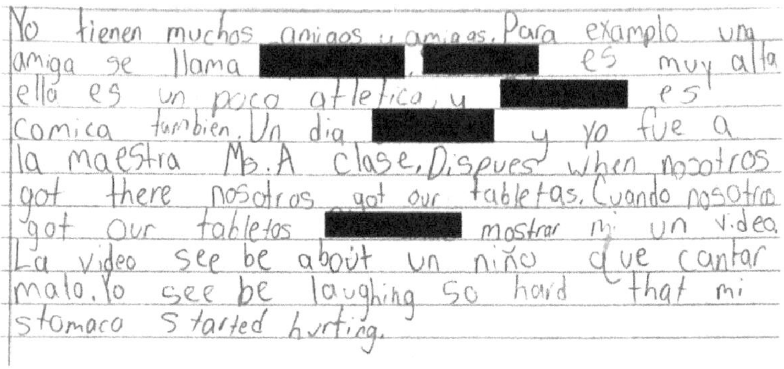

> Yo tienen muchos amigos y amigas. Para examplo un amiga se llama ▓▓▓. ▓▓▓ es muy alta ella es un poco atletico, y ▓▓▓ es comica tambien. Un dia ▓▓▓ y yo fue a la maestra Ms. A clase. Dispues when nosotros got there nosotros got our tabletas. Cuando nosotros got our tabletos ▓▓▓ mostrar mi un video. La video see be about un niño que cantar malo. Yo see be laughing so hard that mi stomaco started hurting.

Figure 2.1 Roberto's writing.

In Figure 2.1, we see that Roberto wrote comfortably about one of his friends. He describes her and some characteristics and traits she possesses, like being tall, athletic, and funny. To elaborate on how she is funny, Roberto describes how she showed him a funny video in class and how watching this video made him laugh so hard that his stomach started to hurt. We can see that Roberto seamlessly uses his entire repertoire to convey his message.

Similarly, Tracy (see Figure 2.2) used her entire repertoire to share about her BFF (best friend forever). Tracy shares that her friendship is nuanced and complicated. She writes that they went on vacation together, but despite that, she wonders if they are friends sometimes. She also shared that her parents sometimes like her friend, which indicates that it

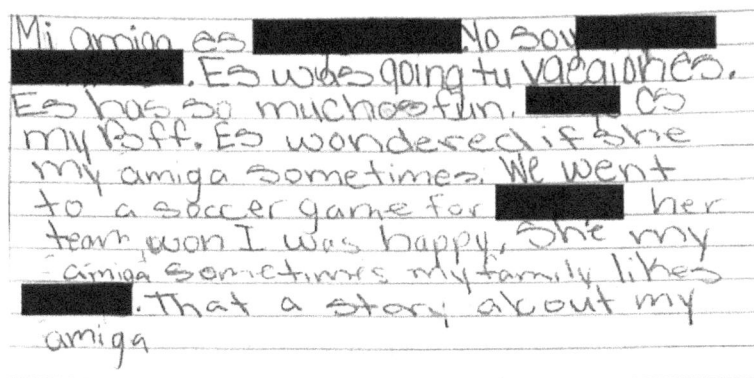

Figure 2.2 Tracy's writing.

is possible that sometimes they do not like her. What we see here is that the student uses her full linguistic repertoire to explore and express these aspects of her friendship and her feelings toward her friend. Roberto and Tracy could have selected to write entirely in one named language or another, as some of their peers did, yet they chose to explore their ideas, feelings, and relationships using their idiolects. We learn about the characteristics of their friendships and the ways these friendships are important in their lives.

One challenge in creating spaces for translingual writing is understanding and supporting students' use of idiolects—especially when some or all of their languaging practices may be unfamiliar to the teacher. We draw on other authors and projects that help shed light on this important concern (CUNY-NYSIEB, Espinosa & Ascenzi-Moreno, 2021; García et al., 2017). The City University of New York, New York State Initiative on Emergent Bilinguals, www.cuny-nysieb.org, provides a wealth of experiences and examples for educators to learn from. For example, their classroom video series on teaching bilinguals (even if you are not one) shares how monolingual teachers provide spaces for multilingual communication, thinking, learning, and writing. In this video series, Ms. Chapman-Santiago shares her experiences as a middle school teacher who does not share the same linguistic background as her students, yet still encourages translingual writing, which allows dynamic languaging practices (García et al., 2017). She describes this as part of the process of getting to know her students. Finally, Espinosa and Ascenzi-Moreno (2021) provide guidance for teachers on how to cultivate multilingual reading and writing spaces—they describe multiple strategies, activities, and suggestions for professional development to employ translanguaging pedagogy in collaboration with teacher colleagues, professionals, families, and community members.

Taking a Strengths-Based Lens to Assess Translingual Writing

When we genuinely strive to learn about and understand students' languaging as part of their identity, we frame our writing instruction and assessment practices with a strengths-based lens. By seeing and teaching the whole person, we understand the limitations of the boxes and squares of traditional rubrics that call for writing in only one language. We recognize that these rubrics do not capture MLs' full essence. As part of an ongoing professional development project, Margarita worked with a dual-language Catholic K-8 school to develop strengths-based writing instruction and assessment (Gómez & Collins, 2021; Gómez & Collins, 2022; Gómez Zisselsberger & Ramos González, 2019). Teachers, paraprofessionals, administrators, and Margarita engaged in professional development sessions focused on addressing both the academic and sociocultural aspects of writing. We examined characteristics of parallel bilingualism (Escamilla et al., 2014) and delved into translanguaging to move beyond the named languages. Teachers worked to examine rubrics that might capture the "both/and" they were seeing in students' writing (as illustrated in the samples above). Initially, teachers adapted rubrics that identified writing traits (Spandel, 2012) in both languages separately and included checklist items from the Literacy Squared project (Escamilla et al., 2014) (see Gómez Zisselsberger & Ramos González, 2019 for specific examples). In the last year of the project, some teachers moved toward adding spaces within the rubrics to document how students were languaging, noticing similarities and differences among traits, and using the rubric spaces to capture dynamic language use in a different way (see Table 2.1 as an example, and for more on this work and the rubric created see Gómez & Collins, 2022).

Table 2.1 Writing Assessment Rubric With Spaces for Learner Input and Co-Assessment

	Develops ideas fully through: • details • examples • reasons • explanations	Provides some: • details • examples • reasons • explanations	Provides few: • details • examples • reasons • explanations	Does not develop: • details • examples • reasons • explanations
Ideas				
Cultural Funds of Knowledge Present				
Organization	• clear focus, easily read, fluent • logical organization	• generally focused • logical organization	• limited focus • weakness in organization	• does not maintain clear focus • lacks a plan of organization
Cultural Organization Patterns Present				
Sentence Fluency & Word Choice	• varied sentence structure • vivid language/vocabulary • Takes risks with sophisticated vocabulary	• some sentence variety • appropriate language	• simple sentences • occasionally uses inaccurate language	• lack of sentence structure • frequently uses inaccurate language
Code Meshing				
Mechanics	• Makes few or no errors in spelling, grammar, and punctuation	• Makes minor errors in spelling, grammar, and punctuation that do not interfere with communication	• Makes errors in spelling, grammar, and punctuation that interfere with communication	• Makes errors in spelling, grammar, and punctuation that seriously interfere with communication
Phonetic & Syntactic Transference				

To assess MLs' writing with an equity focus, we must evaluate whether assessment tools separate language(s) from students' "funds of knowledge", "funds of identity", and unique meaning-making practices, or idiolects. Writing rubrics, checklists, graphic organizers, and supports should reflect the purpose and needs of the multilingual writer. When assessments focus on named languages separately, they bifurcate the unique linguistic profile of MLs, fragmenting their potential for full meaning-making and expression—and ultimately constrain what students may produce. Instead, we advocate for teachers to think about modifying or creating their own rubrics to include spaces that reflect students' unique idiolects. Rubrics often include traits of writing, such as ideas/content, organization, voice, word choice, sentence fluency, and grammar (Spandel, 2012). However, to recognize MLs' full authentic selves, assessments must include flexibility. To expand writing assessment in ways that fully capture students' writing development and leverage their potential, we can engage in joint assessment with students to identify:

- How MLs generate their ideas
- What cultural and linguistic features shape the organization of their writing to meet its purpose
- How MLs' use of idiolects enhances and conveys their true voice and influences their word choice
- What aspects of languaging are evident in sentence fluency
- How MLs use grammar to convey meaning

MLs benefit from more open, flexible instruction and assessment practices that cultivate their full humanity and identity. This requires teachers to reimagine writing assessments to capture students' idiolects and reflect anti-racist and anti-biased language ideologies.

Conclusion

In this chapter, we propose approaching writing instruction and assessment from a translanguaging CHWP perspective. When we take this perspective, we embrace MLs' use of their full cultural and linguistic repertoire and their idiolect to see each ML's full humanity as writers. To employ this writing pedagogy, we must develop a translanguaging stance—one that understands idiolects and languaging from an expansive framework, and cultivate strengths-based language ideologies that normalize and value multilingualism.

We can begin by asking ourselves some important questions:

(1) What might it look like if students were encouraged to use their full linguistic repertoires in their writing?
(2) How would the classroom environment become more welcoming for all learners if multilingual writing were evident in labels, anchor charts, bookshelves, and displays?
(3) What message is the student trying to share through their writing, and how can I partner with them to assess how well it meets their goals and speaks to their audience?
(4) How can I assess translingual writing through a lens of equity and justice—one that centers students' strengths, identities, and intentions?
(5) How do I co-create meaningful assessments with and for student writers?

In addition, the book's companion website offers further resources to support teachers in addressing questions such as: What do I do if I don't share the same linguistic repertoires as my students? How do I set up and support multilingual students' full use of their linguistic repertoires and identities? How can I start thinking about the assessment of writing from a strengths-based lens? And what are ways to engage with my colleagues about examining our raciolinguistic ideologies?

In closing, translanguaging CHWP is dynamic and requires teachers' openness and linguistic flexibility to cultivate a strong translanguaging corriente—the natural ebbs and flows of language use—that embraces multilingualism as a resource and norm. When teachers approach writing instruction with a translanguaging framework, they expand writing and learning opportunities for all students, especially MLs. We believe teaching writing through a translanguaging stance actively counters deficit-based educational practices and policies, expands MLs' access to and engagement with meaningful writing opportunities, and honors their funds of knowledge and identity. By taking a critical humanizing translanguaging approach to writing instruction, educators center social and linguistic justice in the curriculum—reimagining classrooms as spaces where all students can write, thrive, and be fully seen.

References

Athanases, S. Z., Wahleithner, J. M., & Bennett, L. H. (2013). Learning about English learners' content understandings through teacher inquiry: Focus on writing. *The New Educator, 9,* 304–327.

Athanases, S. Z., Banes, L. C., & Wong, J. W. (2015). Diverse language profiles: Leveraging resources of potential teachers of color. *Bilingual Research Journal, 38*(1), 65–87. https://doi.org/10.1080/15235882.2015.1017622

Athanases, S. Z., Wong, J. W., & Banes, L. C. (2016). Self-reflexive inquiry in teacher education for diversity: Tapping and leveraging resources for future language teaching. In P. Hayworth & C. Craig (Eds.), *The career trajectories of English language teachers* (pp. 115–128). Symposium Books.

Athanases, S. Z., Banes, L. C., Wong, J. W., & Martinez, D. C. (2019). Exploring linguistic diversity from the inside out: Implications of self-reflexive inquiry for teacher education. *Journal of Teacher Education, 70*(5), 581–596. https://doi.org/10.1177/0022487118778838

Baker-Bell, A. (2020). *Linguistic justice: Black language, literacy, identity, and pedagogy.* Routledge.

Banes, L. C., Martinez, D. C., Athanases, S., & Wong, J. W. (2016). Self-reflexive inquiry into language use and beliefs: Toward more expansive language ideologies. *International Multilingual Research Journal, 10*(3), 168–187.

Beeman, K., & Urow, C. (2013). *Teaching for biliteracy: Strengthening bridges between languages.* Philadelphia, PA: Caslon Publishing.

Bishop, R. S. (1990). Mirrors, windows, and sliding glass doors. *Perspectives: Choosing and Using Books for the Classroom, 6*(3), ix–xi.

Edelsky, C. (1986). *Writing in a bilingual program: Había una vez.* Ablex Publishing Corporation.

Escamilla, K., Hopewell, S., Butvilofsky, S., Sparrow, W., Soltero-González, L., Ruiz-Figueroa, O., & Escamilla, M. (2014). *Biliteracy from the start: Literacy squared in action.* Caslon Publishing.

Espinosa, C. M., & Ascenzi-Moreno, L. (2021). *Rooted in strength: Using translanguaging to grow multilingual readers and writers.* Scholastic.

Esteban-Guitart, M., & Moll, L. C. (2014). Funds of identity: A new concept based on the funds of knowledge approach. *Culture & Psychology, 20*(1), 31–48.

Federal Interagency Forum on Child and Family Statistics. *Languages spoken at home and difficulty speaking English.* www.childstats.gov/americaschildren/tables/fam5.asp

Flores, N. (2020). From academic language to language architecture: Challenging raciolinguistic ideologies in research and practice. *Theory into Practice*, 59(1), 22–31. https://doi.org/10.1080/00405841.2019.1665411

Flores, N., & Rosa, J. (2015). Undoing appropriateness: Raciolinguistic ideologies and language diversity in education. *Harvard Educational Review*, 85(2), 149–171.

Freire, P. (2005). *Pedagogy of the oppressed* (30th anniv. ed.; M. B. Ramos, Trans.). New York, NY: Continuum.

Fu, D. (2009). *Writing between languages: How English language learners make the transition to fluency*. Heinemann.

García, O. (2009). Emergent Bilinguals and TESOL: What's in a Name?. *Tesol Quarterly*, 43(2), 322–326.

García, O. (2024). *Beyond the puntos y rayas: Translanguaging and texts*. Literacy Research Association Conference, Atlanta, GA, United States.

García, O., Johnson, S. I., & Seltzer, K. (2017). *The translanguaging classroom: Leveraging student bilingualism for learning*. Caslon.

García-Mateus, S., Henderson, K. L., Téllez-Arsté, M., & Palmer, D. K. (2022). An experienced bilingual Latina teacher and Pre-K Latinx students in the borderlands: Tranalanguagingas humanizing pedagogy. In M. T. Sánchez & O. García (Eds.), *Sin Miedo: Transformative translanguaging espacios: Latinx students and their teachers rompiendo fronteras sin miedo* (pp. 156–179). Multilingual Matters.

Gómez, M., & Collins, K. (2021). Who gets to count as emerging bilinguals? Adapting a holistic writing rubric for all. In N. Flores, A. Tseng, & N. Subtirelu (Eds.), *Bilingualism for all? Raciolinguistic perspectives on dual language education in the United States* (pp. 220–243). Multilingual Matters.

Gómez, M. & Collins, K. (2022). Reimagining writing assessment for socio-and racio-linguistic justice: Acknowledging the use of linguistic repertoires for Black and Latinx students. In Tracey S. Hodges (Ed.), *Handbook of research on writing instruction practices for equitable and effective teaching* (pp. 1–22). IGI Global.

Gómez Zisselsberger, M., & Ramos González, G. (2019). Building teacher capacity using critical reflection. In M. Scanlan, C. Hunter, & E. R. Howard (Eds.), *Culturally and linguistically responsive education: Designing networks that transform schools* (pp. 95–116). Harvard Education Press.

Hudelson, S. (1984). Kan yu ret an rayt en ingles: Children become literate in English as a second language. *TESOL Quarterly*, 18(2), 221–238.

Kinloch, V. (2018). Necessary disruptions: Examining justice, engagement, and humanizing approaches to teaching and teacher education. *Teaching Works*. https://www.teachingworks.org/images/files/TeachingWorks_Kinloch.pdf

Kroskrity, P. V. (2004). Language ideologies. In A. Duranti (Ed.), *A companion to linguistic anthropology* (pp. 496–517). Blackwell.

Laman, T. T. (2013). *From ideas to words: Writing strategies for English language learners*. Heinemann.

Land, C. L. (2022). Recentering purpose and audience as part of a critical, humanizing approach to writing instruction. *Reading Research Quarterly*, 57(1), 37–58.

Leider, C. M., & Proctor, C. P. (2024). Toward a dynamic idiolect: Multilingual perspectives on the "science of reading". *Educational Psychologist*, 59(4), 250–262.

Lippi-Green, R. (2011). *English with an accent: Language, ideology, and discrimination in the United States* (2nd ed.). Routledge.

McCarthey, S. J. (2008). The impact of No Child Left Behind on teachers' writing instruction. *Written Communication*, 25(4), 462–505.

Menken, K. (2006). Teaching to the test: How No Child Left Behind impacts language policy, curriculum, and instruction for English language learners. *Bilingual Research Journal*, 30(2), 521–546.

Migration Policy Institute. (2024, May). *Young dual language learners in the United States and by state*. www.migrationpolicy.org/programs/data-hub/charts/us-state-profiles-young-dls

Moll, L. C., Amanti, C., Neff, D., & Gonzalez, N. (1992). Funds of knowledge for teaching: Using a qualitative approach to connect homes and classrooms. *Theory into Practice*, XXXI(2), 132–141.

Muhammad, G. E. (2022). Cultivating genius and joy in education through historically responsive literacy. *Language Arts*, 99(3), 195–204.

National Center for Education Statistics. (2024). English Learners in public schools. Condition of education. U.S. Department of Education, Institute of Education Sciences, https://nces.ed.gov/programs/coe/indicator/cgf

Nieto, S., & Bode, P. (2012). *Affirming diversity: The sociopolitical context of education*. Pearson.

Nuñez, I. (2019). "Le hacemos la lucha": Learning from madres Mexicanas' multimodal approaches to raising bilingual, biliterate children. *Language Arts*, 97(1), 7–16.

Otheguy, R., García, O., & Reid, W. (2015). Clarifying translanguaging and deconstructing named languages: A perspective from linguistics. *Applied Linguistics Review*, 6(3), 281–307.

Paris, D. (2012). Culturally sustaining pedagogy: A needed change in stance, terminology, and practice. *Educational Researcher*, 41(3), 93–97.

Reyes, M. (1991). A process approach to literacy using dialogue journals and literature logs with second language learners. *Research in the Teaching of English*, 25(3), 291–313.

Salmerón, C. (2022). Elementary translanguaging writing pedagogy: A literature review. *Journal of Literacy Research*, 54(3), 222–246.

Samway, K. (2006). *When English language learners write*. Heinemann.

Schieffelin, B. B., Woolard, K. A., & Kroskrity, P. V. (Eds.). (1998). *Language ideologies: Practice and theory* (Vol. 16). Oxford University Press.

Spandel, V. (2012). *Creating writers: 6 traits, process, workshop, and literature* (6th ed.). Pearson Higher Ed.

Tan, A. (1999). Mother tongue. In S. Gillespie & R. Singleton (Eds.), *Across cultures* (pp. 26–31). Allyn and Bacon.

Tian, Z. (2022). Challenging the 'Dual': Designing translanguaging spaces in a Mandarin-English dual language bilingual education program. *Journal of Multilingual and Multicultural Development*, 43(6), 534–553. https://doi.org/10.1080/01434632.2022.2085732

Tian, Z., & Lau, S. M. C. (2022). Translanguaging flows in Chinese word instruction: Potential critical sociolinguistic engagement with children's artistic representations of Chinese characters. *Pedagogies: An International Journal*, 17(4), 282–302. https://doi.org/10.1080/1554480X.2022.2139261

Wong, J. W. (2016). Leveraging hidden resources to navigate tensions and challenges in writing: A case study of a fourth-grade emergent bilingual student. In L. C. D. Oliveira & T. Silva (Eds.), *Second language writing in elementary classrooms: Instructional issues, content-area writing and teacher education* (pp. 47–66). Palgrave Macmillan.

Wong, J. W. (2023, April). Teachers' Evolving Raciolinguistic Ideologies for Culturally Sustaining Writing Pedagogy [Paper presentation]. American Education Research Association Annual Conference 2023, Chicago, IL.

Wong, J. W., Athanases, S., & Banes, L. C. (2020). Developing as an agentive bilingual teacher: Self-reflexive and student-learning inquiry as teacher education resources. *International Journal of Bilingual Education and Bilingualism*, 23(2), 153–169.

Wong, J. W., Athanases, S., & Houk, J. (2024). From deficit to assets-based perspectives on multilingual learners: A critical inquiry in teacher education. *The Teacher Educator*, https://doi.org/10.1080/08878730.2024.2377778

Woolard, K. A., & Schieffelin, B. B. (1994). Language ideology. *Annual Review of Anthropology*, 23, 55–82.

Wright, W. E., & Choi, D. (2006). The impact of language and high-stakes testing policies on elementary school English language learners in Arizona. *Education Policy Analysis Archives*, 14(13), 1–75.

Zapata, A., & Laman, T. T. (2016). "I write to show how beautiful my languages are": Translingual writing instruction in English-dominant classrooms. *Language Arts*, 93(5), 366–378.

Zisselsberger, M. (2016). Toward a humanizing pedagogy: Leveling the cultural and linguistic capital in a fifth-grade writing classroom. *Bilingual Research Journal*, 39(2), 121–137.

3

Raciolinguistics
Centering Cultural Language as Resistance, Belonging, and Affirmation

Roberta Price Gardner and Sanjuana C. Rodriguez

In the author's note of *The Rock in My Throat*, an episodic picture book memoir by Kao Kalia Yang and illustrated by Jiemei Lin, Yang reflects on her childhood experience of becoming a selective mute. She explains that she stopped speaking English as a form of resistance to the dehumanizing erasure and voicelessness she witnessed being imposed on her mother. Yang writes, "As a child, I saw the people who spoke fluent English walk away from your efforts to be understood, and I felt your pain. I couldn't protect you, so I did the only thing I knew to do: I stopped talking in English. It was my great revolution against a world I knew was not listening to you." She continues, "I felt sad and sorry that I couldn't speak for myself or you for many years. But those years have come and gone. I know that sometimes the words I cannot speak into the world, I can write in it" (Yang, 2024, n.p).

Illustrator Jiemei Lin uses various techniques—such as scale, proximity, and a recurring feather motif—to visually counter the heaviness of the metaphorical "rock in one's throat". Lin's choice of earthy tones—brown, red, orange, grey, black, and blue—captures Kao's emotional burden as she navigates the challenges of translating the school curriculum and the mixed, sometimes unwelcoming reactions of teachers, classmates, and even a cashier. In the end, Kao breaks her silence through writing.

Kao's experience highlights the vital role of engaging with critical cultural language in the classroom through reading and writing. This chapter focuses on critical cultural language, particularly on *raciolinguistics*, which explores how cultural and racialized language experiences in reading and writing serve as essential tools for cultural expression, resistance, belonging, affirmation, and voice.

Challenging Linguistic Hierarchies Through Critical Cultural Language

Raciolinguistics examines the intersection of language, race, and societal power (Alim, 2016a). It looks at how language is shaped by race and, in turn, how race influences language. Central to this field are questions like, "What does it mean to speak, or be spoken about, as a racialized subject?" (Alim, 2016b, p. 1). In the context of education, linguist Geneva Smitherman emphasizes the vital role of language because it reflects a culture's worldview. She argues that "language is critical in talking about the education of a people because it represents a people's theory of reality; it explains, interprets, constructs, and reproduces that reality" (1998, p. 154). Despite resistance to diversity, equity, and inclusion initiatives in education, during the second term of the Trump administration, the realities and questions about race, culture, and language remain central to classroom practices of reading, writing, speaking, and listening.

We emphasize the necessity of teachers fundamentally grounding their teaching in revolutionary love (Braden et al., 2024; Wynter-Hoyte et al., 2022) and offer strategies to help young writers use critical cultural language as a form of resistance to racial and linguistic hierarchies. We provide recommendations for writing instruction, using culturally conscious children's literature (Bishop, 1990) that explores race, language, and visual social semiotics (how symbols and language are interpreted and understood in relation to cultural, social, and historical contexts). Finally, we conclude with writing and drawing prompts, book suggestions, and reflective questions to encourage deeper engagement, centering cultural language through expressive writing, drawing, and reading explorations.

Critical cultural language authenticates lived experiences, particularly unfair social norms and stereotypes about race, gender, class, language, and other identities. It is not just about the specific words used but about how they are used—incorporating diverse languages, dialects, vocabulary, accents, and visual symbols that reflect cultural histories, beliefs, and realities. It is a teaching stance that requires considering how languages are spoken, written, and read in classrooms and the stylistic choices, descriptions, and ideas that are validated and welcomed.

We emphasize the importance of respecting and engaging with multiple languages while highlighting Black Language as a key point of reference. In this context, we draw upon Baker-Bell's (2020) concept of "critical linguistic awareness", which challenges the conventional linguistic hierarchies that often dictate what we think students need in their language education (p. 8). Teachers should ask themselves how language variations are used throughout the literacy block and across all subjects to convey ideas, emotions, facts, and characterizations of people and places—both in students' experiences and the larger world. Additionally, educators should consider how creators of culturally conscious, diverse books use language to enrich students' understanding of these connections.

In the next section, we center on Black Language, acknowledging that it is often seen as an inferior linguistic practice in schools, which is assumed to require remediation. However, we aim to shift this perspective. As Teaira McMurtry (as cited in Windsor, 2021) asserts, "Black Language is an art form, not something to be eradicated." It is a vibrant, legitimate expression that should be celebrated, not diminished. Rather than viewing Black Language as undesirable, we argue that it needs to be highlighted in classrooms through literature, just as it is commonplace in many students' daily lives. Baker-Bell (2020), drawing from Smitherman (1981), reminds us that Black Language is a rule-governed, culturally rich linguistic system. Throughout this discussion, we emphasize the critical role that Black Language and multiple languages play in writing pedagogy.

Black Language as Resistance

Black Language is a contested language, particularly within schools. It is a marker of anti-Black linguistic racism. The negation of Black Language includes deficit connotations about social class, region, and intellectual ability. Due to the hierarchical status of White Mainstream English and its use as a potential for upward mobility, some Black people within the Black community also subscribe to the idea of suppressing and remediating Black Language. Teachers must be conscious that the linguistic racism surrounding Black Language devalues the personal, cultural, and historical aspects of this language (Baker-Bell, 2020; Woodson, 1933/2006; Lyiscott, 2014) and stigmatizes the humanity of Black people. As Baker-Bell (2020) asserted, "the way Black Language is devalued in schools reflects how Black lives are devalued in the world" (pp. 2-3). Whether a student uses Black Language to reflect understanding in math, science, or social studies, Black Language scholar Tiera McMurtry (2024) emphasizes that teachers should always emphasize connection over correction. Doing so affirms students' sense of belonging and confidence.

Language shapes perceptions about who belongs, who has power, and who gets silenced. As educators, it's important to pay attention to the social and racialized dimensions of language—how it impacts students' sense of self and place in society. To be sure, the ways we support students when they speak, express themselves, or share their stories influence students' self-perceptions and their sense of agency to impact their world. They should feel empowered as writers to name, script, and describe it the way they see and experience it.

Black Language is rooted in the oral tradition, including dialectal and tonal variations, unique vocabulary, and cultural shifts in meaning (e.g., saying "I'm straight" in Black Language means you are okay, or that things in your universe are good/sufficient). In the context of Black children's literature, including Black Language is an essential tool for conveying cultural identity, pride, and resilience. Black Language is not just a linguistic choice but a powerful cultural expression that reflects Black communities' lived experiences and sensibilities. According to Geneva Smitherman (1977), Black Language is central to Black identity. It offers various rhetorical features such as wordplay and rhythm, just some of the linguistic qualities integral to how Black people communicate and express themselves. In culturally conscious Black children's books, these linguistic features are often woven into the narrative to provide a more authentic portrayal of Black experiences, particularly for young readers who may see and hear themselves reflected in the characters and their voices.

The use of Black Language in literature, particularly in children's books, can manifest in several ways, including through dialogue, narration, or even the overall sensibility of the work. As noted by Sims (1982), Black Language can appear in the way characters speak and the narrative voice, shaping how the story is told. This inclusion of Black Language can serve multiple functions: It can highlight the cultural specificity of the characters, offer a sense of belonging for Black readers, and foster a deeper connection to the book's themes. Moreover, the rhetorical qualities of Black Language—such as rhythm, repetition, and expressive phrasing—enhance the story's emotional resonance and allow readers to engage with it on a more visceral level.

A prime example of using Black Language in children's literature is *I Am Every Good Thing* by Derrick Barnes (2020). In this book, the narrator uses Black Language in simultaneously humble, boastful, and resistant ways. The narrator's voice is infused with a dynamic energy reflecting the character's belief in his identity and self-worth. For instance, the line "I am the BOOM BAP-BOOM-BOOM-BAP when the bass line thumps and the kick drum jumps" (Barnes, 2020) encapsulates the rhythmic and vibrant nature of Black culture, drawing a direct connection between the narrator's identity and the powerful, driving force of music. The use of sound here emphasizes the narrator's self-awareness and creates a sense of celebration and pride. Furthermore, the book's narrator engages in resistance through language. He states, "I am not what they might call me, and I will not answer to any name that is not my own." This declaration serves as a rejection of harmful stereotypes and an assertion of self-determination. It is a powerful affirmation of the narrator's right to define himself, free from the impositions of societal labels. This resistance reflects the narrator's inner strength. It expresses the broader Black community's ongoing struggle to claim agency over their identities, free from the distortions and dehumanizations imposed by external forces.

By incorporating Black Language into children's literature, authors like Barnes provide young readers—especially Black children—with a model of linguistic and cultural pride. The use of this language, with its layers of meaning and cultural significance, serves as a form of self-expression that transcends mere communication, becoming an act of cultural and personal affirmation.

Our suggestions for writing and using mentor texts that reflect critical cultural language serve as consciousness-raising tools. They are reminders that language isn't neutral—it serves as a critical site for antiracism practice in reading and writing. Since all teachers are also language teachers, it's crucial to consider how students express the cultural and linguistic aspects of their world. In order to support students in using writing to express their full humanity (Muhammad, 2020), teachers must interrogate their beliefs and biases to consider how forms of linguistic racism shape their instructional practices.

Revolutionary Love

This work is founded upon Revolutionary Love (RL), a framework that was developed and influenced by the traditions of loving and liberatory beliefs and practices of Black and Latinx teachers (Acosta et al., 2018; Foster, 1997; King & Swartz, 2016; Lesesne, 2020; Walker, 1996). RL requires teachers to have an understanding of three key ideas. Revolutionary-loving teachers must:

1. Know themselves and their students in the contexts of their cultural identities, family, and community.
2. Know policies, laws, and school-based practices that place Black and Latinx children at a disadvantage.
3. Know literacy instruction and curriculum.

Viewing students, families, and communities through an asset-based lens means teachers must have an in-depth knowledge of their own identities. It is also necessary to understand the root causes of the social, economic, health care, and educational challenges that students of color face. Understanding the systems, policies, and processes that harm Black and Latinx children prevents us from blaming students and families for the consequences of racism. This, coupled with knowledge of literacy development, content, and curriculum, ensures that educators affirm students' identities and cultural and linguistic resources and that educators remain critically conscious of systems that do not support students. Revolution-loving teachers acknowledge how language and power intersect and use this knowledge to design curriculum that demonstrates this understanding.

Teachers who embrace RL also understand "that the literacy curriculum that they create with and for children should be designed to make spaces for children to live their lives out loud on the pages of their journals or notebooks" (Wynter-Hoyte et al., 2022, p. 157). More about the RL framework will be described by Myers, one of the authors of *Revolutionary Love: Creating a Culturally Inclusive Literacy Classroom*, in Chapter 10. To strengthen language consciousness, educators must engage in intentional reflection (McMurtry, 2021), and diverse children's literature serves as a powerful site for identifying and expanding this awareness.

Illuminate How Visual and Written Language Conveys Identity

Teachers who want to illuminate how visual and written language convey identity in texts can encourage students to analyze picture books' visual and textual elements. For instance, in the picture book *I Am From*, Gray's verse narration—paired with Oge Mora's visual language—uses Black Language, dialectical specificity, dialogue, and geographical and cultural references. Together, the text and visuals offer a powerful mentor text for reading, modeling, and writing critical cultural language experiences. It is a visual narration and a subtle nod to George Ella Lyon's poem, "Where I'm From" (2011). Throughout Gray's semi-autobiographical poem (he is a Black male from Nova Scotia), he uses culturally distinct language (e.g., to describe the hairstyles of his peers, "cotton candy hair, razor-sharp line-ups, and laid edges" (n.p)) and Black linguistic tones. Black Language serves as a narrative device to demonstrate identity, point of view, setting, plot, and power dynamics, which are conveyed through visual and written language that is critical and culturally distinct. The central character consistently speaks back to the reductive societal attempts to frame his identity as a Black male as he affirms the joyful aspects of where he is from.

Gary R. Gray, Jr. and Oge Mora lure readers into the fascinating everyday world of a nameless Black boy using energized text and brightly colored illustrations that feature the young boy's favorite toys, food, and homelife. It also includes a long bus ride to the other side of town (where his culture is less prominent), and the stir and animation of his school day, which includes "dusty classics" and only a few books he can relate to. The young Black child is from a place where "notebooks and stubby pencils are used to draw his heroes and write his own stories" (n.p). He asserts pride in where he is from, particularly after encountering a series of stereotypical tropes at school, "Can I touch your HAIR? You don't sound BLACK. Do you play BASKETBALL?" (n.p). The disturbed facial expression of the central character conveys the jarring internal sentiment he feels as he is dehumanized by the assertions. The idea that he doesn't "sound Black" defies presumptive ideas about "normative language" as a trait of Black identity. The bright colors and self-assured response to the offensive and limiting assumptions articulated by his peers (presumably white) defy the racialized presumptions. The next page reads, "I'm from Honey, whatchu want?" It is a prideful dialectical shift and cultural response that helps to blunt the crude reality of the systematic and ideological racism that he navigates at school. Like Kao, Gray is also writing to the child within. He is writing to activate his voice and make right the wrongs of his past.

Identifying culturally specific written and visual language within diverse literature allows readers and writers to deepen their comprehension, meaning, including identifying hierarchies, perspectives, power dynamics, value, and narrative tone. Such modalities of meaning include images, typography, shapes, dialogue boxes, color, size, proximity, and other stylistic devices (Serafini, 2014; Serafini & Clausen, 2012). In *I'm From*, the words **HAIR**, **BLACK**, and **BASKETBALL** are in all caps and bold type zig-zagged across the page. The audaciousness of the bold and erect typeface distinctly emerges from the page. It highlights the emotional jolt the character felt navigating these tropes. The craft move reflects the affective experience of being racially stereotyped. Exposure to mentor texts to support critical language experiences through writing expands opportunities to deepen conceptual knowledge about themes, ideas, experiences, and the use of language as a structural and emotive tool in writing.

Broaden Explorations of How Language Functions as a Cultural Tool for Expression

Teachers can center cultural language in the classroom through engaging in an analysis of both visual and written elements in picture books. The picture book *Separate is Never Equal: Sylvia Mendez and Her Family's Fight for Desegregation*, written and illustrated by Duncan Tonatiuh, details the story of the *Mendez v. Westminster* case that helped end school segregation in California in 1947. The visual storytelling by Tonatiuh expands the meaning of the texts. One of the features that Tonatiuh uses in his book is the intentional use of Spanish throughout the book. Tonatiuh only uses Spanish when Sylvia's parents are speaking in the book to say something meaningful or important. For example, when Sylvia is questioning why she has to go to school where she is not wanted, her mother shares: "Sylvia, no sables porque luchamos" [don't you know that is why we fought]. Duncan's illustrations also show a contrast in the use of the color palette for the different scenes. For example, he uses bright colors to show the school where the white students attend. One example is the blue of the school uniforms worn by white students. In contrast, a more subdued color palette is used for the "Mexican school". These visual contrasts underscore the segregation depicted in the story and subtly highlight the differences in treatment between the Mexican-American students and their white peers.

Reading books that expose students to writing reflecting their home language—such as *Still Dreaming*—provides valuable opportunities for teachers to demonstrate the interconnectedness of culture, race, language, themes, and literary devices (e.g., plot, characterization, perspective, symbols, and geographies). This approach allows students to explore how these elements are deeply intertwined in storytelling.

It is essential to offer exposure to writing that includes critical cultural language experiences. This is particularly crucial considering the ongoing discourses around the *Science of Reading* (SOR) and *Science of Writing* (SOW), which continue to influence the adoption of instructional curricula and writing programs. These discourses often assume a neutral raciolinguistic subjectivity for students and teachers (Haddix, 2016). As Haddix emphasizes, empathy, rapport, and a deep understanding of students' unique needs are essential for teachers who strive to support the literacy development of all students. However, demonstrating these qualities is not a race or culturally neutral endeavor. Traditional curricula typically center on white, standard English and cultural norms while banning diverse, culturally relevant perspectives.

The Science of Reading/Science of Writing discourses claim to rely on interdisciplinary evidence-based approaches to reading instruction and must better reflect the inclusion of linguistically and culturally inclusive literature and methods. Acknowledging that language comprehension—an essential component of this approach—must include students' cultural knowledge and linguistic skills. This aligns with the upper strand components of Scarborough's *Reading Rope* (2001), which identifies language comprehension as involving background knowledge, vocabulary, language structure (syntax and semantics), verbal reasoning (including inference and metaphor), and literacy knowledge. Given this, as an example in writing instruction, how might teachers leverage the linguistic competencies and strengths of Black children, who often exhibit exceptional dexterity in oral language and storytelling abilities (Gardner-Neblett, De Marco, & Ebright, 2023; Gardner-Neblett & Lopez Alvarez, 2024)? Engaging with the rich cultural and linguistic assets of all children is critical to fostering their reading and writing development in an inclusive, meaningful way.

Pedagogical Practices

In this section, we highlight the pedagogical practices of using visual language in diverse picture books and highlight the importance of helping students analyze how visual and written elements work together to convey identity, culture, and resistance. Teachers can guide students in examining culturally significant visual iconography, such as murals and public art, to explore how these images reinforce themes of pride and belonging in marginalized communities. Through mentor texts like *I Too Am America* and *I Am From*, students can analyze authorial choices in language and typography that reflect nuanced cultural identities and challenge racialized assumptions. Additionally, books like *Separate is Never Equal* showcase how language and color choices in illustrations underscore racial inequities, providing opportunities for critical discussions about race, power, and identity. By incorporating these texts, teachers can broaden students' understanding of how language functions as a cultural tool, encouraging them to engage critically with issues of representation, equity, and belonging.

Centering Critical Cultural Language Experience in Writing Instruction Through Diverse Picture Books

One of the ways in which teachers can ground their writing instruction is through the use of culturally conscious, diverse picture books. As teachers consider what books to use to display critical cultural language, they should look for books that provide a context for these pedagogical practices. Table 3.1 provides books that can support teachers in engaging with visual language in picture books. This is not an exhaustive list, but rather provides some example texts that can be used. We then provide examples of mini-lessons and mentor texts centering on critical cultural language experiences. These books can provide a start for teachers wanting to engage in this work with students.

In addition to including books that center critical language experiences, teachers can engage students in learning about using these books as springboards for writing through specific mini-lessons.

Table 3.1 Critical Cultural Language Experience Themes and Books

Critical Cultural Language Experience Themes	Book	Summary of the Book	Possible Writing Teaching Opportunity
Communal memories, Black geographies, and family histories	Grant, S. (2009). *Up home* (S. Tooke, Illus.). Nimbus Publishing.	Explores the themes of home, belonging, the power of place, and cultural heritage among Blacks and the importance of preserving geographies and family legacies.	Grant includes the names of gospel groups, special community locations. Have students consider how to include detailed memories that their families or community share, use the book to prompt students to list places important to who they are, and stories about where they come from. Details, like the songs they sing or the neighborhoods they walk through, can bring their writing to life and show others what matters to them and their community.
Strategic use of Spanish	Tonatiuh, D. (2010). *Dear primo: A letter to my cousin*. Abrams Books for Young Readers.	This book showcases two cousins—one living in Mexico and one living in the U.S. who write letters to each other about their daily lives. This is a bilingual book, and the author has chosen to include Spanish words in the English text.	Have students consider how they can enhance their writing by strategically incorporating Spanish vocabulary to reflect cultural authenticity, enrich descriptions, and connect with diverse readers.

Critical Cultural Language Experience Themes	Book	Summary of the Book	Possible Writing Teaching Opportunity
Use of images/signs in the picture book that expand understanding of the racial and cultural experiences	Martinez, C. (2023). *Still dreaming / Seguimos soñando* (M. Mora, Illus.) Lee and Low Books.	This book details the story of one family's journey as they are forced to return to Mexico during the Mexican Repatriation.	Have students consider how to use visual details, such as images, signs, and symbols, in their writing or storytelling to highlight and deepen their understanding of racial and cultural experiences. Share how pictures or signs in a story can say things words cannot. They can show us the history, pride, or challenges of a community.
Black Language, resistance to anti-black racism	Gray, G. (2023). *I'm from* (O.Mora, Illus.). Balzer + Bray.	A young Black boy describes his routine by using the frame "I come from," answering the question "where are you from?".	Have students explore how to include Black Language in their writing to honor culture and resist linguistic racism and limitations of Black geographies by sharing stories that celebrate Black joy, community, and resilience. Writing in their own voice is a way to show the world that their stories matter.
Black Language, affirmations of identity, and language	Barnes, D. (2020). *I am every good thing* (G. James, Illus.). Nancy Paulsen Books.	A young Black boy is proud and celebrates his strengths, joys, and dreams.	Have students notice the lines in the book that affirm identity and challenge stereotypes. After pointing this out, have the students write affirmations that reflect their identities.
Visual depiction of language, multilingualism	Menon, U. (2024). *My mother's tongue: A weaving of languages* (Jomepour Bell, Illus.). Candlewick Press.	This book celebrates bilingualism as a little girl tells the story of her mother's bilingualism and her own realization that being multilingual is a superpower.	Invite students to share their own personal language journeys and to reflect on the cultural significance of their home languages. After having this discussion, have students visually represent the languages in their lives by creating a language heart with different sections for each language (or way of speaking) that they connect with.

Writing Mini Lesson 1: Connecting Visual and Linguistic Elements: Critical Reader Response to *I Am Ruby Bridges*

Reader response theory emphasizes that a book's meaning and interpretation should center around the reader. A response that focuses on cultural language experiences recognizes literature's emotive, cultural, and racial implications, including the intersectional aspects of identity (Brooks & Browne, 2012; Gardner, 2017; Gardner et al., 2021). This approach acknowledges that literature has the power to shape and reflect the complexities of race, culture, and identity.

This mini-lesson guides students to engage critically with literature's visual and linguistic elements. By using interactive, guided instruction, we help students connect the pictures in a book with its linguistic components, deepening their understanding of the text. Students are often drawn to the images in picture books but may overlook the powerful language that drives the narrative (Beck & McKeown, 2001; Gardner, 2017). By emphasizing critical cultural language and integrating both aspects, we encourage students to explore how words and images work together to create a fuller understanding of the experiences portrayed in the story.

For this lesson, we use *I Am Ruby Bridges* by Ruby Bridges, illustrated by Nikkolas Smith. This book offers a compelling narrative in which Ruby reflects on her experience as the first Black student to integrate an all-white school. Written from the perspective of her 6-year-old self, Ruby invites readers into her world as she grapples with the challenges of being "the first" and navigating racism. The artwork by Nikkolas Smith complements Ruby's words, offering powerful metaphors, such as illustrating Ruby as a literal bridge between Black and White people. Teachers can discuss this metaphor and show the corresponding image to clarify its significance while teaching words like segregation and discrimination (both are in the glossary). The illustrations gradually reveal the deeper meaning of Ruby's experience, such as a poignant visual series highlighting Ruby's realization of what it truly means to be the first when she does not see any other Black students.

Smith's art encourages readers to "envision" their opportunities and think about how they can contribute to a more just and equal world. To deepen this engagement, students can work in small groups to identify quotes or images from the book that resonated with them—whether those elements made them feel uncomfortable, affirmed, or angry. This activity helps students analyze the book through a lens that considers the intersectionality of race, culture, and identity, fostering a deeper understanding of the text.

A key feature of this lesson is the glossary at the back of the book, which Ruby Bridges provides to expand students' vocabulary and deepen their connections to the story's themes. Using the glossary, students can engage with words related to justice and equality—central themes in Ruby's narrative—and brainstorm ways these concepts can be applied in their lives. This guided approach to responding to literature, which centers on both images and language, helps students grasp how written and visual language play a crucial role in shaping our understanding of social issues. The teacher's role is key in facilitating discussions and guiding students to reflect through interactive writing or journal responses. Thought-provoking questions can be used to prompt students' responses, such as:

- How is Ruby's school experience similar to or different from your own?
- What emotions did you feel when you listened to Ruby's story?
- Were there any images or words in the book that stood out to you? Why?
- Draw or write about how you've served as a bridge, helping others to come together through differences or challenges.

Through these activities, students develop a richer understanding of literature by examining both the visual and linguistic aspects of the text, fostering critical thinking and empathy in the process.

Mini Lesson 2: Writing Informational Sentence Stems

To help students develop structured and meaningful informational writing, guide them in using sentence stems. For this mini-lesson, have students write informational sentence stems—statements, descriptions, ideas, and feelings about history, objects, cultural experiences, or identity, using sentence stems, then go deeper by adding specific details to create a structure for writing.

Students can write informational texts by writing a clear and concise lead sentence. Throughout *Fry Bread*, the author used bold red statements that served as clear statements to convey key ideas and themes that upheld cultural values while also guiding readers' understanding regarding the symbolism and significance of fry bread across place and time. "Fry Bread is Nation" is followed by substantive information and background that describes how fry bread represents Indigenous nationality and sovereignty. Students can use this model by writing their own informational texts with a strong lead statement and then expanding on it with detailed explanations about that lead statement. As teachers engage students in thinking about ways in which they can do this, they can provide some lead sentences that can then be used by students as they write their own ideas. Teachers can use the following statements as a guide for students who need more guidance:

- Language is legacy ...
- Hair is heritage ...
- Food is family ...
- Holiday [insert specific holiday] is memory ...

Other examples of books centering a language of resistance using sentence frames that can be modeled include *Yes We Will: Asian Americans Who Shaped this Country* (Yang, 2022). This book uses one-line biographies to highlight the stories of Asian Americans. The book may be used as an example of how sentence frames connect the actions of individuals to their stories. The book provides a clear framework for students to examine how language itself can be a form of resistance in writing.

Mini Lesson 3: Writing Dedications

In this lesson, teachers can explore how writers use dedications to affirm and sustain cultural, racial, and linguistic histories, family members, and values. Dedications are often more than simple acknowledgments—they're powerful spaces for honoring heritage and showing gratitude. Through carefully chosen language, writers can convey deep respect, love, and pride in the people, places, and traditions that shape them. As a part of this mini-lesson, teachers can point out powerful dedications that focus on authors honoring their heritage.

One example of this is the dedication written by Juana Martinez-Neal for the book *Fry Bread*. In this dedication, Martinez-Neal writes "Para

Gladys, mi mama and keeper of all recipes," and Kevin Noble Maillard wrote, "To Irs, Nan and all the women who teach us stuff." Both creators use cultural references and language of endearment to hold the women in their family in high esteem. Language is modeled as a tool for affirming all women. In *Show the World!* (Dalton, 2022), illustrator, Daria Peoples, writes, "For the children of Oakland. Y'all better show them!" She uses informal vernacular to encourage Black youth from Oakland to be an instrument in the world in any way they imagine, including posing, writing, dancing, singing, or waiting, for language that makes you feel something: "that makes you think something; that makes you do something" (n.p).

Another poignant dedication example appears in the book, *Still Dreaming/Seguimos Soñando*, Claudia Guadalupe Martínez writes, "To my Apá—who made the first of my willing and unwilling journeys to and from the US as a boy in the 1940s—and to my Amá—who took a leap of faith to join him in Tejas to raise a family" [Para mi Apá, que durante su infancia, en los años cuarenta, hizo muchos viajes voluntarios e involuntarios de ida y vuelta a los Estados Unidos. Y para mi Amá, que, como un acto de fe, viajó a Tejas con él, para formar una familia] (n.p). The first thing to note is that the dedication is written in both English and Spanish, which signals the importance of both languages for the author and resists the prominence of English-only texts. In the dedication, the author uses the endearing terms Apá and Amá, which are both tender and loving terms to refer to father and mother in Spanish.

Finally, in her dedication in the book *Up Home*, Shauntay Grant simply writes, "To the children of North Preston, with much love." Preston was the largest Black settlement in Canada. Preston remains a city comprising Black migrants and refugees from the 1800s. The first page reads, "I remember ..." After reading the book, use Grant's opening words to serve as a provocation for young writers to reminisce, recall and remember a family event, special place, story, music, sounds in their home, and so on. In the book, Grant writes, "I remember Sunday mornings Shirley Caesar, Deniece Williams, The Winans vibration' the walls ..." Model writing about a community event, family celebration, or other memory. What other examples can you locate of language that reflects racial and cultural sustenance and affirmation? Invite students to consider writing dedications routinely to allow students to culturally and racially affirm people, places, and values they uphold. Figure 3.1 is a sample anchor chart that you can use as you teach this lesson.

Figure 3.1 Writing powerful dedications.

By Gardner & Rodriguez.

Conferencing to Assess and Support Linguistic Freedom

According to Evangeline Harris Stefanakis (2002), "The word assess comes from the Latin assidere, which means to sit beside. Literally then, to assess means to sit beside the learner" (p. 9). Assessment in writing requires that teachers sit beside the student, look closely at student writing, consider what they are doing well, and how they may move the student to the next steps in writing. In considering assessments, it is also important to remember that these conversations are happening with students who have so much to teach us about their writing process.

In his discussion about creating culturally relevant assessments for students Gibson (2020) walks us through his process of realizing that a part of implementing culturally relevant assessment instruction required him to build relationships, "It finally hit me that I needed to understand my students *first* and use my own classroom assessments to accurately understand their knowledge. I wasn't able to effectively help them in the classroom until I understood them as people and understood their culture" (n.p). As teachers, it's important to guide students in developing their writing by encouraging them to consider how language reflects deeper cultural, historical, and emotional contexts. The following set of questions offers an insightful framework for assessing students' writing, prompting them to think critically about the choices they make in their own writing. These questions ask students to explore how specific details—such as sights, sounds, language shifts, and cultural references—can enrich their writing and help convey more complex ideas. By having students consider these questions, teachers can help students' understanding of these aspects of writing.

- How does the written or visual language reflect the experience of the people represented in the narrative or informational text? What are the specific sights or sounds associated with a geographic place? What are the objects, names, and unique features of the time and place?
- What specific language or dialogue was used? When reading books with multiple languages, when does the language shift? How does the shift in language convey power or resistance? What opportunities exist to make language shifts in your writing?
- How can specific details reveal the cultural, historical, or emotional depth of your topic? What symbols, typeface, language, or imagery can you add to make your writing more meaningful to you or your culture?

Key Considerations for Teachers When Selecting Books That Include Cultural and Racialized Language

When selecting texts that include critical cultural language experiences, consider how the language functions as a cultural tool for expression. For example, How is the language of race, culture, place, and nationality represented? How is the language used to convey emotion and experience? How are visual images used as writing to convey culturally affirming ideas or resistance to white supremacy? We also believe that it is important to consider who the author and illustrator of the book are and their relationship to the topic or narrative. Teachers should consider the following questions: Who is the author? Who is the illustrator? Is the language representation authentic to the author or illustrator? As it pertains to language authenticity, relative to Black Language, we embrace the definition of Pittman et al. (2024), who assert, "the concept of authenticity means that readers who speak Black Language will identify with the language and know whether the language usage is accurate in the texts and thus be affirmed by the text" (p. 157). However, in order to effectively support language variation, educators must be aware of the linguistic features of Black Language, White Mainstream English (see Pittman et al., 2024), the geographic nuances of Black Language, and stylistic approaches used by diverse authors and illustrators across the Black diaspora. For example, Dinah Johnson's poetic picture book *Indigo Dreaming* (2022) opens with the line, "Every morning at day-clean, I wonder if there is a girl like me, across an ocean or sea" (n.p). The term "day-clean" is commonly used in Jamaican and Gullah Geechee cultures to refer to dawn, when the sun rises, or the beginning of a new day. Although *She Come Bringing that Little Baby Girl* (Greenfield, 1974) also uses Black Language, Greenfield uses Black southern grammatical shifts and dialectical references, whereas Johnson's Black Language reference reflects coastal Caribbean and West African Black Language. When writers incorporate culturally distinct phrases and vocabulary, they offer valuable nuanced insights into the people, geographies, histories, and worldviews that shape the meaning and messages within their stories.

Navigating cultural and racialized language of experience can be uncomfortable for some educators. In methods courses for pre-service teachers, we use audiobooks with native speakers as models for pronouncing words and language we are challenged by. As mentioned earlier, teachers who embrace a Revolutionary Love framework must know themselves, the systems in which schooling operates, and their literacy instruction and curriculum. One of those key tenets in understanding literacy instruction and curriculum is to take steps that counter systems of racism that have been embedded in the literacy curriculum. That involves understanding the topics, knowing how to analyze the language used in books, and taking "intentional steps to counter oppressive and marginalizing linguistic practices that are deeply embedded in school systems and our classrooms" (Wynter-Hoyte et al., 2022, p. 106). Selecting books in which writers use language to resist, reveal, and empower is a critical step in this process and practice.

Closing

Race and culture have distinct characteristics associated with language, and such characteristics are part of narrating informational and imaginative writing. Critical cultural language, which includes written and visual storytelling in picture books, provides valuable tools for affirming identities, challenging dominant language ideologies, and helping students to consider forms of resistance through writing. It's vital for teachers to use mentor texts that illuminate how language intersects with race, culture, and identity, and consider how these texts can be a vehicle for writing opportunities for students to resist erasure and silence. These books can help students to explore their own cultural linguistic narratives while also providing an opportunity for them to broaden their understanding of others. The pedagogical strategies that we have outlined in this chapter are grounded in Revolutionary Love, an approach to teaching literacy that asks educators to consider ways to affirm and amplify the voices of students. Exposure to a critical cultural language of experience resists colonization, the pervasiveness of white norms, and the consistent erasures of nonwhite experiences that limit youths' ideological possibilities for writing. All students' literacy experiences are being censored to protect a perceived harm to white children with little or no regard for the wounds, anguish, and continued implications born out of the erasure and suppression of individual, ideological, and systemic exclusion of nonwhite children and their communities.

Providing exposure to critical cultural language experiences across multiple genres can help students locate cultural experiences to support their emerging identities and resist racist structures. Reading and writing their worlds helps them to embrace who they are and envisage other worlds. Award-winning author Zetta Elliot noted that as a young Black writer, she wrote many stories of fantasy that erased her racial identity because she didn't believe she could exist in those worlds. She stated, "I had been invisible for so long that I automatically erased myself without ever considering I had a right to create and inhabit magical worlds" (Elliot, 2019). Whether students write about speculative worlds, information, or personal narratives, mentor texts that reflect racial and cultural identities and the linguistic experiences and sentiments of their cultural and racialized worlds can serve as resources for enriching expression, narrative, and informational understanding, cultural and personal pride. We offer the following questions as you engage in putting critical cultural language experience into practice in your classroom.

Reflective Questions

1. In what ways do you create classroom spaces that provide opportunities for students to write about their linguistic and cultural identities?
2. How does the language in your children's literature selections serve as linguistic "mirrors, windows, or sliding glass doors" (Bishop, 1990) for students?
3. What are the racial and cultural identities of the authors on your shelf, and how does language, dialect, nationality, race, place, and ethnicity function in their writing?

References

Acosta, M. M., Foster, M., & Houchen, D. F. (2018). "Why seek the living among the dead?" African American pedagogical excellence: Exemplar practice for teacher education. *Journal of Teacher Education*, 69(4), 341–353.

Alim, H. S. (2016a). Who's afraid of the transracial subject? Raciolinguistics and the political project of transracialization. In H. S. Alim, J. R. Rickford,

& A. F. Ball (Eds.), *Raciolinguistics: How language shapes our ideas about race* (pp. 33–50). New York: Oxford University Press.

Alim, H. S. (2016b). Introducing raciolinguistics. Racing language and languaging race in hyperracial times. In H. S. Alim, J. R. Rickford, & A. F. Ball (Eds.), *Raciolinguistics: How language shapes our ideas about race* (pp. 1–30). New York, NY: Oxford University Press.

Arizpe, E. (2020). Sharing visual experiences of a new culture: Immigrant children's responses to picturebooks and other visual texts. In J. Evans (Ed.), *Talking beyond the page* (pp. 134–151). Routledge.

Arizpe, E., Farrell, M., & McAdam, J. (2013). Opening the classroom door to children's literature: A review of research. In *International handbook of research on children's literacy, learning, and culture* (pp. 241–257). Wiley.

Arizpe, E., & Styles, M. (2015). *Children reading picturebooks: Interpreting visual texts*. Routledge.

Arizpe, E., Colomer, T., & Martínez-Roldán, C. (2014). *Visual journeys through wordless narratives: An international inquiry with immigrant children and the arrival*. A&C Black.

Baker-Bell, A. (2020). *Linguistic justice: Black language, literacy, identity, and pedagogy*. Routledge.

Barnes, D. (2020). *I am every good thing*. (C. J. Gordon, Illus.). Paulsen Books.

Beck, I. L., & McKeown, M. G. (2001). Text talk: Capturing the benefits of read-aloud experiences for young children. *The Reading Teacher*, 55(1), 10–20.

Bishop, R. S. (1990). Mirrors, windows, and sliding glass doors. *Perspectives*, 6(3), ix–xi.

Braden, E., Myers, M., Thornton, N., Rodriguez, S., & Wynter-Hoyte, K. (2024). Revolutionary love: Centering the full humanity of children in the literacy curriculum. *Reading Research Quarterly*, 60(1). https://doi.org/10.1002/rrq.592

Brooks, W., & Browne, S. (2012). Towards a culturally situated reader response theory. *Chldren's Literature in Education*, 43, 74–85. https://doi.org/10.1007/s10583-011-9154-z

Collins, P. H. (1999). Reflections on the outsider within. *Journal of Career Development*, 26(1), 85–88.

Cueto, D., & Brooks, W. (2019). *Drawing Humanity: How picturebooks illustrations counter antiblackness*. Routledge.

Dalton, A. (2022). *Show the world!* (D. Peoples, Illus.). Viking Books for Young Readers.

Elliot, Z. (2019, January 4). When writing fantasy, Black Magic Matters, says Zetta Elliott. *Toronto Star*. www.thestar.com/entertainment/books/when-writing-fantasy-black-magic-matters-says-zetta-elliott/article_767229cf-ace5-5fe7-a9ce-3053f17d9250.html

España, C., & Herrera, L. Y. (2020). *En comunidad: Lessons for centering the voices and experiences of bilingual Latinx students.* Heinemann.

Espinosa, C. M., & Ascenzi-Moreno, L. (2021). *Rooted in strength: Growing multilingual readers and writers through translanguaging.* Scholastic.

Farrell, M., Arizpe, E., & McAdam, J. (2010). Journeys across visual borders: Annotated spreads of 'The Arrival' by Shaun Tan as a method for understanding pupils' creation of meaning through visual images. *Australian Journal of Language and Literacy, 33*(3), 198–210.

Foster, M. (1997). *Black teachers on teaching.* New York: New Press.

Gardner, R. P. (2017). Unforgivable blackness: Visual rhetoric, reader response, and critical racial literacy. *Children's Literature in Education, 48,* 119–133.

Gardner, R. P., Osorio, S. L., & McCormack, S. (2021). Creating spaces for emotional justice in culturally sustaining literacy education: Implications for policy & practice. *Theory Into Practice, 60*(3), 301–311. https://doi.org/10.1080/00405841.2021.1911578

Gardner-Neblett, N., & Alvarez, D. L. (2024). Sharing stories versus explaining facts: Comparing African American children's microstructure performance across fictional narrative, informational, and procedural discourse. *Journal of Speech, Language, and Hearing Research, 67*(11), 4431–4445.

Gardner-Neblett, N., De Marco, A., & Ebright, B. D. (2023). Do Katie and Connor tell better stories than Aaliyah and Jamaal? Teachers' perceptions of children's oral narratives as a function of race and narrative quality. *Early Childhood Research Quarterly, 62*(1), 115–128.

Gibson, V. (February, 2020). Working Toward Culturally Relevant Assessment Practices. National Council of Teachers of English blog, https://ncte.org/blog/2020/02/working-toward-culturally-responsive-assessment-practices/

Grant, S. (2009). *Up home* (S. Tooke, Illus.). Nimbus Publishing.

Greenfield, E. (1974). *She come bringing me that little baby girl* (J. Steptoe, Illus.). HarperCollins.

Haddix, M. M. (2016). *Cultivating racial and linguistic diversity in literacy teacher education: Teachers like me.* Routledge.

King, J. E., & Swartz, E. E. (2016). *The Afrocentric Praxis of Teaching for Freedom: Connecting Culture to Learning.* Routledge Taylor & Francis Group.

Lesesne, P. J. (2020). A sistah circle of seven: Black women's self-perceptions of their teach for America (TFA) experiences in the U.S. Mid-Atlantic Region (147) [Doctoral dissertation, University of Pennsylvania].

Lyiscott, J. (2019). *Black appetite. White food: Issues of race, voice, and justice within and beyond the classroom.* Routledge.

Martin, M. (2004). *Brown gold: Milestones of African American children's picture books, 1845–2002.* Routledge.

Martinez, C. (2023). *Still dreaming / Seguimos soñando* (M. Mora, Illus.) Lee and Low Books.

Martínez-Roldán, C. M. (2013). The representation of Latinos and the use of Spanish: A critical content analysis of Skippyjon Jones. *Journal of Children's Literature, 39*(1), 5.

McMurtry, T. (2021). With liberty and black linguistic justice for all: Pledging allegiance to anti-racist language pedagogy. *Journal of Adolescent & Adult Literacy, 65*(2), 175–178.

McMurtry, T. (2024). We BEEN Knowin: Black Women Teachers (Re)member that Our Language is a Living Legacy. *Research Journal of the National Association for the Teaching of English, 58*(1), 6–22.

Mendez v. Westminster, 64 F. Supp. 544 (S.D. Cal. 1946).

Mendoza, J., & Reese, D. (2001). Examining multicultural picture books for the early childhood classroom: Possibilities and pitfalls. *Early Childhood Research & Practice, 3*(2), n2.

Menon, U. (2024). *My mother's tongue: A weaving of languages* (Jomepour Bell, Illus.). Candlewick Press.

Muhammad, G. (2020). *Cultivating genius: An equity framework for culturally and historically responsive literacy.* Scholastic.

Pérez Huber, L., Camargo Gonzalez, L., & Solórzano, D. G. (2023). Theorizing a critical race content analysis for children's literature about people of color. *Urban Education, 58*(10), 2437–2461.

Pittman, R. T., Piper, R. E., McCoy, W., & Alanis, M. (2024). African American Language in Children's Literature. *Journal of Literacy Research, 56*(2), 157–183. https://doi.org/10.1177/1086296X241244702

Serafini, F. (2014). *Reading the visual: An introduction to teaching multimodal literacy.* Teachers College Press.

Serafini, F., & Clausen, J. (2012). Typography as semiotic resource. *Journal of Visual Literacy, 31*(2), 1–16.

Sims, R. (1982). *Shadow and substance: Afro-American experience in contemporary children's fiction.* National Council of Teachers of English.

Sipe, L. R. (2008). Learning from illustrations in picturebooks. In N. Frey & D. Fisher (Eds.), *Teaching visual literacy: Using comic books, graphic novels, anime, cartoons, and more to develop comprehension and thinking skills* (pp. 131–148). Sage.

Smitherman, G. (1977). *Takin and Testifying.* Detroit, MI: Wayne State University Press.

Smitherman, G. (1981). "What Go Round Come Round": King in Perspective. *Harvard Educational Review, 51*(1), 40–56.

Smitherman, G. (1998). Ebonics, King, and Oakland: Some folk don't believe fat meat is greasy. *Journal of English Linguistics, 26*(2), 97–107.

Stefanakis, E. H. (2002). *Multiple intelligences and portfolios: A window into the learner's mind.* Heinemann Educational Books.

Tonatiuh, D. (2010). *Dear primo: A letter to my cousin.* Abrams Books for Young Readers.

Walker, V. (1996). *Their highest potential: An African American school community in the segregated south.* University of North Carolina Press.

Windsor, M. (2021, October 1). Helping teachers see the beauty in Black language. *UAB Reporter.* https://digitalcommons.library.uab.edu/all-news/14685/

Woodson, C. (1933/2006). *The Mis-Education of the Negro.* Trenton, NJ: Africa World Press.

Wynter-Hoyte, K., Braden, E. G., Myers, M., Rodriguez, S., Thornton, N., & Boutte, G. (2022). *Revolutionary love: Creating a culturally inclusive literacy classroom.* Scholastic Incorporated.

Yang, K. (2022). *Yes we will: Asian Americans who shaped this country* (Illustrated by various artists). Dial Books.

Children's Books Cited

Bridges, R., & Smith, N. (2022). *I am Ruby Bridges.* Orchard Books.

Grant, S. (2009). *Up home* (S. Tooke, Illus.). Nimbus Publishing.

Gray, G. (2023). *I'm from* (O. Mora, Illus.). Balzer + Bray.

Martinez, C. (2022). *Still dreaming/Seguimos soñando* (M. Mora, Illus.). Lee and Low Books.

Tonatiuh, D. (2010). *Dear primo: A letter to my cousin.* Abrams Books for Young Readers.

Tonatiuh, D. (2014). *Separate is never equal: Sylvia Mendez and her family's fight for desegregation.* Abrams Books for Young Readers.

Yang, K. K. (2024). *The rock in my throat* (J. Lin, Illus.). Carolrhoda Books.

4

Trauma

"We go through a story together": Considering Trauma in Critical, Humanizing Writing Classrooms

Elizabeth Dutro

As the storyteller and the listener, we go through a story together.
~Maxine Hong Kingston

Be it grand or slender, burrowing, blasting, or refusing to sanctify; whether it laughs out loud or is a cry without an alphabet, the choice word, the chosen silence, unmolested language surges toward knowledge, not its destruction.
~Toni Morrison, Nobel Prize Lecture (1993)

As storytellers and listeners, to invoke Kingston, there is no shortage of difficult stories that humans may go through together in classrooms. Children and adults are always holders of stories of joy, challenge, security, precarity, peace, connection, loss, anxiety, harm, and healing. Stories, some, as Morrison writes, that "cry without an alphabet", are always present in educational spaces. The stories of experience, of history, that humans hold in and through the body speak to the fact of students' wholeness, richness, and knowledge. Some of that experience and knowledge is painful. When any of us feel the traumas of life pulsing as we cross a classroom threshold, it's an open question whether we, the whole person, will feel welcome. So, if we stipulate that students' (and teachers') difficult stories are always present, we then also have to acknowledge that those experiences, the ones that fuel so much of what a person knows, and impact how they are making sense of the world, must be considered at the heart of school writing. We know that vibrant learning is fueled when children feel that their lived stories are seen, heard, and valued as sources of knowledge and resources for school literacies. However, as teachers, we may rarely have opportunities, whether in preservice preparation or professional development, to learn critical, humanizing principles and practices to take children's traumas into account in the day-to-day teaching and learning in our classrooms.

Fortunately, this landscape is shifting, as the idea of trauma in schools, the complex and important dimensions of what that word needs to mean (and not mean), has burgeoned as a focus of conversation. Importantly, those discussions increasingly include the critical and humanizing ways educators can consider and approach difficult experiences in the writing classroom. I believe school writing provides a particularly bountiful context for critically and responsively integrating attention to challenging life experiences into our teaching. *How* to honor the hard aspects of experience in a humanizing way is far from straightforward, though. Too often, discussions about children's trauma are disconnected from the relationships and connections with others and with texts that are already ever-present in the literacies we engage in our classrooms. When a hard experience spontaneously arises in children's writing, teachers may feel overwhelmed and unsure of whether and how to respond. Also, when attention to trauma arises related to schooling, the information that frames those conversations can slip into damage-centered narratives about children. As Love (2019) and others have emphasized, those pathologizing narratives about students' trauma often aim, explicitly or implicitly, at children who are already marginalized in schooling through long histories of injustice in educational systems, including students of color, English Language Learners, students from immigrant backgrounds, and those facing poverty or economic struggle.

Given my positionality, these are not impacts I have to weather as a white cis straight economically secure woman, current professor, and former elementary teacher in southern California. I have collaborated with many children and teachers in my inquiries over time and, in this work, I position myself as ally to children and colleagues of color and to my family members, including my children, both of whom are queer biracial Asian Americans.

What do these crucial complexities surrounding trauma suggest for writing classrooms? I hope it convinces each of us of the necessity of committing to the principles that guide this book. These are principles that can fuel the daily joys that come when the knowledges we hold most tenderly, most deeply, are welcome in learning spaces, and remind us of the fierce commitments to justice and advocacy that are required at every turn. Many of the chapters in this book hold crucial implications for crafting writing classrooms that honor students' lives and their experiences that are highly relevant to supporting critical, humanizing, and antiracist approaches to trauma, so I encourage readers to attend to those overlaps among chapters. We know from research and from our own experience that teachers and students can craft classroom communities centered on care, compassion, and criticality. In the context of those rich and relational spaces, literacy educators can invite and value difficult experiences to live and breathe in the writing classroom (Dutro, 2019).

This chapter will explore how writing classrooms can serve as sites of testimony and witness where hard stories—traumas of life, in their various forms and impacts—are valued and honored. I will first discuss some of the principles that are common across critical work related to trauma that are applicable to writing classrooms. Next, I turn to a framework to support incorporating humanizing approaches to trauma into the writing classroom, followed by an illustration from a classroom. I then discuss several of the stances and practices from that teacher's lesson and writing classroom, as well as examples of children's writing. It goes without saying that hard things are already in the room when humans, children, and adults enter a shared space. The question is whether they are acknowledged and viewed as fuel for pedagogical approaches that center student knowledge, connection to others, and to literacies, and support justice goals in literacy teaching and learning. Without doubt, the answer to that question can and must be "yes", so we can support one another as educators to live that commitment.

Central Principles: Trauma and Critical Humanizing Approaches

In this section, I discuss three central principles I see in the scholarship in critical, humanizing approaches to the presence of trauma in schools and literacy classrooms. For one, trauma takes many intersecting forms that demand critical recognition, including trauma wielded through structural, systemic oppressions. Second, across those forms, the difficult stories students hold speak to children's wholeness, wisdom, and insight in the midst of pain or harm—and never to damage or brokenness. Third, attention to care, love, and agency, as well as honoring the knowledge and histories students (and their teachers) embody, must be part of what we do in the day-to-day of writing classrooms, not an add-on or an exercise in a "trauma-informed" curriculum.

Trauma as Systemic and Multifaceted

Attuning to trauma in humanizing ways in writing classrooms requires understanding trauma as complex and both systemic and multifaceted. In writing classrooms, trauma encompasses both personal and shared experiences; it is a fundamental part of the human condition, but also systemically targeted and often exacerbated by schools themselves. For instance, the prevalence of school shootings represents a shared trauma that impacts society as a whole, yet students, families, and educators feel its weight in deeply personal ways, viewing each incident through the lens of "it could be me or my child." While loss and pain are universal experiences, many traumas are intensified by oppressive systems. Trauma-informed education often focuses on trauma as something students bring into schools, with limited attention to schools as sources of trauma. Historically and currently, Black, Brown, Indigenous, and queer students are more likely to face institutional harm than their straight, cisgendered white peers (Khasnabis & Goldin, 2020; Donisch et al., 2020). As Alvarez (2020) emphasizes, we must center race in trauma discussions, cautioning that failing to do so can lead to the criminalization or pathologizing of trauma-exposed Black and Brown youth.

Attending to these intersecting ways that trauma manifests in lives and schools means holding two truths at once, not as binaries in opposition, but as always enmeshed: recognizing the ongoing oppressions and persistent material and rhetorical violence that are realities we must keep centrally in our sights and actions, *and* the joys, connections, brilliant insights, and everyday ordinary moments that children are always bringing with them to the page.

Trauma as Children's Knowledge, Not Damaged Children

Children in writing classrooms may experience wounds across those complex ways that trauma can fall into their lives. Although all resources available should aim to support and care for students in the midst of harm or loss, the knowledges and perspectives those experiences represent deserve to be honored, rather than framed as brokenness or damage to be fixed (Goldin et al., 2023).

Why parse words like "wound" versus "damage"? Though they may seem similar, these terms carry distinct meanings and imply different narratives about students. When discussing trauma in classrooms, it's essential to consider the nuances of the language we use to describe students and their experiences. Critical educators, particularly educators of color, have shown how terms like "grit", "resilience", and "mindfulness" can become racialized within schools with histories of systemic racism, framing children—especially children of color and those facing economic hardship—as needing traits they're assumed to lack (Goodman, 2018; Love, 2019; Pettway, 2017; Simmons, 2019). Similarly, terms like "cognitive damage" or "brokenness" often reflect deficit-based assumptions about trauma and can attach negatively to certain students. If our approach to trauma reinforces deficit labels, we must rethink our language and approach. Sociopolitical awareness is essential when addressing trauma in writing classrooms.

Trauma Responsiveness as Threaded into the Tapestry of Writing Classrooms

Researchers have emphasized how critical, humanizing approaches to trauma need to be part of an ethos that is reflected day-to-day in writing classrooms. We should expect writing classrooms to be contexts that are always humming with all aspects of life as children attempt to make their own connections with the content, genres, and instruction they are encountering (e.g., Adair & Kim, 2023; Dutro & Pacheco, 2022; Everett, 2021; Savitz & Kane, 2023).

Why is it so vital to focus on the daily unfolding of writing in classrooms? Trauma-informed, humanizing writing pedagogy is a stance—a commitment to honoring students' life experiences, including trauma, even if those experiences are never shared explicitly. As Everett (2021) states, "We need trauma-informed and healing-centered teaching approaches because we do not know our students' trauma histories. We may never know them" (p. 10). This approach requires embracing the complexity and nuance of trauma in teaching, as Duane and Venet (2022) write, "We can embrace the mess and complexity of understanding trauma the same way we lean into the nuance with our content every day" (p. 14). Creating classrooms that honor the full range of children's experiences isn't a straightforward process. Recognizing the layered meanings of trauma assumes the need for classrooms that offer all children—and whatever they choose to write—a soft place to land (Leonardi & Staley, 2022). As I describe below, there are particular ways our humanizing response to trauma must show up for children to honor their right to bring the fullness of their loss, love, pain, and joy to their writing, but those pedagogies are inseparable from the larger tapestry.

Children's writing reminds us how central their knowing must be to literacy practice. Children's narratives of their experiences are crucial to what is possible to know about the experience of living in fragile human bodies, as well as in worlds in which the injustice of systems and the power adults exert over children fuel hardship and pain for some children. In the following sections, I build on the principles discussed above to consider the implications of those foundational commitments and stances for pedagogical practice. I start with a particular framework for conceptualizing writing pedagogy in light of the imperative to recognize and honor difficult experiences: testimony and critical witness. I have written about these pedagogies previously and how they arose through learning with children and teacher colleagues in literacy classrooms (Dutro, 2013; 2019). As I discuss, these pedagogies are animated by other researchers' ideas and approaches. I then share an example of a lesson taking up those pedagogies and share examples of student writing. Finally, I highlight a few key ideas that speak to central implications of those pedagogies for writing classrooms, including invitation (never requirement), challenging binaries, and attunement to poetics.

A Framework for Trauma-Informed Writing Pedagogy: Testimony and Critical Witness

In trauma-informed writing classrooms, *testimony* and *witness* are central concepts, illuminating a critical path toward responsive, humanizing pedagogy. Writing classrooms are always spaces of testimony, reflecting the complex lives of students, whether on the page or in subtler ways. *Testimonio*, as defined by scholars, conveys personal experiences connected to larger histories of oppression (Calderón et al., 2012; DeNicolo & Gonzalez, 2015; Saavedra, 2011). Cruz (2017) notes that "testimonio ... positions a listener or an audience for self-reflection" (p. 462). In classrooms that affirm the value of students' lived experiences, including trauma, students may testify through writing or, equally, through non-verbal cues—such as a sigh, a blank page, a turned back, or a slammed door. Such testimonies call for *witnessing* from teachers and peers. The question becomes: What kind of witness will we be to each other's testimonies?

Literacy researchers have theorized testimony and witness as circular and cyclical in classrooms, as a testifier's story is heard, absorbed, and may awaken the witness's empathy and, very often, the pull of connection to their own experiences of loss, fear, pain, and violence (Dutro, 2019; Savitz & Stockwell, 2021). In short, we should expect witnessing others' testimonies to prompt additional testimony, which demands more witnessing, and so on. Imagining testimony and witness as circular among children and their teachers positions children as active participators and agents of that process in writing classrooms. In relation to trauma, children are not simply responders to invitations to make challenging aspects of life part of what matters to school writing but are also important witnesses to their classmates' and teachers' sharing (e.g., Haddix, 2016; Wissman, 2009). As Regidor (2023) notes, stories of trauma can function as "agentive texts" that can transform "how we teach literacy and writing in creating more just and equitable" classrooms (p. 15). In other words, reciprocity is a central aspect of testimony and critical witness to trauma in writing classrooms, which requires teachers to lead the way in showing children that school writing is a space to bring our full selves.

Witnessing children's testimony and inviting them to witness each other's stories is vital, but it's not enough. Witnessing must include action that addresses the sociopolitical contexts shaping children's lives and commitments to justice. Researchers and educators emphasize "worthy witnessing" (Winn & Ubiles, 2011), "faithful witnessing" (Lugones, 2003), and witnessing as an "active ethical stance" (Zembylas, 2016). My own work explores "critical witness" in literacy classrooms, which involves recognizing how children are positioned within power structures and how they actively resist these injustices. Cruz (2017) underscores this, stating, "To be a faithful witness to a story of trauma or oppression, there is a responsibility we owe to the speaker" (p. 468). This aligns with Ginwright's (2015) concept of "healing justice", which seeks to address institutional oppressions that intensify trauma. Critical witness, then, is an ongoing, daily process of holding children's experiences close with care, love, and resonance while, at the same time, holding others' stories at a far enough distance to recognize, analyze, and advocate within the very different ways lives are interpreted and impacted by systemic and sustained oppression. Adair and Kim (2023) capture this well, writing that "Trauma as a racial equity issue in education (Alvarez, 2020) makes the need for critical witnessing all the more urgent. Rather than spaces that overlook, marginalize, or contribute to students' trauma, classrooms must be spaces for all students to narrate themselves and their experiences, including experiences of trauma, on their own terms" (p. 13).

Teacher Commitments and Actionable Practices

What does this look like in practice in a writing classroom? Here, I'll share just one example of many of how a teacher can embed invitations to bring difficult experiences to school writing into day-to-day writing instruction. I'll then discuss the writing instructional practices and stances it illustrates. Finally, I share examples of the ways children took up those invitations across time and genre in classrooms.

~~~~~~~~~

On this day, the second graders in Megan's classroom gathered as usual on the rug for the start of writing time. The class was continuing their personal narrative unit. Megan started the lesson by sharing the story of the day she found out her grandfather had passed away. Megan told the children that the story she was going to write that day was inspired by the stories three children wrote after the class read *Visiting Day* by Jacqueline Woodson, a book about a little girl who visits her father in prison. The rubric they were using to guide their learning of the genre was printed on poster paper and posted in view of the students.

> Megan: Today, I'm gonna write about the time my grandfather passed away. He was very close to me, very special. This was my Dad's dad. I called him Papa.
>
> Turning to the chart paper and holding her pen poised at the top of the page, Megan says,
>
> So, let's say, I'm gonna name it. Gosh, I don't know … It happened in August ….
>
> Juan: My Saddest Time of All.
>
> Emma: Shocking News.
>
> Megan: Hmmm. I think just "The Sad Day." I might go back and change it because sad is kind of a boring word.
>
> Samantha: What about "the tragic day"?
>
> Megan talks through "sad" and "tragic". She tells Samantha,
>
> Tragic is a great adjective. Tragic … Hmmm. I'm not sure it was tragic … I'm going to think about it, is that ok?
>
> Megan starts to write: It was a sunny, warm August afternoon. My sister.
>
> Jossalyn interjects: Katherine.
>
> Megan: You know what, that's probably better than saying "my sister" since you know her name (crosses out "my sister" and writes "Katherine" and then continues writing). Katherine and I were inside trying to stay cool.
>
> Megan pauses and reads aloud what she has written so far.
>
> Megan: When I write about something like this, when I'm remembering what happened, I feel kind of sad. Does that ever happen to you? When I got this news, I got this really sick feeling in my stomach.
>
> Student: Did you cry?
>
> Megan: I did cry. I get the sick feeling, again. Did you ever get that feeling?

She continues to write and talk aloud about the decisions she makes as she drafts her narrative. When she has filled two pages of the chart paper, she stops.

Megan: So, I'm gonna stop there for today, but let's go to my rubric for a quick second. Where was I for my content?

Several children: 4!

Megan: 4's are kind of reserved for published books. So, I would say it's a 3. My title said, "The Sad Day." Did I write about the sad day? What about my conventions?

She talks about her conventions, pointing to specific examples of spelling, punctuation, and indented paragraphs.

Megan: We have lots of time today to write. Thank you very much for being respectful while I shared that hard story with you. Today, I'm going to invite you, again. If there's something you want to write about that was sad in your life, kinda like I wrote about with my papa, you can write about that. It doesn't have to be about someone dying—maybe your pet got lost and ran away. But maybe there was a time you had that feeling in your stomach, too. But, you don't have to. You can write about something from the weekend, something silly that happened, etc.

This example highlights the kinds of lessons Megan taught throughout the year, mindfully including testimony and critical witness of life experiences that matter and are meaningful, including the hard aspects of life. In what follows, I highlight several of the writing instructional practices and stances visible within this lesson and this writing classroom. In Table 4.2, you will find examples of children's writing in response to these pedagogies.

Foster Joy, Care, and Connection

It is crucial to underscore that this is a joyful classroom. In Megan's classroom, children use descriptors such as "like a family", love, fun, important, and exciting to reflect on their experiences with writing with their teachers and classmates. Black scholars, in particular, argue for the centrality of joy in antiracist literacy pedagogies (Dunn & Love, 2020), and that is central to critical writing pedagogies considering trauma. Indeed, my collaborators and I are arguing in our work together that modeling of testimony to what deeply matters in teachers' and children's lives and attentive witnessing to others fosters joy and connection.

Model Vulnerability

Megan regularly used her own writing as a mentor text for testimony and critical witness, and also incorporated children's literature to provide trauma-sensitive mentor texts (Savitz & Kane, 2023). When asked in conversational interviews toward the end of each school year if they remember times when Megan shared her writing with them, more than half of the children across three years responded with an example of a time she shared an important, deeply felt experience from her life. In Abran's words, "Yeah. It's good [when she models her writing]. Maybe she is trying to tell us that someone died in her family too. She misses some people too." Teachers' intentional testimony positions children as witnesses and serves as invitation and endorsement for drawing on deeply felt life experiences as sources and resources for school writing.

Invite, Never Require

As illustrated in the lesson above, Megan consistently invited children to view life's challenges as valuable knowledge for writing, while making it clear that sharing such experiences was optional. For writing classrooms to be spaces of testimony and critical witness to children's lives, students need to trust that their experiences will be valued and treated with respect and care (Handsfield & Valente, 2016). Writing instruction should authentically invite students to bring their lives to the page, across genres, but never as a requirement. An invitation should always allow students to opt in or out, and if they choose to write about personal experiences, it doesn't mean they must share with others. As Zamora Liu's work with unhoused adults shows, writers may disclose sensitive details without wanting further discussion. Children, likewise, need a sense of control and agency over their writing.

Embrace Complexity and Challenge Assumptions

Consciously or not, as teachers, we may bring our own assumptions about how and when to bring pedagogies of testimony and critical witness to writing instruction. Those assumptions may relate to genre, topics, or children's emotions. But we can remind ourselves and each other to embrace complexity across dimensions of writing practice in ways that are responsive to children's lives and expand their writing opportunities.

Broaden genres for testimony and critical witness. These pedagogies are effective across genres, not just in personal narrative or poetry. Expository writing, too, can connect deeply with children's lives. As teachers, we should set aside assumptions about what topics will resonate with students' experiences. For example, when introducing research reports, I shared a childhood book, *Baby Animals*, gifted by my late brother. I told students how this gift fueled my desire to learn about animals, showing how even informational texts can carry personal meaning. This approach challenges rigid genre boundaries, inviting children to find meaningful connections in any topic, fostering a vibrant, creative learning environment.

Demonstrate that meaningful writing, like all writing, deserves to be revised and improved. Incorporating testimony and critical witness in the ways Megan demonstrates shows how these pedagogies are woven into writing instruction, including skills and processes instruction. In that illustration, the focus on the curricular personal narrative components remains, but the mentor texts and space for connections allow students to explore meaningful experiences. Megan uses the rubric with students to analyze her own writing, demonstrating that even stories of loss can be worked on, revised, and valued as part of a writer's process. Her story is an experience of loss and sadness that belongs on the page, holds meaning for the writer, opens connections for children, and shows how that writing *deserves* to be honed.

Disrupt binary categories of children's emotions. Importantly, each child's writing about difficult experiences held echoes of the more positive dimensions of life, such as connection, love, wishes, and courage, that are enmeshed with hardships. In this way, children's writing about trauma challenges binary categories of happy/sad, connection/disconnection, and pain/joy. For example, the wrenching loss and longing in Naomi's letter (below) about her parents' deportation cannot be detangled from the depths of love, devotion, and connection between parent and child.

Challenge assumptions about what counts as "trauma". Reciprocal testimony and witnessing in writing classrooms involves meaningful sharing and invitation for life to fuel writing in the classroom. For teachers, this requires positioning children as witnesses to teachers' lives, whether or not a teacher would attach an experience to the word trauma.

Further, as teachers we must challenge fears we may hold about whether our stories are "difficult enough" compared to some students' experiences. If you share a story of your sadness when your parents divorced, are you implying that experience is equivalent to a child's loss of a parent to incarceration? No. Rather, in sharing something that mattered in a teacher's life, the possibility has been opened for a child to make their own connections to something that matters deeply to them. Embracing reciprocity is decidedly not about drawing comparisons or equivalencies between experiences.

Highlight Writing That Matters to the Writer

Remind children that investment and connection to writing is central to the writing process. As Megan did in her lesson, teachers can model those investments and underscore that idea in writing conferences or lessons. And as the children's writing shows, they had learned that the modeling and invitation was genuine, and they took it up (or chose not to) in the ways that mattered to them. Time and again, what we noticed was that children connected to the larger themes of struggle, grief, fear, longing, anger, and loss they encountered through witnessing others' writing and, if they chose, would weave those themes into their own writing. In writing conferences, Megan and I often asked children questions aimed at supporting children to keep investment in mind as writers. Now, we imagine using an anchor chart focused on affirming reminders to think about connections to experiences, places, people, things, and ideas that matter to them and not accept disconnection as the way it has to be (see Table 4.1).

Innovate Within Curriculum-Required Writing Instruction

I recognize the constraints many teachers face in supporting writing. When curriculum is scripted or writing is treated as a subset of reading, it can seem hard to implement the pedagogies discussed here. However, small shifts—like using different mentor texts—can create space for children to see their lives, including trauma, as valuable in school literacies. For

Table 4.1 My Writing Should Matter to Me

My Writing Should Matter to Me!	
How am I feeling about this writing I'm doing?	
Am I feeling: Connected, Good, Excited, Interested, Curious, Motivated?	Keep going!
Am I feeling: Bored, Stuck, Unmotivated, Uninterested, Blah?	How can I make this matter more to me?
What could I do to get more interested in this topic/idea?	Read a mentor text; talk with my teacher or classmates
Is there a connection to this topic I can make in my writing or in my mind as a writer?	What might be a big idea in this writing activity or topic that matters to me?

example, if teaching constructed responses, selecting texts that resonate with students' lives can make writing more meaningful. Another way to innovate is to resist "expected responses" in scripted curricula, which often assume whiteness and wealth and limit children's unique perspectives. Instead, we can stay open to their diverse responses, which can be far richer than a teacher's guide predicts.

Separate Conventions from Other Aspects of Writing

Research shows that many assessment practices, from standardized tests to some classroom assessments, are biased by race, culture, wealth, and identity factors like gender (e.g., Shear, 2022) and assessors' unconscious biases. It's helpful to separate feedback on content from feedback on structure and conventions in writing—and to explain this distinction to students. When a child's grammar or spelling obscures their ideas, especially when they respond to invitations to write about difficult topics, transcribing their work with conventional grammar can allow us to better appreciate their content and craft. Why is it worth it to adopt this practice in assessment? I find that explicitly reminding myself and children that conventions are just one of many important aspects of writing, helps to reposition children as knowledgeable writers whose ideas, regardless of skill level, deserve careful attention. This attunement—especially when a child has experienced trauma—allows us to respond more meaningfully to their work, noticing what, how, and even whether they write, and discerning what those choices may signify.

Approach Children's Writing Through a Literary Lens

When we view children's writing with the same attentiveness we give published authors, we recognize their work as rich with aesthetic features—not just as therapeutic exercises. Children's writing, especially about difficult experiences, reveals that emotions like joy and sadness, connection and disconnection, and wounding and healing are interconnected. By focusing on their use of imagery, metaphor, and phrasing, we see the depth of their craft. Approaching children's writing with an assumption of their brilliance allows us to notice their poetic choices. While it's challenging to deeply analyze each piece in a busy classroom, we can carry the mindset that all children bring artistry to writing about meaningful topics. As an example, Daniel's poem about his pet turtle's death uses a refrain, "I can see you," and a vow, "I will never forget you," that resonate with universal feelings of loss (see Table 4.2). I feel that vow to my bones. Joey, the beloved turtle, connects to my own losses of beloved family members and friends. Will some children's writing make their poetics more obvious on first read? Yes, no doubt. But could I find poetics in each and every writing example I share here? Also, yes. I could and I have. Taking time to linger in children's writing invites us to puzzle through and attune to poetics across genres, but what we can know is that they are always bringing craft to their writing of meaningful topics (Dutro & Caasi, 2022). Attuning to poetics is a stance, as much as it is a practice.

Take a Long View of Children's Testimony to Trauma

When children feel invited to bring their life experiences into their writing, we can observe an arc in their work throughout the school year. My research in humanizing literacy classrooms shows that a significant experience in a child's life can subtly echo across different genres and pieces over the course of a school year. For instance, Malina's story expressing

Table 4.2 Examples Across Genres of Children's Writing in Response to Pedagogies of Testimony and Critical Witness

Dear Dad,	**The Cancer Trip**	**My Grandpa Died**
I hope I am going to heaven like you did and we could meet roads, like me and you were walking by ourselves on a road and you were one block away from me and then I ran up and hugged you. *Love,* *Abran*	My brother had cancer. About the last day the doctor asked "What's your wish? Going to Disney World or Disneyland? If you don't want to go to those you can pick any place." My brother said, excited, "Disney World!" By Sonia	I went with my dad to the hospital! I wasn't allowed to see him for a long time. He died. We went to the funeral for a lot of days. We dug him in the dirt. I felt sad for a long time. By Julianna
My Dad was in jail. I was sad and mad because my Dad is always being a bad Dad and I do not like it. I wish he was not a bad person. Then I would be proud of him. But I am not proud of him. I am angry at my bad dad. That is why my mom does not let us see our dad. The End. By Malina	**Joey (a poem about a pet turtle)** I'm sad because you are not alive anymore I can see you in my dreams And I can see you in my window in my imagination I will never forget you, not even once I will never forget you. By Daniel	Dear Papa, I wish you and my mom weren't deported cause sometimes I miss you when I'm at school. I wish my mom and you can see me cause I miss you and I care about you and I can't stop saying I love you cause I love you so much. Love, Naomi

Vroom Vroom we were going back home. When we got there I looked over at my Dad. I knew that my Dad was sick. My Dad said he will be in the hospital for ten days. I said why are you going in the hospital. For I can be good and to check my tummy.
When the ten days were finished me and my family went to see my dad in the hospital. The nurse said you can go back with your family, but you can't ever do drugs anymore.
By Javier

My Dog Angel

I have a dog
She is big
I love
She is awesome
I love her best.
I will call my dog
She comes to me.
I am so mad
Because my mom
Gave away my dog
I am mad.
My mom gave it to my stepmom.
She gave it to my grandma.
By Lily (Bold text is in original)

I Miss My Uncle

One afternoon I was watching a movie. I heard a knock at the door. 'Dad, there's someone at the door!' My Dad came running to the door. They were at the door. They said my uncle died. My stomach lurched. I started to cry. I ran to my dad and hugged him. The next day I packed my bags. We were driving to Kansas. I waited for four hours. We were there before I knew it. We were at the funeral. The End. By Shania

Source: For many more examples, see Dutro (2019).

anger with her father (see Table 4.2) was joined by other writing across genres that explicitly invoked her father, as well as writing focused on her mother—gratitude for her presence and stories of everyday life in their home—that held echoes of her frustration with her absent father. From personal narratives to research reports, themes of loss or trauma often surface, even if they are not immediately obvious.

Closing Thoughts

I close with this reflection. Recently, I reread an article a colleague and I wrote about children's writing—stories of loss, connection, political threat, and agency woven through their school literacies. We addressed the material threats and rhetorical violence faced by children of color, especially those navigating life across borders and languages, in the wake of the 2016 U.S. presidential election. Now, as I finish this chapter after another election, the brutality seems even worse. Dehumanizing rhetoric and policies targeting women, Black, Brown, queer, and trans people permeate society, intensifying trauma for many children, their families, and teachers. If I grasp for hope, I can find it in this book's pages, full of commitments and actionable ways to move toward justice in constrained and oppressive times. For writing teachers who wish to be change-agents toward social justice in schools, infusing humanizing pedagogies that are responsive to trauma with the other commitments and practices shared across this book will lead to creative, caring, and critical approaches beyond what I have explored here. Teachers and teacher educators can shape and reshape the dimensions of testimony and critical witness that can animate writing pedagogy. This is always both heartwork steeped in human connection *and* fiercely critical and analytical work, brewed in the deepest commitments to folding children into loving classrooms and pursuing action and advocacy for their right to be seen, represented, and exist.

Questions for Reflection and Discussion

What is a difficult experience you carry? How has it shaped who you are in the world? How has it impacted your relationships with others (whether or not that experience is ever shared or spoken)? What forms of trauma are you considering as you think about this? How does your positionality (race, gender, sexuality, economic situation, language) shape the forms of trauma you have or have not experienced? When, if ever, do you find that experience coming up for you in your teaching life?

What are some ways educators might innovate within writing instruction to support students to see their lives, including trauma, as crucial and valued resources for school writing? What resonates with you about the approaches discussed in this chapter? What additional approaches have you taken or can you imagine taking that fuel critical, humanizing pedagogies that honor children's knowledge and experiences related to trauma?

How can teachers lean into reciprocity as a humanizing pedagogical practice in writing classrooms? What forms can this take?

Consider an informational genre and topic that might appear in literacy curricula. How might you connect to it, launch it through your own testimony in a lesson, and present your own story of why that topic is important to you? Take up this thought experiment with other genres too.

References

Adair, L., & Kim, G. M. (2023). Critical witnessing as a critical literacy practice in secondary English education. *The New Educator*, 19, 33–54. https://doi.org/10.1080/1547688X.2023.2172243

Alvarez, Adam (2020). Seeing race in the research on youth trauma and education: A critical review. *Review of Educational Research*, 90, 583–626.

Calderón, D., Bernal, D. D., Huber, L. P., Malagón, M., & Vélez, V. N. (2012). A Chicana feminist epistemology revisited: Cultivating ideas a generation later. *Harvard Educational Review*, 82(4), 513–539.

Cruz, C. (2017). Making curriculum from scratch: Testimonio in an urban classroom. In D. Bernal, R. Burciaga, & J. Carmona (Eds.), *Chicana/Latina testimonios as pedagogical, methodological, and activist approaches to social justice* (pp. 109–120). Routledge.

DeNicolo, C. P., & Gónzalez, M. (2015). Testimoniando en Nepantla: Using testimonio as a pedagogical tool for exploring embodied literacies and bilingualism. *Journal of Language and Literacy Education*, 11(1), 109–126.

Donisch, K., Ake, G., Halladay Goldman, J., Trunzo, C. P., Agosti, J., & Houston, F. (2022). *National Child Traumatic Stress Network's Breakthrough Series Collaborative Schools Brief: A Focus on Trauma-Informed Practices*. Los Angeles, CA, & Durham, NC: National Center for Child Traumatic Stress.

Duane, A., & Venet, S. V. (2022). Thirteen ways of looking at trauma: Possibilities and considerations in trauma theory for ELA educators. In Elizabeth Dutro & Bre Pacheco (Eds.), *Trauma-Informed Teaching*, Volume 2 (pp. 13–23). Urbana, IL: National Council of Teachers of English.

Dunn, D., & Love, B. L. (2020). Antiracist language arts pedagogy is incomplete without Black joy. *Research in the Teaching of English*, 55(2), 190–192.

Dutro, E. (2013). Toward a pedagogy of the incomprehensible: Trauma and the imperative of critical witness in literacy classrooms. *Pedagogies: An International Journal*, 8(4), 301–315.

Dutro, E. (2019). *The vulnerable heart of literacy: Centering trauma as powerful pedagogy*. New York: Teachers College Press.

Dutro, E., & Pacheco, B. (Eds.). (2022). *Trauma-informed teaching: Toward responsive, humanizing classrooms*. Champaign, IL: National Council of Teachers of English.

Everett, S. (Ed.). (2021). *Trauma-Informed Teaching*, Volume 1. National Council of Teachers of English, Urbana, IL.

Farinde-Wu, A., Alvarez, A., & Kunimoto, N. (2023). Teach like a black woman: A trauma-informed black feminist praxis. *Urban Education*, 60(3), 761–791. https://doi.org/10.1177/00420859231175669.

Fisher, D., Frey, N., & Savitz, R. S. (2020). *Teaching hope and resilience for students experiencing trauma: Creating safe and nurturing classrooms for learning*. Teachers College Press.

Ginwright, S. (2015). *Hope and healing in urban education: How urban activists and teachers are reclaiming matters of the heart*. Routledge.

Ginwright, Shawn (2018). The future of healing: Shifting from trauma informed care to healing centered engagement. *Occasional Paper*, 25, 25–32.

Goldin, S., Khasnabis, D., Duane, A., & Robertson, K. (2023). Deciphering truth: Teaching about the systemic nature of trauma. *Urban Education*, 60(3), 792–820. https://doi.org/10.1177/00420859231175678.

Goodman, S. (2018). *It's not about grit: Trauma, inequity, and the power of transformative teaching*. Teachers College Press.

Haddix, M. M., & Mardhani-Bayne, A. (2016). Writing our lives: The power of youth literacies and community engagement. In S. Greene, K. J. Burke, & M. K. McKenna (Eds.), *Youth voices, public spaces, and civic engagement* (pp. 131–147). New York, NY: Teachers College Press.

Handsfield, L. J., & Valente, P. (2016). Momentos de cambio: Cultivating bilingual students' epistemic privilege through memoir and testimonio. *International Journal of Multicultural Education*, 18(3), 138–158.

Jones, S. P. (2020). Ending curriculum violence. *Learning for Justice*, 64. www.learningforjustice.org/magazine/spring-2020/ending-curriculum-violence

Jones, S. P. (2022). The language of curriculum violence. *English Journal*, 111, 15–17.

Khasnabis, D., & Goldin, S. (2020). Don't be fooled, trauma is a systemic problem: Trauma as a case of weaponized educational innovation. *Occasional Paper Series*, 43, 5.

Leonardi, B., & Staley, S. (2022). Disrupting damage-centered approaches to LGBTQ+ inclusion: Finding queer possibilities. In Elizabeth Dutro &

Bre Pacheco (Eds.), *Trauma-Informed Teaching*, Volume 2 (pp. 34–40). Urbana, IL: National Council of Teachers of English.

Love, B. (2019, February 12). "Grit is in our DNA": Why teaching grit is inherently anti-Black. *Education Week*. www.edweek.org/leadership/opinion-grit-is-in-our-dna-why-teaching-grit-is-inherently-anti-black/2019/02

Lugones, M. (2003). *Pilgrimages/peregrinajes: Theorizing coalition against multiple oppressions*. Rowman & Littlefield Publishers.

Morrison, T. (1993, December). Nobel Lecture. Nobel Prize in Literature. Lecture presented at 1993 Nobel Lecture, Stockholm, Sweden.

National Child Traumatic Stress Network, Justice Consortium, Schools Committee, and Culture Consortium. (2017). *Addressing Race and Trauma in the Classroom: A Resource for Educators*. Los Angeles, CA, and Durham, NC: National Center for Child Traumatic Stress.

Ohito, E. O., Watson, W., Lyiscott, J., & Sealey-Ruiz, Y. (2019). Postscript: Visions of love in urban schooling, or a love letter from the editors. *The Urban Review*, 51, 146–148.

Pettway, A. (2017). Mindful of equity: Practices that help students control their impulses can also mask systemic failures. *Learning for Justice*, 57. www.learningforjustice.org/magazine/fall-2017/mindful-of-equity

Regidor, M. P. C. (2023). "I'm a Bad Writer": Latina college students' traumatic literacy experiences. *College English*, 86(1), 9–35.

Rossina Zamora Liu (2019). Humanizing the practice of witnessing trauma narratives. *Journal of Adolescent & Adult Literacy*, 63(3), 347–350.

Saavedra, C. M. (2011). Language and Literacy in the Borderlands: Acting upon the World through "Testimonios". *Language Arts*, 88(4), 261–269.

Saleem, F. T., Howard, T. C., & Langley, A. K. (2022). Understanding and addressing racial stress and trauma in schools: A pathway toward resistance and healing. *Psychology in the Schools*, 59(12), 2506–2521.

Savitz, R. S., & Kane, B. D. (2023). *Trauma-sensitive literacy instruction: Building student resilience in English-language arts classrooms*. Teachers College Press.

Savitz, R. S., & Stockwell, D. (2021). Student Voice is Power: Incorporating Critical Witness and Testimony in Middle-School Classrooms. In Jason DeHart, Carla K. Meyer, & Katie Walker (Eds.), *Connecting theory and practice in middle school literacy* (pp. 25–41). Routledge.

Shear, B. R. (2023). Gender bias in test item formats: Evidence from PISA 2009, 2012, and 2015 math and reading tests. *Journal of Educational Measurement*, 60(4), 676–696.

Simmons, D. (2019, April 1). Why we can't afford Whitewashed social-emotional learning. *ASCD*. www.ascd.org/el/articles/why-we-cant-afford-whitewashed-social-emotional-learning

Winn, M. T., & Ubiles, J. R. (2011). Worthy witnessing. *Studying diversity in teacher education, 295.*

Wissman, K. (2009). Reading and becoming living authors: Urban girls pursuing a poetry of self-definition. *English Journal*, 98(3), 39–45.

Zembylas, M. (2016). Emotion, trauma, and critical pedagogy: Implications for critical peace education. In M. Bajoj & M. Hantzopoulos (Eds.), *Peace education: International perspectives* (pp. 19–34).

5

Multimodality

The Power and Promise of Multimodal Composition for Enacting Critical Humanizing Writing Pedagogies

Shawna Coppola

Beginning in the 1930s, a "new" form of composition—of meaning-making via text—began to gather steam. This compositional form was, and remains, multimodal in nature (Figure 5.1), making use of written, visual, and spatial text to both (1) communicate fans' fascination, admiration, and interpretation of science fiction, and (2) showcase original works written in the genre. These *zines* (short for "fanzine") were self-published, minimally circulated, and often free—especially for science fiction fan club members.

Importantly, this form of composition was inspired by the "amateur press movement" of the 1920s, when "small groups of Black artists and writers used the *little magazine* ... to undermine the established literary system" (Coleman, 2023, emphasis added). Throughout the twentieth century, the popularity of the zine ebbed and flowed, most notably during the punk music scene of the 1970s/1980s and the "Riot Grrrl" movement of the 1990s.

Figure 5.1 Assortment of zines.
By A Small Cinema (Flickr).

Inherent in its multimodality, the zine was, and continues to be, a symbol of protest and anti-establishmentism in its privileging of counternarratives and its circumventing of "traditional" channels of communication or paths to publication.

This is not exclusive to the zine format; it's true of many multimodal forms of composition. The first comics that arrived on the American scene around the turn of the twentieth century, for example—among them Richard Outcault's *Hogan's Alley* (featuring its scrappy young protagonist, Mickey Dugan)—served to offer its readers a dose of scathing social criticism through a format that also made use of written, visual, and spatial text. The political commentary Mickey's adventures illuminated was that which "engag[ed] with issues of immigration, nativism, and xenophobia" through "the plight of Irish Catholics" within the tenements of New York City (Abate, 2021). Although published conventionally, Outcault's comic—while itself littered with crude exaggerations and problematic tropes—served as an important counternarrative to that of the "American Dream" that President Grover Cleveland promised would offer folks both "enlightenment" and freedom from "the darkness of ignorance" (which, in reality, welcomed certain immigrants to the country and excluded and/or demonized others).

Around this same time, a call by members of the Black press went out to artists interested in helping to "counter the misrepresentations of African American life that circulated in popular media" through this same multimodal form. Comics, they recognized, served as an apt "platform" for social discourse—including, according to Whitted (2023), conversations around "the so-called race problem" throughout the first half of the twentieth century (p. 3).

The Power and Promise of Multimodality

These examples help elucidate how powerful multimodal composition can be in a world that continues to privilege monomodal writing practices—specifically, those that exclusively make use of alphabetic, or print, text. This is particularly the case for the kinds of literacy practices that are most often centered in K-12 school spaces (Coppola, 2019; Stockman, 2023), where the motivation to write school-sanctioned texts trends down as students move through the grades (Bruning et al., 2013; Koster et al., 2015) and where "academic" essays, personal narratives, and the like proliferate.

In this chapter, I will make a case for the need for educators to intentionally incorporate opportunities for students to compose multimodal texts, consider some of the ways we might do so, and explain how such modifications to our practice can ultimately provide our learners with a more critical, inclusive, and humanizing experience within the K-12 writing classroom.

As I have argued elsewhere, it is not that print-heavy texts—like the one you currently hold in your hands, as it happens!—are *themselves* problematic. From the nineteenth century onward, we have had the capacity to democratize both knowledge consumption and knowledge creation as a direct result of the technology that made the printing press possible—as well as that which, in more recent years, has made digital consumption and composition more accessible to the masses. What *is* problematic is the ideological hierarchy that has positioned exclusively written (i.e., printed) text above all others:

> [A]s some historians have argued, ... the dominance of print texts in society, and therefore in most schools and classrooms, has oftentimes

> served as a way for those with a disproportionate amount of social and political capital to determine the "acceptability" of individuals' levels of literacy—and consequently, in many cases, their very *personhood*.
>
> (Coppola, 2023, p. 102)

While this (often implicit) positioning of print text may seem like a benign issue to some, what often remains unspoken—and unacknowledged—is the connection between this positioning and the centering of literacy compositional practices that are steeped in White, colonialist, patriarchal ideologies.

Although the most frequently cited scholarship around multimodal composition does not always explicitly name this connection, it does often theorize how providing students with opportunities to compose multimodal texts, both analog and digital, can offer them a more inclusive, humanizing, and globalized educational experience. In their groundbreaking piece "A Pedagogy of Multiliteracies: Designing Social Futures" (1996), the New London Group argues about the need to broaden our pedagogy around the reading and composition of texts to "account for the context of our culturally and linguistically diverse" society and "ensure that differences of culture, language, and gender are not barriers to educational success" (p. 61). Likewise, Ball, Sheppard, and Arola (2018) write that "[b]y learning to compose multimodal texts instead of rehashing the limited use of written essays, writer/designers can communicate in more globally aware, digitally driven, ethical, and accessible ways, making our society a better place." They offer readers dozens of examples from real-life classrooms that demonstrate how multimodal composing can assist us, alongside our students, in "(re)mak[ing] our social futures" and "remind[ing] us that we are all on this planet together" (pp. 6–7).

Perhaps unsurprisingly, however, it is most frequently scholars of Color—particularly Black, Brown, and/or Indigenous scholars—who *explicitly* name the ties that bind the mode of text most often centered in school spaces and the urge to protect dominant (i.e., White, Eurocentric) literacy practices. In doing so, many argue, our educational system effectively gatekeeps who is "proficiently" literate under a cloak of "objectivity". In their study of the multimodal compositional practices of Black elementary and middle school-aged youth, for example, Griffin and Turner (2021) assert that "[l]iteracy curricula in particular have long been claimed as white property":

These curricula often focus so closely on monolithic school-based notions of literacy at the expense of incorporating the varied literacy practices of Black students that by relying on it, some educators intentionally and strategically belittle and erase the contributions, experiences, and knowledge of Black folks. (441)

Desireé B. Stephens, author of the e-book *Dismantling Supremacy Culture: Understanding and Overcoming Its 15 Pillars*, explains how this monolithic paradigm reflects dominant society's "Worship of the Written Word," a tenet of White Supremacy Culture first identified by Jones and Okun (2003). By design, this particular characteristic diminishes and erases other forms of meaning-making via "text":

> The written word ... is quite often in contrast with our indigenous ways of spoken heritage and familial lore. This juxtaposition invites us to question and explore how our reverence for written communication is often at the expense of other diverse forms of communication, knowledge, and lived experiences, which opens us up to collective memory and reconnection.
>
> (2003, para. 2)

Vanessa Angélica Villarreal (2024) recently wrote about this phenomenon in a thread on X, arguing that the lack of diversity around texts and the "inaccessible language" of those that are both monolingual and print-heavy "structure early antagonisms" toward literacy for students who come to school often inexperienced in the literacy practices of White, middle-class Americans (Figure 5.2).

Fortunately, there are many ways we can revise our practices as educators that can at least *start* to mitigate—and even, eventually, to dismantle—the oppressive chokehold that monolingual, alphabetic

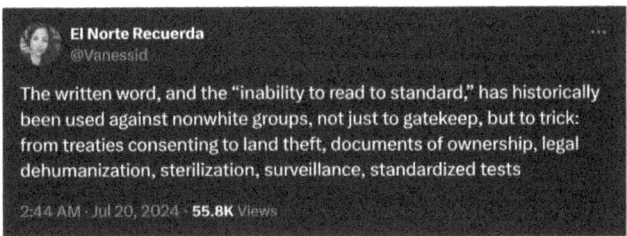

Figure 5.2 Villarreal's post on X.

By Vanessa Angélica Villarreal.

print texts have had on decades of school-age children, including (and especially) those unprotected by the cloak of whiteness. First, however, let's consider how doing so will benefit all those with whom we work.

Toward a More Inclusive, More Humanizing Pedagogical Practice

As many proponents of multimodal composition and digital literacy practices have maintained for decades, providing our students with opportunities to move away from more dominant writing practices—i.e., to compose multimodally and/or using digital technologies—offers us the potential to increase student agency, provide them with a more inclusive educational experience, and resist (and perhaps even transcend) White, colonialist ideologies around text, literacy, and learning. However, a caveat: We must be careful not to assume that simply inviting our students to engage in compositional practices that utilize a variety of modes (e.g., alphabetic, visual, aural, spatial, and/or gestural) will help us achieve these ends. Just as the practice of engaging in print-heavy forms of composition is not always *in and of itself* oppressive or reflective of the institutional marginalization of Black, Brown, Indigenous, disabled, and/or LGBTQIA+ children and youth, inviting students to compose multimodally is not *itself* sufficient to mitigate the harms enacted by an unwavering focus on traditionally school-sanctioned writing pedagogies.

As we seek to incorporate more opportunities for our students to compose multimodal and/or digital texts, we must consider inviting them to do so within the context of enacting what Kline and Kang (2022) call "transformative and humanizing Critical writing pedagog[ies]". Within this paradigm, literacy educators are urged to "reflect, reimagine, and revisit" their practices while pursuing a thread of professional inquiry that includes reflecting on questions like, "How can [we] invite students to compose in a broad range of forms and provide opportunities for students to write for purposes of advocacy, action, and justice?," and "How can [we] expand [our] use of technologies to connect students with broader audiences and open up spaces for Critical discourse?" Doing so, they write, can "help us see what we privilege and what we neglect when making conscious pedagogical decisions for our students," resisting the potential harms enacted by an uncritical adherence to White, neurotypical literacy norms (pp. 301–309).

Taking a Critical Stance Toward Multimodal Scholarship

In my book *Literacy for All: A Framework for Anti-Oppressive Teaching* (2023), I make the argument that while increasing students' opportunities to compose using a variety of modes and forms of text can benefit all students, there is a wealth of research, both empirical and anecdotal, that demonstrates that such opportunities are especially beneficial for (1) students who have been identified with a language-based learning disability, (2) emergent bilingual and multilingual students, and (3) immigrant children and youth (see, for example, the work of Bui, 2012; Ghiso, 2016; Mills & Dooley, 2019; Veum et al., 2021; Whitney, 2016).

However, we must be both *discerning about* and *inclusive of* those whose scholarship around multimodality—digital or otherwise—we acknowledge, amplify, and learn from as practitioners. Davis (2015) zeroes in on the cultural homogeneity of the field of multimodal composition, and cautions against allowing a lack of criticality to taint the pedagogical practices that we most often amplify. Upon examining some of the most cited, and thus most valued, "touchstone" texts in the field, Davis, perhaps not unsurprisingly, found them lacking in the acknowledgment of nondominant, nonlinear forms of multimodal composition and, in particular, in the multimodal compositional practices characteristic of Black communities. She warns that, without an acknowledgment of this gap in scholarly representation and of diverse communities' ways of composing,

> we ultimately risk normalizing a discourse that will continue to limit students [to] screen-mediated, digital, print-based essayistic modes of meaning-making instead of exploring and gaining experience with the vastly multimediated, multimodal communicative systems provided by the multicultural discourses found in our public spheres.
>
> (p. 24)

Learning About Multimodality and Digital Literacy from Scholars of Color

Our own exploration around multimodal scholarship (and in the ways that this scholarship can inform—i.e., *reflect, reimagine,* and *revisit*—our pedagogical practice) ought to include learning from folks like Adam J. Banks. For example, in his work advocating for a sustained focus on African American oral tradition and multimedia creation—specifically, DJing—in English composition courses, Banks points out that such a focus can provide students with

> a wealth of content reflecting black epistemologies and ontologies, ways of knowing and being in the world ... that begin with the assumption of black humanity [and] provide examples of the wide continuum from access to, participation in, and resistance of broader narratives and structures. (2011, p. 32)

Additionally, in their literature review of the research specific to Black girls' literacies, Muhammad and Haddix (2016) remind us of their "multidimensional, layered, nuanced, and complex" nature that frequently makes use of "the reading and creation of texts across multiple modes". For these students, they write, engaging in digital literacy practices "has the potential to enable collaboration, relationship building, participation in sociopolitical thought" and can provide them with "a safe space ... [to draw] from their own narratives and of others to express their subjectivities among dominant discourses" (pp. 301–309). In short, broadening our literacy pedagogy in order to provide our students with opportunities to compose multimodally using a critically-conscious lens—specifically as a way to confront racial inequities and anti-Blackness—can help "center and affirm" what Griffin and Turner (2021) call "Black Livingness," a way of thinking that "(re)assert[s] Black life and declar[es] the fullness of Black humanity" (p. 450).

Echoing these Black scholars' pleas to educators to embrace modes of text/composition beyond the alphabetic mode, Medina (2018) illustrates how digital/multimodal composition that *also* makes use of culturally relevant storytelling—such as the Latin American *testimonio*, a form of composition that traditionally "bring[s] to light a wrong, a point of view, or an urgent call for action" (Reyes & Rodríguez, 2012, p. 525)"—can promote student engagement and agency by "broadening audiences' perspectives" and "communicate experiences about which they have previously been silenced by the limited intended audience of monomodal writing" (para. 6). At the same time, the digital *testimonio* also provides a means for children and youth to engage in collaborative writing that makes use of linguistic, visual, gestural, and aural modes of text:

> [it] presents a complex knot of literacies, modes, and cultural practices paralleling preexisting understandings of multimodal possibilities ... [and] creates a culturally relevant space for Latinx students while providing non-Latinx students a similar space to address their own subjectivity and how they can be allies. (paras. 24–28)

As these and many other scholars of Color have demonstrated, the question is not *whether* to integrate multimodal composition into our pedagogical practice (or, as Kang and Kline write, to consider it an "add-on" [2020]); rather, the question is how we can ever justify *not* doing so knowing the impact it can have on so many of our students—particularly, on our students of Color.

Taking a Critical Stance Toward Digital Tech/Tools

Just as we ought to question whose scholarship we most often amplify, we must call into question the tendency for many multimodal and/or "new media" scholars to conflate all multimodal composing practices with the (uncritical) use of digital technology. While many opportunities to compose texts using a variety of modes do include using digital technologies, not *all* multimodal composing practices do—or frankly, *should*. We would be wise to learn from colleagues like Jason "J" Palmeri, who urges educators to "remain vigilant" about how digital literacy practices might be used to "reinforce both problematic pedagogical practices ... and material inequalities of race, class, gender, and disability ... " (2012, p. 10). We have witnessed this play out time and time again, most recently during the start of the COVID-19 pandemic and schools' hasty pivot to using digital literacy tools in order to mimic the experience of being "in person". These tools were often incorporated without educators first stopping to consider whether these tools, and their varying affordances, align with equity- and access-focused pedagogical principles (Coppola et al., 2021).

Likewise, Gleason and Mehta (2022) point out how technology is often inaccurately framed as a "neutral tool" that fails to consider "the social, cultural, political, and historical contexts in which technology is produced, mobilized, and repurposed" (p. 5). While they focus mainly on the use of technology within online learning models, their argument is relevant to the call to *critically* incorporate the use of digital tools, both in-person and online, as part of our desire to provide our students with a more humanizing and culturally responsive experience as learners (and for our specific purposes here, as composers of text).

For example, consider what it might look like to teach or encourage students to use a popular online design platform like Canva to create multimodal texts—an infographic explaining the inaccessible design of many playgrounds, for instance, or a short video discussing the impacts of climate change on various animal populations. On a platform like this, students would have access to a library of hundreds of thousands of free graphics—more, if they have access to a premium subscription—that they can choose from to help create their composition. But what kind of graphics would they discover? Which graphics are pushed to the top of a search on a platform such as this?

The short answer is that many platforms like Canva amplify graphics and images that fit dominant cultural and societal ideals, perpetuating the idea that experiencing life outside of these ideals is somehow wrong or unusual. If we were to search for graphics that fit the concept of "family", for example, we would find that traditionally nuclear, mostly White (or racially ambiguous) families centered around cishetero couples are those that are amplified. Scroll down through the dozens of graphics that Canva offers, and we might see a family that features a mother wearing a hijab. Scroll even further down, and we may happen upon a graphic representing "family" that includes a single parent. However, one would have to scroll for what feels like forever to find a graphic depicting a family centered around a (presumed) gay couple or to see families with members who have a visible disability (or diverse body types, for that matter). What kind of message does this send?

Here's another example: Let's imagine that we are teaching students how to create short videos of book recommendations (perhaps like the ones many Gen X'ers like me loved to watch on *Reading Rainbow* once upon a time), and we're looking for some mentors on TikTok to show students as examples. Many educators may not be aware of the fact that internal documents leaked in late 2024 reveal that the company tweaks its algorithm to amplify the videos of people who meet a particular beauty "norm" (Patterson, 2024). Who do we imagine is likely to be included in—and more importantly, to be *excluded from*—that norm? Whose #kidbooktok videos, then, do we think would be more or less visible to audiences, and thus more likely to be used as a mentor "text" for students to emulate?

This is not to imply, necessarily, that because of issues like these, we ought to abandon using digital tools altogether. However, without a critical eye toward the digital and/or multimodal texts and tools we choose to utilize, and without teaching our students to *also* view these through a critical lens, the road toward enacting more critical humanizing writing pedagogies might as well be paved with spikes.

Concretizing This Work

At this point it should be clear that multiple truths can exist at the same time:

- integrating opportunities for students to compose multimodal and/or digital texts into our practice is essential to enacting a more humanizing writing pedagogy;
- in seeking to do so, it's important to acknowledge the whiteness of multimodal scholarship as a whole and to consider, if not prioritize, the scholarship of those whose literacies and languages are often the most marginalized in school spaces;
- the use of digital tools, if not incorporated into our practice using a critical lens, can perpetuate the same cultural and social marginalization/erasure that multimodal scholars seek to mitigate in school spaces.

How do we then hold tight to these multiple truths as we seek to revise our pedagogical practices? What might "broaden[ing] conceptions of traditional composing" and acknowledging the value of the varied and complex ways that students communicate their meaning-making (Kline & Kang, 2022, p. 303) *actually* look like in a classroom? Consider the following ideas to inspire your own practice working with student writers.

IDEA #1: Invite students to compose infographics—or perhaps a short video—in lieu of writing a research essay

Many teachers like me often find themselves bound to district, school, or department mandates regarding the forms of writing we must teach our students to write. One of these forms, of course, regardless of the age of the students we teach (except for, perhaps, our youngest learners) is the research essay.

Due to the ubiquity of the form in school spaces—not just in language arts classrooms, but in nearly all classrooms and subject areas—our students will have more than enough practice learning to compose this type of print-heavy text. But let's boil this ubiquitous form into the skills we want our student writers to demonstrate. In essence, the typical research essay is designed to assess how well students can do one or more of the following:

- Summarize what they've learned about a topic or subject;
- Provide an analysis of the topic/subject;
- Communicate their summary/analysis with an audience in a clear, concise, and organized manner;
- Properly cite the sources they used throughout their research;
- Demonstrate their understanding of the spelling and grammar conventions of White Mainstream English throughout their composition.

Without delving into the problematic assumptions inherent in some of these ideas (e.g., what is considered "White Mainstream" or "standard" or "conventional" English), the point I wish to make is that we don't need to force students to write in an essay format time and time again in order to demonstrate the above skills. What we can do is explicitly teach students to demonstrate their grasp of a subject or topic using multimodal forms of composition—forms like the infographic or the video essay, for instance—both of which make use of multiple modes of text.

For example, a co-teacher and I asked upper elementary students to compose an infographic as a way to share their knowledge gained from a week-long exploration around environmental justice, food justice, and water justice (see Figure 5.3)—and at the same time, propose a "call to action" for their readers. I have also, in my work at many grade levels

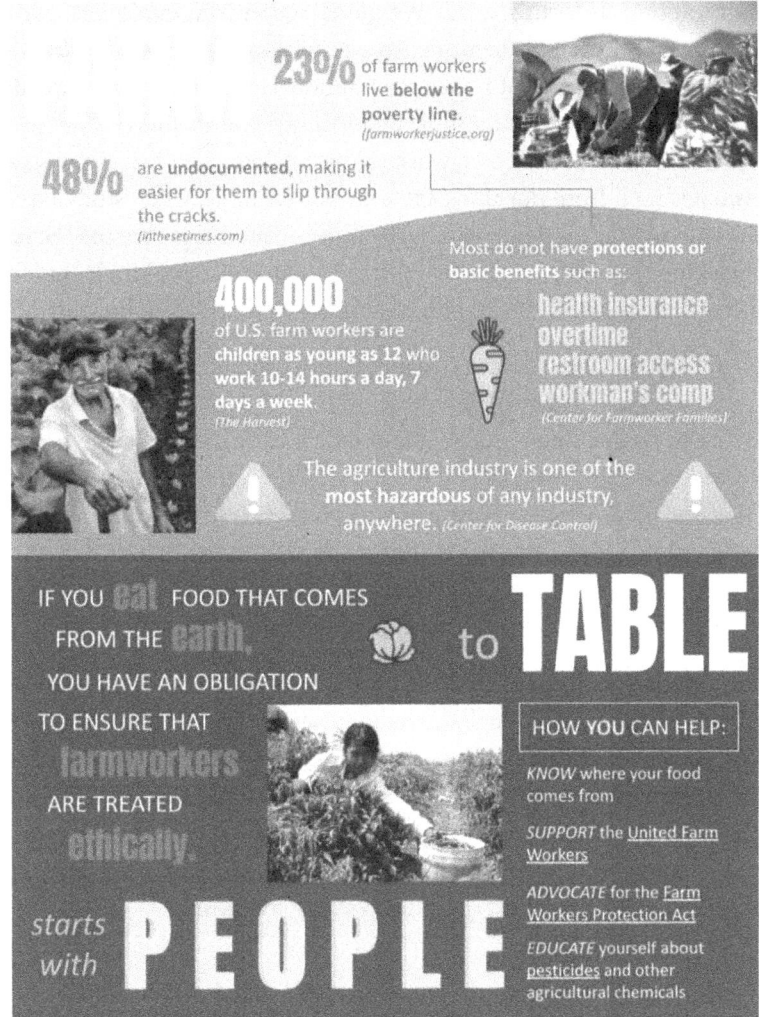

Figure 5.3 "Farm to Table" mentor infographic.
By Shawna Coppola.

(e.g., 3–12), encouraged students to create short video essays in order to share their knowledge around a research topic of social and/or cultural significance. With either form, students are tasked not only with composing alphabetic text to help inform their audience about their research topic, but visual text and—in the case of video essays—aural text as well.

Whether teaching students how to compose these forms using digital and/or analog tools and materials, my colleagues and I typically take an inquiry approach to this work. We guide students in exploring a wide and inclusive variety of mentors; we ask questions that lead students to identify the defining features and common elements of these mentor examples; and we provide multiple opportunities for them to try out these features/elements in their own work, gathering lots of feedback from their classmates (and from us) along the way. For example, when studying the short video format as demonstrated by those created as part of the "Nature Is Speaking" series (www.conservation.org/nature-is-speaking), students noticed that each of the examples we viewed included the following:

- minimal alphabetic text (usually an important fact or something for viewers to ponder over);
- clear, compelling visual text that relates to the topic (in the form of video and/or images);
- transitions between most pieces of visual text (e.g., a fade out);
- aural text (i.e., a voiceover written/spoken in first person point-of-view as well as appropriate background music);
- a title image.

These common elements served as a checklist of sorts indicating what their own short videos should include. In addition, we had several discussions about the way that these mentors served to inform their audience about an environmental "issue" through the use of narrative, or story. Despite never having created such a complex multimodal text before, students as young as nine-years-old were able to effectively share the research they had done through the short video essays they composed.

IDEA #2: Create a repository of digital videos featuring student-created spoken word that families can access and enjoy

Spoken word, for those unfamiliar with the form, makes use of poetry, aural, and gestural text (e.g., facial and body movements) and is rooted in what scholar Maisha T. Winn refers to as African Diaspora Participatory Literacy Communities (ADPLCs). Primarily existing in out-of-school or after-school settings, spoken word is a culturally sustaining compositional form that is often used as a way to (1) support "shared knowledge" within ADPLCs, (2) expand and deepen the literacy skills of both its performers and its audiences, (3) provide those "who have been traditionally silenced or ignored to present their lives and experiences," and (4) promote a call to action (Winn, 2003, p. 364).

This historically and culturally situated multimodal literacy practice, while an essential curricular component to include for the benefit of the Black students we teach in our schools and classrooms, is also an important communicative practice to highlight for students of all races, ethnicities, and cultures. As Woodard and Coppola (2018) have demonstrated, exploring this particular form of composition with students has benefits that transcend beyond the writers themselves. Because it is a form that makes use of authentic audiences through "slams" (where the poets competitively perform their work from memory in front of their peers and other community members) and/or non-competitive "open mics", spoken word also offers educators the opportunity to teach students about composing supportive "reader" responses, which include the use of both embodied responses in the moment (e.g., snaps, smiles, laughter, and other verbalized feedback) as well as written or verbal responses to the authors' work that address things like content, performance style/technique, and the effectiveness of their rhetorical appeal(s). Although different spoken word events traditionally have "varying rules of engagement", Winn writes, one that is nonnegotiable across contexts "is for the audience to listen with an open mind. There is a fundamental belief that everyone has something important to say and deserves active listening" (2003, p. 366).

For those who've taught students to compose poetry in a more traditional way, this shift to spoken word is unlikely to be too overwhelming. Again, it would be essential to begin by finding a diverse set of mentors (see "Additional Resources to Explore" on the Writing Reimagined companion website) that students can spend time exploring, as part of a small group or a whole-class inquiry, to identify the kinds of elements that make spoken word the unique multimodal form of composition that it is—as opposed to, say, a simple verbal reading of a poem.

Because not every family or caretaker works the same kind of shift, or is able to take time off of work to attend a slam or open mic event held during the school day, students of all ages can be shown how to record and upload their spoken word performance to a digital platform like Padlet, which can act as a secure repository for families and caretakers to peruse at their leisure (and where they can upload their own "reader"/listener/viewer responses to their child's performance using the commenting tool).

IDEA #3: Encourage students to use the comic or zine format to compose narratives that also inform and/or push back against harmful ideas

As I mentioned at the start of this chapter, the creation of both zines and comics have historically served as a way for members of traditionally marginalized groups to challenge the status quo and to share their stories and lived experiences using a combination of alphabetic, visual, and spatial text. Although many readers will be familiar with the comic form, fewer will have come across a zine, which is traditionally created using paper, a writing instrument, tape or glue, and scissors. The most common zine format, an eight-page zine, can be created using any paper size, although I have always favored using 11 × 17 paper for the compositional space it offers.

Once students have come up with a topic idea for their zine, I usually encourage them to create a rough sketch, or "mockup", which illustrates how the content they intend to include will be laid out on each page (including the front and back cover; see Figures 5.4 & 5.5). The most liberating aspect of composing a zine, as any exploration of mentor zines will illuminate, is that creators may decide to include photos, photocopied images, illustrations, borders, charts, tables, handwritten or typed text, or whatever else will effectively communicate their story/message to their readers. Some of what I have taught to students in my own classroom who have created zines include lessons on layout and the use of white space, word art, collage techniques (useful for creating interesting backdrops on which to glue or tape typed alphabetic text!), and brevity (due to the form's limited space). After assembling all of their content, zine-makers typically photocopy and distribute (or trade) their work with other creators, opening up a perfect opportunity for students to share their learning with one another in an authentic way.

A Note on Assessment

Regardless of the multimodal form(s) and/or digital media we want to integrate into our work with student writers, the ways in which we assess their compositional practices ought to take, as I suggest in my book *Writing,*

Multiodality 141

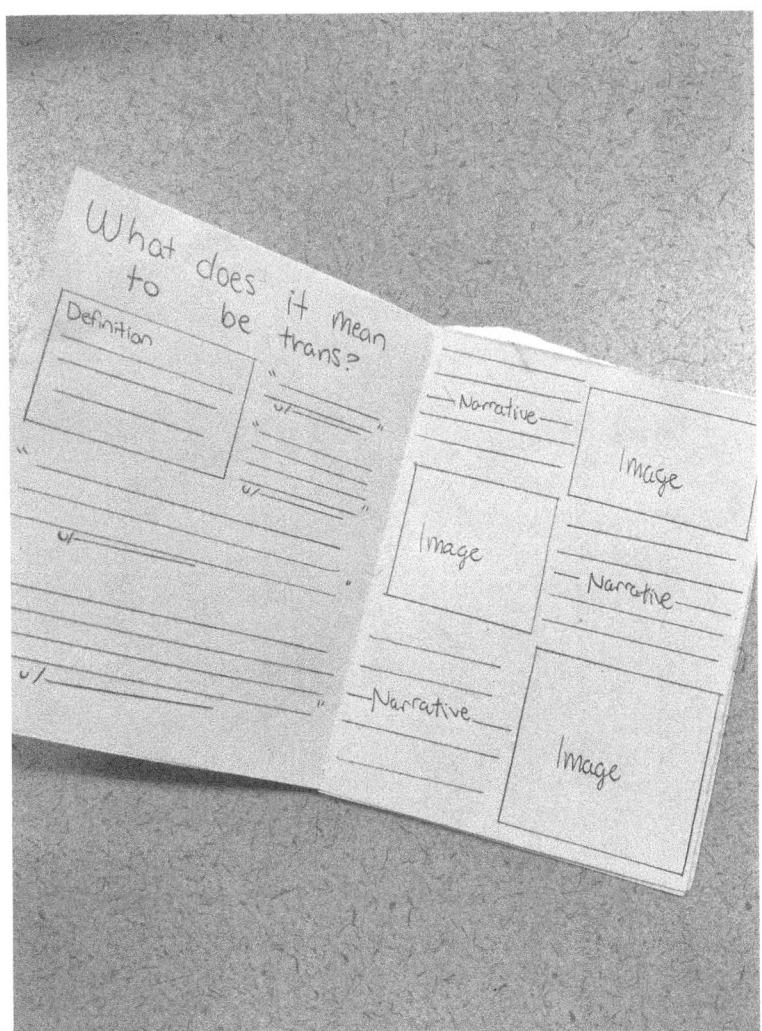

Figure 5.4 Student zine in progress.
By Leo.

Redefined: Broadening Our Idea of What It Means to Compose (2019), a three-pronged approach that includes students' own self-assessment or reflections, peer-to-peer feedback, and teacher assessment. Ideally, each of these assessment practices would be developed using criteria set forth during the instructional/inquiry process itself, which would include the common elements that were collectively identified during the initial exploration of the form.

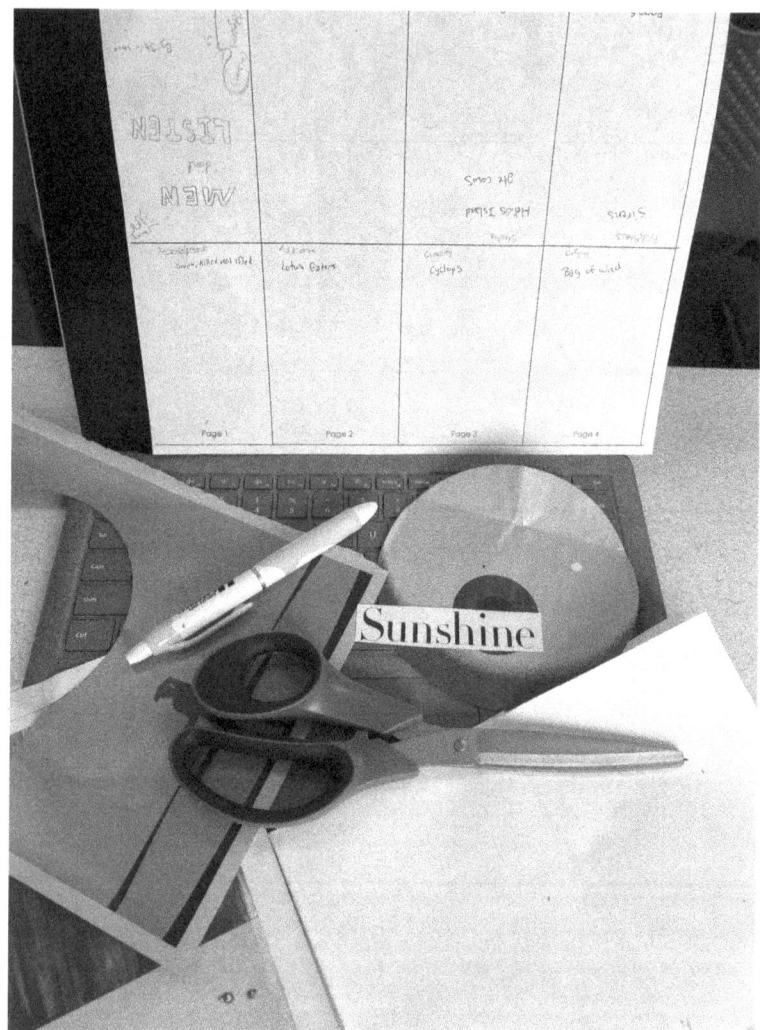

Figure 5.5 Student zine in progress.
By Trevor.

This approach that I've developed for use in my classrooms over the past decade not only leads students to engage in thoughtful, collaborative discussions about these compositional forms, but becomes the basis for how I ultimately assess their products—*if* that is the end goal. In some cases, the end goal is not to craft an "audience-ready" *product*, but rather to spend some time in a supportive, playful, and low-risk environment moving through a *process* that, regardless of the outcome, helps further their development as writers of multimodal and/or digital texts.

As with any set of teaching suggestions, how they are ultimately implemented is dependent on the context within which you work—*your* students, *your* institution, *your* level of autonomy. However, it is never too soon to revise our practices around teaching writing in school spaces which, for far too long, have privileged the literacies of too few at the expense of too many. Will we continue to be complicit in essentially delegitimizing many of the ways that diverse communities—particularly communities of Color—engage in compositional meaning-making? Do we still wish to hold tightly to the notion that "text" refers only to printed text, when one glance around us in any space (within *or* outside of school) utterly destroys that notion? If so—we must ask ourselves why. What is it we're protecting?

In this chapter I have offered my colleagues more than just a justification for decentering dominant writing pedagogies in our classrooms. I have also laid out a number of ideas to help guide us on our journey toward embracing a more critical, more humanizing practice through the integration of opportunities for students to engage in multimodal composition.

Where will you go from here?

Conclusion and Reflective Questions

1. Consider the decisions that are made when writing a "traditional", print-heavy text, such as an essay or short story. How are these decisions *similar to* and/or *different from* those we might make when composing a multimodal text (e.g., a digital story, podcast, or comic)?
2. What were your initial reactions to the idea of "worship of the written word" being a tenet of White Supremacy Culture? Do you believe this to be true? How might your reaction(s) reflect your cultural identities and/or the ways you were socialized, particularly in school spaces?
3. Reflect on your experience as a teacher and/or a student. How many opportunities did you/your students have to compose using a variety of textual modes? Where can you envision integrating multimodal and/or digital composition into your (or your colleagues') practice?

4. When it comes to offering students more opportunities for multimodal composition in school spaces, what feels most exciting? Most concerning? Who might we partner with or lean on for support as we *reflect, reimagine,* and *revisit* our pedagogical practices?

References

Abate, M. (2021). The yellow kid and the yellow peril: R. F. Outcault's comics series, Asian caricature, and Chinese exclusion. *ImageTexT*, https://imagetextjournal.com/The-yellow-kid-and-the-yellow-peril-r-f-outcaults-comics-series-asian-caricature-and-chinese-exclusion/

Ball, C. E., Sheppard, J., & Arola, K. L. (2018). *Writer/designer: A guide to making multimodal projects*. Bedford/St. Martin's.

Banks, A. J. (2011). *Digital Griots: African American Rhetoric in a Multimedia Age*. Southern Illinois University Press.

Bruning, R., Dempsey, M., Kauffman, D. F., McKim, C., & Zumbrunn, S. (2013). Examining dimensions of self-efficacy for writing. *Journal of Educational Psychology*, 105(1), 25–38.

Bui, T. (2012). Immigrant students use cartoons to share their journeys. *What kids can do*, www.whatkidscando.org/featurestories/2012/03_oakland_international/index.html

Cleveland, G. (1886, October 28). Remarks on the unveiling of the Statue of Liberty in New York City. *The American Presidency Project*, www.presidency.ucsb.edu/node/363222

Coleman, S. (2023). Zines and self-published materials: Timeline of zine history. *The Library of Virginia*, https://lva-virginia.libguides.com/c.php?g=1332410&p=9812968

Coppola, S. (2019). *Writing, redefined: Broadening our ideas of what it means to compose*. Stenhouse.

Coppola, S. (2023). *Literacy for all: A framework for anti-oppressive teaching*. Routledge.

Coppola, S., Magnifico, A., & Smith, L. (2021, November 12). Digital literacies: Surviving and thriving in classroom spaces. *The Educator Collaborative Community Blog*, https://community.theeducatorcollaborative.com/digital-literacies-surviving-and-thriving-in-classroom-spaces/

Davis, Y. (2015). The normalization process of multimodal composition: "Unseeing" people of color in multimodal composition scholarship. *Electronic Theses and Dissertations*, 658. https://stars.library.ucf.edu/etd/658

Ghiso, M. P. (2016). The laundromat as the transnational local: Young children's literacies of interdependence. *Teachers College Record*, 18(1), 1–46.

Gleason, B., & Mehta, R. (2022). Editorial. A pedagogy of care: Critical humanizing approaches to teaching and learning with technology. *Italian Journal of Educational Technology*, 30(1), 4–17.

Griffin, A. A., & Turner, J. D. (2021). Toward a pedagogy of Black livingness: Black students' creative multimodal renderings of resistance to anti-Blackness. *English Teaching: Practice & Critique*, 20(4), 440–453.

Jones, K., & Okun, T. (2003). Dismantling racism: A workbook for social change groups. *National Child Welfare Workforce Institute*, https://ncwwi.org/document/dismantling-racism-a-resource-book-for-social-change-groups/

Kang, G. & Kline, S. (2020). Critical literacy as a tool for social change: Negotiating tensions in a pre-service teacher education writing course. *Journal of Language and Literacy Education*, 16(2), 1–16.

Kline, S., & Kang, G. (2022). Reflect, reimagine, revisit: A framework for centering critical writing pedagogy. *Language Arts*, 99(5), 300–311.

Koster, M., Tribushinina, E., de Jong, P. F., & van den Bergh, H. (2015). Teaching children to write: A meta-analysis of writing intervention research. *Journal of Writing Research*, 7(2), 249–274.

Medina, C. (2018). Digital latinx storytelling: Testimonio as multimodal resistance. *Computers and Composition Digital Press*, https://ccdigitalpress.org/book/shorthand/chapter_medina.html

Mills, K. A., & Dooley, J. (2019). Sensory ways to Indigenous multimodal literacies: Hands and feet tell the story. In J. Rennie & H. Harper (Eds.), *Literacy Education and Indigenous Australians: Theory, Research, and Practice* (pp. 33–50). Springer.

Muhammad, G. E., & Haddix, M. (2016). Centering Black girls' literacies: A review of literature on the multiple ways of knowing of Black girls. *English Education*, 48(4), 299–336.

New London Group. (1996). A pedagogy of multiliteracies: Designing social futures. *Harvard Educational Review*, 66(1), 60–92.

Palmeri, J. (2012). *Remixing composition: A history of multimodal writing pedagogy*. Southern Illinois University Press.

Patterson, C. (2024, October 17) TikTok's algorithm prioritizes "beautiful" people according to leaked documents. *Dextero*, www.dexerto.com/tiktok/tiktoks-algorithm-prioritizes-beautiful-people-according-to-leaked-documents-2953018/

Purcell-Gates, V., Jacobson, E., & Degener, S. (2004). *Print literacy development: Uniting cognitive and social practice theories*. Cambridge: Harvard University Press.

Reyes, K. B., & Rodríguez, J. E. C. (2012). *Testimonio*: Origins, terms, and resources. *Equity & Excellence in Education*, 45(3), 525–538.

Stephens. D. B. (2023). Unpacking the 15 pillars of supremacy culture: A summary. *Liberation Education Newsletter*, https://desireebstephens.substack.com/p/unpacking-the-15-pillars-of-supremacy

Stockman, A. (2023). *The writing workshop teacher's guide to multimodal composition (K-5)*. Routledge.

Veum, A., Siljan, H. H., & Maagerø, E. (2021). Who am I? How newly arrived immigrant students construct themselves through multimodal texts. *Scandinavian Journal of Educational Research*, 65(6), 1004–1019.

Villarreal, V. A. [@Vanessid]. (2024, July 20). The written word, and the "inability to read to standard," has historically been used against nonwhite groups, not just to ..., *X*. https://x.com/Vanessid/status/1814551935942598881

Whitney, E. H. (2016). Multimodal composition as inclusive pedagogy: An inquiry into the interplay of race, gender, disability and multimodality at an urban middle school. *University of Pennsylvania ProQuest Dissertations & Theses*, 10158583. www.proquest.com/openview/42bac7a6f8260ca07ac0e8ce139dbef1/1?pq-origsite=gscholar&cbl=18750

Whitted, Q. J. (Ed.). (2023). *Desegregating comics: Debating blackness in the golden age of Comics*. Rutgers University Press.

Winn, M. T. (2003). Open mics and open minds: Spoken word poetry in African diaspora participatory literacy communities. *Harvard Educational Review*, 73(3), 362–389.

Woodard, R., & Coppola, R. (2018). More than words: Student writers realizing possibilities through spoken word poetry. *English Journal*, 107(3), 62–67.

6

Pop Culture

Powerful "X-people" and Rhythmic "Teen-age-ers": Popular Culture in Childhood Composing

Anne Haas Dyson

Liliana, a kindergartener I know, loves to sing. During her after-school program, the staff usually plays music videos on a YouTube screen as the children eat their after-school lunch. Almost immediately, Liliana and her peers begin singing and moving to songs as they play out. Consider, for example, this song sample:

Because I'm happy
Clap along if you feel like a room without a roof
Because I'm happy
Clap along if you feel like happiness is the truth. (Williams, 2014)

In musical contrast, Liliana has sung to herself a thematically related but musically quite different one; here is a sample:

If you're happy and you know it
Clap your hands
Clap Clap

> If you're happy and you know it
> Clap your hands
> Clap Clap (Traditional children's song)

Both songs are cheerful and display happiness, and both contain at least some movement, but they are from very different sources in Liliana's social and cultural life. The latter lyric above is from a traditional song for children, one that young children might sing in school. It has a simple, steady beat. Judging from YouTube, it is sung by school children all over the world, including in China, Turkey, Thailand, and, of course, in the U.S.

The former song is an upbeat neo soul song, its rhythmic, syncopated beat accompanied by movement, including, of course, clapping but also hip-hop dance moves—not just the hands clap but the whole body rhythmically moves. In fact, so do almost all the children sitting at the lunch table in Liliana's room whenever a popular song is played. They may be sitting down, but their bodies move, accentuated by their bopping heads and their bent, swaying elbows.

In videos of the Williams' (2014) "Happy" song, people dance in the street, on the sidewalk, in church, in the sunlight, and in the twilight—they dance however the music moves them. One cannot imagine such a reception for a song like the latter one. But the former song's media roots and varied manifestations mark it as a form of popular culture: the Williams song was written for a widely seen movie and then showed up on many YouTube videos enacted by groups of a diversity of ages, occupations, heritages ... all over the country and around the world. And as for those hip-hop dance moves, Liliana explained to me that she learned her moves from social media (i.e., TikTok), but, I should know, "you have to practice."

For young children, popular culture may figure in different ways into their social and cultural lives. While most children will appropriate for their own use some of the appealing symbolic material around them, this universal process is articulated in different ways in different historical, sociopolitical, and economic contexts (Beneke & Love, 2022; Storey, 2024). In Liliana's after-school program, the staff and the children were from an African American neighborhood. In fact, staff members tended to respond to the chosen music and to the children by dancing around the children's table as the little ones ate, sang, and moved. It was a lovely, warm, and happy scene.

In this chapter, I aim to discuss the role of popular culture in childhoods and the pedagogical issues and possibilities it raises. First, though, I need to provide a definition of popular culture and then to discuss the processes through which it becomes embedded in childhood (and, indeed, all) cultures. Because there is a need for both educators' appreciation of, and their need to help children think critically about, the media in their lives, critical pedagogy will figure into this discussion.

Next, to illustrate these concepts, I will draw on vignettes from the ethnographic work (and play) I have had in children's classrooms over many decades. In so doing, I am going to pay particular attention to young children's composing—their intermingled and often playful drawing, talking, and writing; this activity is a prime place where popular culture may take center stage in children's school lives. In making this short chapter manageable, I will focus on children's use of superhero media and of popular music, although the concepts apply broadly to all forms of popular culture. I will bring the discussion to a close by summarizing its implications for our decision-making about the young child composers in our care.

So, let's get started. First, what exactly is popular culture? And then, what is meant by childhood cultures?

Background: Popular Culture in Childhood Cultures

"Popular culture" is not a simple term to describe. As cultural theorists have explained (e.g., Storey, 2024; Marshall & Sensoy, 2016; Jenkins, McPherson, & Shattuc, 2002), there is no one definition of popular culture, nor is its meaning fixed; in different contexts, with different users, its meaning, and its ideations, may differ. We can see this easily over historical time, as particular products have belonged to different peoples and, thus, to different cultural categories.

In a fascinating book by the cultural historian Lawrence Levine (1990), *Highbrow/Lowbrow*, he explains how, in the nineteenth century, Shakespeare's works were indeed popular culture. They were performed across many social classes and ethnicities, and in many public gathering places, from saloons to churches; in attendance, the audience would eagerly participate, hissing or clapping, even reciting dialogue with the actors. However, by the twentieth century, the ruling elite had claimed Shakespeare for themselves, deeming it "high culture". They did this through developing architectural structures and cultural practices (like remaining relatively quiet until "clapping time" arrived); these practices deemed him theirs. Now, young adolescents may have to be in honors English to approach this "difficult" body of work.

Contemporary scholars of everyday cultural practices approach popular culture, not as in opposition to "high culture", but as the meaning-producing practices people engage in with commercial media products from their everyday lives (see Jenkins, McPherson, and Shattuc's "manifesto for a new Cultural Studies" [2002]). Media products are easily available to most children; and thus children selectively engage with material from any available cultural repository in their everyday play and, indeed, in their playful writing. Like us all, they do this through recontextualization processes.

To understand these processes, it helps to imagine children on a landscape of voices. As the Russian language philosopher and literary theorist Bakhtin (1981) explained, characters in novels, like small children, move through time and space by appropriating for themselves available words and genres (i.e., varied kinds of communicative practices). They are not joining a chorus of like voices but entering into dialogues with speakers from the past and from the present time and place. Children are dialoging with the past because people in their milieux have enacted certain social situations in similar ways (i.e., in particular genres). They are dialoging with the present because they are using those words in a particular social situation with others, and so they infuse what they view as expected, socially appropriate words with their own intentions; that is, they recontextualize them.

So children, like us all, appropriate and recontextualize available voices and, thus, articulate their own. You can easily observe children's attention to situated human voices, including those from media, by attending to their play. You will hear children borrowing (appropriating) appealing characters' voices and plot lines as they jointly weave (recontextualize them in) their own stories. (They may appropriate not only voices of course but also bodily movements, ways of dressing, and ways of speaking, along with visual images.) And this may also happen when children playfully compose.

There are of course many media sources, and not all available media material directed toward children becomes a part of their "popular culture". Moreover, popular media may "converge" in Jenkins' (2006) sense; that is, like Williams' "Happy" song, their media platforms may shift (i.e., adapted to film, single release, album, video …). It is not the texts themselves that are "popular culture"; it is those available to and chosen by children and thus used—appropriated and recontextualized—in the practices they enact with others. The media material thus becomes what I call "textual toys", material that spreads among children who use it in their play and in their communication—gestural, oral, drawn, and written (Dyson, 2003, p. 10; 2013; Henward, 2015; Yoon, 2021).

From the beginning of the intense interest in children's writing in the mid-seventies and the eighties, dominant authors left out or explicitly rejected young children's interest in popular culture. Most researchers of child-composing focused only on individual children's literal writing, preferably of the "truth", and, also, on adult-child interaction about that writing (e.g., Graves, 1975; 1983; Bissex, 1980). Moreover, teachers tended to view popular culture, like superheroes or Disney characters, as purely out-of-school material (for examples, see Dyson, 2013; Henward, 2015).

A key challenge to these biases is that, for many young school children, composing becomes a social activity—they provide each other with audience members, potential helpers, and ongoing collaborators. And what those children are likely to have in common are the story materials from their media pleasures (e.g., characters, plots, gripping images, memorable dialogue lines, and sung songs).

Before illustrating in the sections to follow appropriation and recontextualization processes in children's composing, there is one more critical concept to introduce: the ways the material children (and adults) appropriate establish linkages to particular social affiliations (Hanks, 1996; 2010). These affiliations can be used both by children to affiliate with others and by others to situate the users in the social constellations—and the stereotypes—of the powers that be. And this is why critical pedagogy is so important: "Popular culture … is a way for all of us … to reposition ourselves from cogs in the machine to social actors intent on jamming, resisting, and/or rewriting the status quo" of one's everyday media culture (Marshall & Sensoy, 2016, p. 9).

Let me illustrate appropriation, recontextualization, and critical pedagogy below, beginning with an old but clear and still timely example of how young school children appropriated superhero stories in their fiction writing and in their dramatic play (Dyson, 1997). The children grew as players, communicators, writers, and critics informed by social justice. This growth was a response to their dialogic questioning of the standard, beloved, but often stereotypical media stories, that is, by their critical awareness of who was well served by the standard stories and who was not (a dialogic pedagogy for critical action, most famously developed by Paulo Freire, 1970).

Superheroes as Media Characters and as Child Activists

Superhero stories offer children identities as powerful people who do battle against evildoers and win. And yet, children from different socioeconomic, cultural, and gender backgrounds may interpret these stories differently in different contexts. In a socioeconomically diverse, multiracial classroom in which I studied, this was visible and audible in the children's appropriations from, and their recontextualizations in, superhero stories. In a classroom activity called Authors Theater, the 7- and 8-year-old children drew and wrote their own stories (amid much social talk); afterwards, on the classroom rug, they could call on other children to enact their stories. And, among the boys, the most popular stories were of the superhero variety.

Those male authors, on the one hand, crossed racial lines quite readily in offering male roles to boys vying for roles. The pressure from boys led to the frequent choice of X-Men superheroes (Lee, Houston & Meugniot, 1992-1997) because X-Men, unlike the singular superhero, are an interracial, co-ed team (although, at the time, most X-Men were white males, at least in the televised cartoon of the nineties). The significant quality of the male roles was physical power.

On the other hand, the male authors were reluctant to include female roles, especially in their X-Men stories. In a story featuring the Teenage Mutant Ninja Turtles (Wolf, 1987-1996), they might offer the one (non-superhero) female role, April, to a white girl (as April was white). To the boys, the most significant quality of the female role seemed to be physical appearance; indeed, one day Lawrence, who was biracial, said that April *had* to be white, which drew strong objections from children of Color and, also, from Kristin, their white teacher. (At the very moment he said this, Lawrence was drawing the white, bald Professor X of X-Men fame as a Black man with a flat top.)

Girls of Color did strongly vie for active roles in superhero stories. One of those girls was Tina, who decided to write and enact her own such stories. Those stories recontextualized material from varied sources, including but not limited to the heretofore standard classroom superhero fare. In *her* stories, Tina appropriated Black women as *active* superheroes. And this was not the only way that Tina's recontextualizations posed new story possibilities. Consider the following vignette:

> Tina, a Black girl, is quite put out by the fact that, as she said, "the boys doesn't let us play." So she decides to write her own superhero story, featuring active X-Men female characters (but not exclusively). Tina brings her story to Authors Theater. She stands in front of the large rug on which the theater is played out. She calls her actors and begins to read. In her story, the X-Men begin to battle the bad people as usual, but then something quite unprecedented happens: Tina reads, "One of the X-Men *died*." No one dies, and Tina responds:
>
> Tina: (reading) "ONE OF THE X-MEN DIED!" Die! Die!
>
> Tina stares at one character, who eventually "dies". Tina continues reading. "And the rest were very sad. They cried." Everybody cry now, even the *boys*.
>
> At the end of the story, there is a funeral. Tina calls "the singing girls" to the stage, and they sing in honor of the deceased.
>
> After the play was over, James, a boy in the play, complains:
>
> James: You didn't give me no part.
>
> Tina: Your part was to cry and to fight.
>
> James: Uh uh. [No]
>
> Tina: I said *everybody*, including *you*, should cry. *Everybody*, including *you*, should fight.
>
> And that was that. (Capital letters indicate raised volume; italics indicate emphasis.) Tina had been uncomfortable with the identity stereotypes consistent with the boys' superhero stories. She had evaluated the intersecting gender and racial stereotypes, resisted them, and took writing action. In fact, not only did she address such stereotypes, she transformed the usual classroom plot into one that called on different symbolic material. Never before had anyone died in a classroom superhero story, nor, for heaven's sake, had there been a funeral at which there was crying and singing. When questioned about her choices, Tina firmly stood her ground.

As just illustrated, this connection between popular culture and identity stereotypes can become a source of critical pedagogy—*if* educators are sensitive to children's own sense of injustice, of unfairness. Such was the case in this classroom. In fact, in the wider school, children were not allowed to bring their popular culture characters and plots into the classroom; but

Kristin chose to honor the children's perspectives on their chosen topics. (Kristin did not even own a television!) Every day, the children had what amounted to a public forum on theater presentations. Kristin listened, made sure the children listened to each other, and commented herself on the complexities of issues of fairness when they arose.

Indeed, before Tina's superhero story, the children had talked about gender and racial identity issues in theater and had agreed that anyone can play any role. (Recall the peer objections to Lawrence's comment.) They also discussed issues of power. In a superhero story, what did "power" mean? Given that the reference was to physical power, Tina's sense of unfairness was due class respect, as Kristin pointed out to her young students. She asked them to think about a different kind of story, say a true story from our history, and she referenced peace makers that individual children had studied for their classmates. For example:

> Kristin: We talked about Ghandi [whom Rahda had researched] … and [from his pictures, we know] he was a very very thin, small man … But he was able to get all these people to follow him. (from Dyson, 1997, p. 183)
>
> So, Kristin asked, did Ghandi have power? What about Martin Luther King? Did she as teacher have power? Power depends on the story being told, on contextual matters.

The depth of the children's conversations remains the most striking that I have heard in my fifty years with young children. Nowadays, though, it can be difficult to have such critical discussions. The tight focus on mandated, linearly organized, and tested curricular skills tends to "close doors for students by narrowing the curriculum and focusing on test preparation activities" (Datnow, 2024, p. 195). Similarly, the recent upsurge in states banning books and, moreover, banning pedagogies highlighting gender, race, and other grand human issues make the effort of being open to the challenges facing children in our complex society more problematic (Bigelow, Sanchez, & Barbian, 2023; Natanson, Tierney, & Morse, 2024). And yet such issues are an integral part of our lives (not to mention our history and our literature); if we listen to our children, they will pose these issues of civil justice, just as Kristin's children did … if they have a curriculum open to their views and, of course, a socio-critically aware teacher.

Similar issues may arise with music, particularly with the "teen-age-er" music, to use a descriptor coined by Denise and Vanessa, two 6-year-old first graders who will figure into the next section of this discussion. Once again, I illustrate the key concepts of appropriation, recontextualization, and critical pedagogy.

Popular Music and Childhood Identities: Judging "Appropriateness"

Liliana's after-school program is full of music—all kinds. One of the adult staff, Mr. Washington, usually precedes after-school lunch with a quick lesson on the music he's going to play on that day, and he names the music. He has played and named, for example, jazz, R & B, soul, rap, and gospel (which Liliana's daddy listens to, she told me). No matter what the music, the children bop along and often sing, and, any chance they get, try out their hip-hop moves.

Sometimes the songs are full of angst about love gone wrong; sometimes the songs are clearly marketed for children, like the hip-hop song, the *Veggie Dance* (Hollingsworth, 2024). The children seem mainly interested in the rhythm and the movement that music elicits in them and, moreover, the community-building fun of shared music. The children remind me so much of Denice and Vanessa, two music-loving friends, players, and composers I met in a project called *The Brothers and Sisters Learn to Write* (Dyson, 2003). The girls were members of a small group of Black children who comprised a "fake family"—they had the same fake Mama, who apparently kept a tight rein on them, as one said to another, "Remember what Mama said …." The children had been bussed to their elementary school, traveling from a mainly Black neighborhood in the city to a mainly white neighborhood. (Nonetheless, because of "white flight", the dominant school population was Black.)

Music was a major part of the children's lives, all kinds of music, but in this piece I want to bring into focus the fake family's great interest in "teen-age-er music". This music was, they knew, not considered age-appropriate by their parents, as I confirmed in a meeting with the parents! That music, said their "brother" Noah's father, was full of "negative images" and vulgar language. Still the children reported learning the music primarily from radios, radios that were the backdrop to morning routines and daily commutes, that they heard in community center offices and, most of all, that were in the possession of adolescents, cool people they admired. The children sang the choruses of popular songs, made up genre-appropriate songs, and imagined themselves as singing stars. (Although readers may think that surely young children no longer are exposed to the radio, this is not so. American adults listen to far more radio than any other audio source, and the car remains a popular radio stage. [See Roeloffs, 2024].)

One day Denise and Vanessa responded to an assignment to draw and write about themselves as grown-ups by rendering themselves as fancily dressed singers like, they said, Tina Turner. Denise made herself up in a slinky dress and high-heeled shoes. But Vanessa, in a maternal voice (seemingly appropriated from her mom and evidencing her critical awareness), said to her friend:

> I'm not putting high heels on me cause that's too fast, Denise. That's too *fa::st*. We're only 6 and 7. And that is *too fast* (with definiteness). Cause, Denise, I'm sorry if I'm breaking your heart. (Dyson, 2003, p. 39). (Colons indicate that the preceding sound was elongated; italics indicate emphasis.)

This awareness did not mean that the children did not appropriate from teen-age-er music for their own songs, whether orally or in writing. But when they wrote them, they did not put them in their official writing journals, because they explained to me, their teacher, Ms. Rita (a middle-aged white woman), just wasn't "used to" that style of music. Still, out on the playground, Denise and her fake sisters demonstrated their keen knowledge of varied popular genres. They were able to borrow and use (i.e., to appropriate and recontextualize)—not only the words of songs but also their aesthetics, that is, their usual beats and melodic contours, their moods, and the physical arrangements and movements of the singers themselves. They appropriated this material and, simultaneously, recontextualized it in their own social scene.

For example, one day Denise and Vanessa were concerned about a classmate "spying" on them. Denise broke out in a rap (perhaps influenced by MC Lyte's, 1998 *In My Business*). She appropriated and recontextualized the driving beat and aggressive tone of a rap, along with evident efforts to maintain a pattern of syllable stresses and rhyme; those efforts were audible in her invention of words! Listen to a sample of her performance (a slanted line [/] indicates a line pause):

> It's called, "Why You in My Bus'ness?" (said sternly)
> (rapping) Why you in my bus'ness?
> Cause I *got* you/In my far-*is*-mus
> And I *had* you/In my char-*is*-mus/My bus'ness
> Why you gotta be/In the bus'ness? (from Dyson, 2003, p. 45)

On another occasion, Vanessa took the lead in a quite different "make-up [made up] song", one whose aesthetics the children also understood, appropriated, and recontextualized. This was a soulful "love song", with Denise and another "sister", Wenona, as the back-up singers. After some negotiation, they decided that the "backup" would be "baby boy". Here is just a sample of the performance:

> Vanessa: 1, 2, 3. (spoken)
> Nobody can tell me
> to tell me who I see
> to tell me when I move
> OO oo::
> …And the backup soon comes in soft and smooth:
> Denise & Wenona: *Ba: by* boy

This music was not the kind of fare associated with 6-year-olds, but it was evidence of the children's voice-filled landscape and their flexibility on that landscape.

In the Denise and Vanessa vignettes, the children were not just developing options for a singular event as in the superhero data. Rather, they were developing a rich repertoire, particularly but not exclusively in the area of popular songs. Moreover, the compositional competence and confidence developed in their music-making did become recontextualizable in their official work, particularly their official composing.

To briefly illustrate, late in their first-grade year, the two friends collaborated on an official journal entry in a process similar to their recess composing play. Just as they negotiated the backup voice of their soulful "love song", they negotiated their collaborative production of a scary story inspired by the *Goosebumps* television show (Forte, 1995–1998, reruns until 2001). Below is just one excerpt from their lengthy collaboration; in this excerpt, they are trying to decide on a title:

> Vanessa: What's the title going to be?
> …
> Denise: "One Boy and Two Girls."
> Vanessa: That's not good.
> Denise: What should it be then? "The Man and Two Women."
> Vanessa: That's not good either.
> Denise tries a more theme-sensitive title:
> Denise: "The Happy Scary Thing."
> Vanessa is still not satisfied. But then—
> Vanessa: Wait! It should be, "Be Careful What You Wish For." This appeals to Denise:
> Denise: And a girl could say, "I wish I was a vampire." And she could turn into a vampire!

And then they were off writing … and continued negotiating about vocal parts, what lines would sound good when, and scary-enough words. They appropriated unofficial media materials into their official concerns as first graders: like Rita, they considered if what they had written "made sense" and attended to text details like "titles" and "endings". The recontextualization of resources from diverse cultural practices yielded sophisticated composing.

The stories of Denise and Vanessa illustrate the essence of the appropriation and recontextualization processes that thread this chapter together. These processes involve active constructing from mutually engaged participants, improvising as needed to fit the social situation. The common fear that children *just* copy from media sources is not true. Nor is the pervasive notion that children acquire literacy skills linearly, progressing up a ladder toward eventual mastery. As the language and literary scholar and philosopher Bakhtin's (1981, p. 426) dialogic theory reveals, any individual utterance, any speaker or writer's text, can "only be understood as part of a greater whole", that is, as negotiated in response to others in some particular situation, against some particular cultural landscape of voices.

These children, like all their "brothers and sisters", had adults in their lives who were alert to their musical soundscapes. As a "brother's" mother told me,

If we're driving down the street and we hear something [on the radio] that I don't particularly find appropriate, then I hear [my kids] singing it ... I'll ask them, "So what do you think that means? What does that word mean? ... Do you think that everybody thinks like that? What is your opinion? Because my opinion is blah blah blah ... You know what is appropriate in this house ... You have to form your own opinion with music, with TV, with what you see in the news, with what your friends are doing."

As illustrated earlier, the children's brother and sister play reiterated their "Mama's" talk while also reflecting their critical awareness and their acknowledgement of age and race—matters that were, in fact, as important as what music they were to sing. They all agreed that the Barney song was a "preschool" song and that "teen-age-er" music was "too fast", but still, they got into its rhythms and melodies. And when they together voiced certain popular music lyrics as a group (always from Black musical artists), neighborhood white children were not expected to join in. The brothers and sisters expressed their care and concern for their teacher Rita (whom they explicitly "loved") by being careful what they exposed her to. But, at the same time, they always recontextualized material from popular genres (especially "love songs" and "rap") with an emphasis on the rhythmic and melodic aspects; their lyrics were recontextualized in their own social play. You might recall Denise's "Why You in My Bus'ness?" My favorite example is when the brothers and sisters chanted a Tupac Shakur lyric (1996)—"They got an APB out on my thug family"—as "I'm gonna ABC for my fam-i-ly."

As with Kristin and the children's dialogues about story and power, Rita too played a critical role in the children's dialogues about music and its recontextualization in their joint lives. They were aware, and respectful, of adults' concerns about appropriateness, but they also felt free in Rita's classroom to express their attraction to music—indeed sometimes all the sisters and brothers would burst into a "love song" as they worked, get sidetracked into a discussion of its age, gender, and even racial appeal, and then, sometimes at Ms. Rita's suggestion, start singing a thematic song related to their assigned task.

Ms. Rita shared all kinds of music with her class, from Afro-beat to jazz and classical orchestral music too. And, like Kristin, she talked to the children about racial issues that arose and gender ones too (see Dyson, 2003). Finally, again like Kristin, she assigned all sorts of compositional genres, but she had a daily time when children could choose their own topics and inform her of what they were thinking about.

In the closing section of this chapter, I will bring together the pedagogical implications embedded in the above two classroom illustrations and, more broadly, the qualities of classrooms that allow children to bring the pleasures—and develop a critical awareness—of popular culture into their classrooms. And I'll leave you with some questions that have guided my own reflections herein.

So How Should Teachers Respond to Children's Participation in Popular Culture?

I wrote this chapter while the 2024 Democratic Convention was taking place. A big theme of that convention was Americans' desire for freedom. So, in terms of this chapter, what does freedom mean for children and for their use of popular culture?

For children, freedom is a verb, a becoming, an expanded sense of agency and of the possibilities of choice and action. As children compose alongside each other, they may draw on the stories, songs, games they share with their friends, and one powerful source of that material is their engagement with popular culture. Through joining with their friends in pleasurable, imagined worlds, Tina and Denise, Vanessa, and their "siblings" could assume powerful roles and have fun as well. At the same time that those texts could be socially valuable, they were also ideologically drenched. As the children herein demonstrated, popular texts are infused with values and beliefs, that is, with assumptions about how those texts may position one in the world as a person of a particular gender, race, age, culture, and so on. Centering popular culture is essential to every aspect of Critical Humanizing Writing Pedagogy. It is at the core of being an educator who embraces critical and humanizing perspectives.

Thus a major implication of this chapter is that it is in conversation, dialogue with others differently positioned in the world, that children's assumptions about how the world works—about good and evil, about proper "boys" and "girls", about power and its manifestations—can become "dialogized", as Bakhtin (1981, p. 426) would say. That is, in Kristin's and Rita's classrooms, dialogue allowed children's taken-for-granted assumptions to be rendered as options, contextualized options in an ever-changing world. The assumptions about characters and plots, about "too fast" music and fashion, about singing and age, race, and gender could open up in interactional space. That space was created when children were faced with those differently positioned in the world, be they in interaction with parents, teachers, or peers.

This critical space would not have opened up without the attentiveness of both Kristin and Rita to the children's talk. They knew, as Jimmy Britton (1970, p. 29) said years ago, writing happens "on a sea of talk". So both had designated times when children would share and discuss their work, along with the expectation that they would seek help from, collaborate with, and simply talk about their work with each other. Too often writing is associated, not with talk, but with silence. And that may be superficially true for older writers when they seek a quiet place to hear themselves think through, respond to, and reflect on the voices in their minds; but young children, still developing the use of inner speech (Vygotsky, 1962), are often quite audible drawers and writers. Teachers may worry about channeling the children's talk, but, like Kristin and Rita, not silencing it.

It was the talk children did with each other on their own and when guided by Kristin that accounts for the expansion that occurred in their writing over time and, most relevant for this chapter, for their critical insights. It was the talk among Tina and her close friends, and her own indignation at the boys' stories that led to her powerful and groundbreaking X-Men story. (It even led her peer Sammy to refer, not to X-Men, but to "X-people".) It was the talk between Denice and Vanessa, in the musical contexts of Rita's room, that allowed for the flexibility of their composing in diverse genres; thus they had diverse resources to draw upon for their sophisticated collaboration in composing their (official) horror story. This link between literacy and community was implicit in the vignettes shared herein.

We as teachers of writing must begin with whatever is familiar and comfortable for our children, be that the symbolic tools accessible to them (like drawing or dramatic play), supportive social structures (like composing with friends), and familiar cultural symbols (like popular stories and songs). But that does not mean that we abandon our responsibility to make judgments ourselves about extending children's literacy interests or about the appropriateness of certain material, which may be blatantly offensive (e.g., containing racist or sexist material) or well beyond their experience level.

Still, as demonstrated herein, children respond to what Vivian Paley (1987) once called the children's "3 Rs"—the realms of fantasy, fairness, and friendship. And given that the focal teachers herein provided open-ended composing activities, regular classroom sharing of texts, and class discussions of those texts, they did indeed discuss, not just the clarity of their prose (as in traditional writing workshop approaches), but their sense of what was fair—to the characters in a child's text and also to themselves as community members.

Clearly the possibilities and challenges that will face teachers and their children in writing instruction will vary depending on the sociocultural nature of the people in each classroom (Dyson, 2021). Both Kristin and Rita were aided in their teaching by the cultural diversity of their children. But, in any classroom, children come with a myriad of diverse resources, imaginations, and expressive desires. And the way they weave themselves into a community of writers, guided by their responsive teacher, is a joy available to all who teach. Teachers might consider these questions as they respond to their students' appropriation of material from their participation in popular culture:

1. What aspects of popular culture do I participate in? What aspects did I participate in as a child? What role has it played in my own life and that of my friends and family?
2. Observe your students in their talk and play with each other, in the classroom, and on the playground. How does popular culture figure into their lives together? How do their interests promote inclusion? exclusion? curiosity?
3. How do children draw on their participation in popular culture when they write? For example, do they draw on characters, plots, songs, techniques (e.g., dialogue bubbles, comic boxes, graphic manipulations of letters, as in BOOOOO or *sorry*)? How might you extend their efforts?

4. How do children respond when they share their writing? Do they appreciate and support each other? Do they articulate how they may want to write their own related story differently? Do they, or you, discuss issues of fairness, in terms of who is represented in their stories and, in an Authors Theater situation, who gets to play out someone's narrative story and who may be feeling left out? (Think in terms of group identities, as to race, gender, language, and any other groups relevant to your class.)

I want to close with another story from Liliana, a child now on first-grade's door step, like other children at the center. I had started a composing (drawing, writing) group with the children, as I feared that writing meant "handwriting" to them, not meaning-making. The children could be a tad reluctant when we started, not sure of what they were to do. But not Liliana, whose enthusiasm soon infused the group. As earlier noted, Liliana and her peers were terrific dancers, especially with hip-hop dance moves. And, to our great delight, one of Liliana's very first compositions drew on this pleasure (and skill). On her paper, she drew three boys on one side of the top blank space on her paper, three girls on the other. And on the lines on the bottom, she wrote: *3 boys vs 3 girls*. And when she stood up to share, she explained that the children were "going to have a dance contest". We were anxious to hear how the contest turned out! Maybe it would end with a tie or a call for a rematch! And Liliana was on her way as a composer.

I wish for the readers of this chapter their own satisfying engagements with lively children, children who know they have playful imaginations, plenty of resources, and the pleasure of appreciative companions for the sometimes challenging, but ultimately rewarding work and play of composing. Enjoy!

References

Bakhtin, M. (1981). Discourse in the novel (M. Holquist, Trans.). In M. Holquist & C. Emerson (Eds.), *The Dialogic Imagination: Four essays by M. Bakhtin* (254–422). University of Texas Press.

Beneke, M. R., & Love, H. R. (2022). A DisCrit analysis of quality in early childhood: Toward pedagogies of wholeness, access, and interdependence. *Teachers College Record*, 24(12), 192–219.

Bigelow, B., Sanchez, A., & Barbian, E. (2023). Love, solidarity, and defiance. *Rethinking Schools, 38*(1), 4–6.

Bissex, G. (1980). *GYNS at work*. Harvard University Press.

Britton, J. N. (1970). *Language and learning*. University of Miami Press.

Datnow, A. (2024). Education reform, past and present: Asking equity questions and looking for hope. *Educational Researcher, 53*(4), 193–200. https://doi.org/10.3102/0013189X241228255

Dyson, A. Haas. (1997). *Writing superheroes: Contemporary childhood, popular culture, and classroom literacy*. Teachers College Press.

Dyson, A. Haas. (2003). *The brothers and sisters learn to write: Popular literacies in childhood and school cultures*. Teachers College Press.

Dyson, A. Haas. (2013). *ReWRITING the basics: Literacy learning in children's cultures*. Teachers College Press.

Dyson, A. Haas. (2021). *Writing the school house blues: Literacy, equity, and belonging in a child's early schooling*. Teachers College Press.

Forte, D. (Executive Producer). (1995–1998, reruns until 2001). *Goosebumps* [TV series]. Protocol Entertainment.

Freire, P. (1970). *Pedagogy of the oppressed*. Seabury Press.

Graves, D. (1975). An examination of the writing processes of seven-year-old children. *Research in the Teaching of English, 9*(3), 227–241.

Graves, D. (1983). *Writing: Teachers and children at work*. Heinemann.

Hanks, W. F. (1996). *Language and communicative practices*. Westview.

Hanks, W. F. (2010). *Converting words. Maya in the Age of the Cross*. University of California Press.

Henward, A. S. (2015). "She don't know I got it. You ain't gonna tell her, are you?": Popular culture as resistance in American preschools. *Anthropology & Education Quarterly, 46*(3), 208–223.

Hollingsworth, J. (Composer). (2024). Veggie dance [Video on *Gracie's Corner* channel]. You Tube.

Jenkins, H. (2006). *Convergence culture: Where new and old media collide*. New York University Press.

Jenkins, H., McPherson, T., & Shattuc, J. (2002). Defining popular culture. In H. Jenkins, T. McPherson, & J. Shattuc (Eds.), *Hop on pop: The politics and pleasures of popular culture* (26–46). Duke University Press.

Lee, S. (Author & Illustrator), Houston, L, & Meugniot, W. (Producers). (1992–1997). *X-Men: The animated series* [TV series]. Fox Kids Network. (Currently owned and distributed by The Walt Disney Company.)

Levine, L. W. (1990). *Highbrow/lowbrow: The emergence of cultural hierarchy in America*. Harvard University Press.

Lyte, MC. (1998). In my business [Song]. On *Seven & seven*. Elecktra Entertainment.

Marshall, E., & Sensoy, O. (Eds.). (2016). *Rethinking popular culture and media* (2nd ed.). Rethinking Schools.

Natanson, H., Tierney, L., & Morse, O. E. (2024, April 4). America has legislated itself into competing red, blue versions of education. *The Washington Post*. https://washingtonpost.com/education/2024/04/04/education-laws-red-blue-divide

Paley, V. (1987). *Wally's Stories*. Harvard University Press.

Roeloffs, M. W. (2024, May 4). Americans listen to far more radio than podcasts—even young people, new data shows. *Forbes* Newsletter. www.forbes.com/sites/maryroeloffs/2024/04/30/americans-listen-to-far-more-radio-than-podcasts-even-young-people-new-data-shows

Shakur, T. (1996). Hail Mary [Song/Rap]. On *Don Killuminati: The 7 day theory*. Can-Am Studios.

Storey, J. (2024). *Cultural theory and popular culture: An introduction* (10th ed.). Routledge.

Vygotsky, L. S. (1962). *Thought and language*. The M.I.T. Press.

Williams, P. (2014). Happy [Official Music Video for Song]. YouTube.

Wolf, F. (Producer). (1987–1996). *Teenage mutant ninja series* [First TV series]. Eyemark Entertainment.

Yoon, H. (2021). Stars, rainbows, and Michael Myers: The carnivalesque intersection of play and horror in kindergarteners' (trade)marking and (copy)writing. *Teachers College Record*, 123(3), 1–22. https://doi.org/10.1177/016146812112300303

7

Play

Storying Identity as Curricular Practice: The Multimodal Resonances of Play and Writing

Haeny S. Yoon

Introduction

Jalen was a kindergartener in New York City and an avid fan of Teenage Mutant Ninja Turtles (TMNT)—Leonardo was his favorite and uncannily similar to Jalen's disposition. Leonardo is widely known as the leader of the turtles, often taking the place of Master Splinter if unavailable. He organizes the ninjas as they fight the Foot Clan—he is viewed as more disciplined than the other turtles, who also have distinct personalities of their own. Leonardo is a "take-charge" sort of ninja and commands the rest of the group. Therefore, it is not surprising that Jalen would take up this persona as a leader and choreographer of his friends' play. Like Leonardo, Jalen was confident, commanding, and sophisticated in how he enacted and wrote TMNT into the social landscape at school (see Figure 7.1). He directed many play scenarios in the classroom, even pointing out when other children did not play the TMNT storyline "correctly". When

Figure 7.1 Jalen's Teenage Mutant Ninja Turtle drawing, complete with labels of characters and references to the show on Nickelodeon.
By Jalen.

classmate Trevor simply wanted to pretend "fight" and deviate from the storyline, Jalen declared, "No, they fight the Shredder. They only fight the Shredder." On the one hand, Jalen was silly and fun, yet engaged and serious about his play. On the other hand, he was steadfast—even inflexible—in how such play was organized and enacted.

Jalen was more than a fan. His identity and presence in the classroom centered around TMNT; it was important, then, to get this *right* and to claim authority when it came to this topic. Others would have their realm of expertise as well, and children's involvement in one another's play was a reciprocal act—one that acknowledged and elevated expert identities. Consequently, other children engaged with the TMNT franchise, yet TMNT (not necessarily the most popular television series in the media landscape at the time) had particular affordance and capital in this classroom because of Jalen's popularity. TMNT became central figures as characters for play, as inspiration for writing, as a means for social connection. Jalen's TMNT text, displayed prominently by classroom teachers for others to see, made visible utilitarian dexterity with rudimentary literacy marks (e.g., spelling, fine motor skills, alphabetic principles, labeling, color) while at the same time it was an identity text, sedimenting his status within childhood cultures (Wohlwend, 2009). In other words, children reveal parts of themselves obscured by attention to only routinized and rudimentary demands of school literacy.

Writing served as a tool for Jalen to shape and guide his play, just as it does for many children. While sophisticated in and of itself, Jalen's written text is a visual document recounting classroom life. The real richness came from how he acted out the stories—through role-playing, staged fight scenes, and embodied actions. Together, these multiple modes contributed to how he brought TMNT to life. His writing didn't exist in isolation, but as part of a larger, multi-layered experience that combined written words, gestures, and physical action. Therefore, what remains on paper is a still image of the larger multimodal resonances of children's play.

Children are making sense of their world through play, yet the times we take their ideas seriously are often viewed through the lens of reading and writing basics (Dyson, 2013b) rather than literacy as a social construction, rooted in knowledge, identity, and being (Street, 2003). We expect children to communicate the deepest parts of themselves through writing (hooks, 2006) focused on utilitarian skills: sound/letter correspondence, sentence structure, phonemic awareness, and alphabetic principles. While these are important, we tend to cast aside what children might be telling us about who they are and how they situate themselves in the cultural landscape. In turn, children—knowing full well what is valued in their writing—reveal little about themselves even in writing that purports to center personal narratives. How can writing be a form of play? How can play foster utilitarian and practical skills while amplifying childhood cultures and mobilizing identity formation? How do children mobilize writing to develop social relationships, as a means for social positioning, and to participate in community life—including but not limited to school? I turn to Jalen and his peers to illustrate the entanglements between play and writing.

Background

Early writing research considers the reciprocal relationship between writing and play, taking seriously the intellectual, social, and political work of children's mark-making (Dyson, 1993; Wohlwend, 2011; Yoon, 2020). Children's writing reveals the creative, multimodal, and affective dimensions of their social beings—that is, what gets left on their paper are residual effects that reverberate far beyond what remains on the page (Bomer & Laman, 2004). Writing can be (as we know, even as adults) magical, soulful, and moving (hooks, 2000). Communities form around stories (e.g,. book clubs), demonstrating the power of written words in conveying collective and shared experiences. At the same time, writing can also be visceral, disturbing, and inflammatory (Collins & Blot, 2003; Luke, 2018; Prendergast, 2003). Beyond the scope of this chapter, but relevant to writing studies, is that writing is not always neat, tidy, and "brilliant". There are many instances of writing (both kid writing and adult writing) that disturb us, that mobilize harmful political rhetoric, or that dehumanize groups and people—literacy has the power to include and exclude (Adger et al., 2014; Alim et al., 2016; Flores & Rosa, 2015; Ladson-Billings, 2021). Hence, "sticks and stones may break my bones, but words can never hurt me" might not actually be as robust an adage as we assumed. Words do matter. They can uplift and they can hurt.

A wealth of research expands definitions of literacy to include communicative competence across settings (Adger et al., 2014; Heath, 1983), experiential and cultural knowledge (Kwon, 2021; Orellana, 2001), embodied actions (Thiel, 2020; Wohlwend, 2020), multimodal and multimedia constructions (Vasudevan, 2011; Wargo, 2015), and translanguaging (Garcia & Kleifgen, 2019). Undergirding this line of inquiry are authentic relationships between children and teachers with mutual regard for what makes us fully human. Culturally sustaining and humanizing pedagogies center young people's lived experience—engaging children with ideas, content, and practices that amplify their cultural knowledge (Alim et al., 2020; Ladson-Billings, 2021). In this way, scholars point toward children's sociocultural entanglements as important to classroom instruction.

Play and Writing: Childhood Cultures in Curriculum and Pedagogy

Enacting critical pedagogies is more than addressing critical topics, but creating the space and conditions for children's layered identity constructions. That is, beyond racial, gendered, and ethnic affiliations, children also possess interests, passions, and desires that surface in playful interactions with adults and peers (Yoon, 2021). For instance, while Jalen is a Black boy with disability labels, he is also a ninja turtle expert and a social leader in play events. His identity is not reduced to visible markers. Consequently, just as much as writing can be about social action, writing can also be about awakening and validating a part of oneself that is obscured in places like school, where skills are valued over meaning-making. When teachers ask children to write themselves into texts, children reveal personal and critical connections about their status in the world at the intersection of race, class, gender, and so on (Johnson & Sullivan, 2020). At the same time, when we consider children as truly human and whole, we should also take seriously what appears to be un/critical, risky, and tenuous experimentations during play (Sicart, 2014; Trammell, 2023). Instead of dismissing their social worlds, these playful acts provide a lens for examining the "multi" cultural lives of children's living and being.

In reality, the demarcation between play and writing is not so distinct. The boundaries are arbitrary, created by schools that surveil and bound children's movements by subjects, skill level, time, and completion of tasks/activities. For young children, these boundaries are loose and permeable (Dyson, 1993), suggesting that play is ever-present in the center to the edges of teaching and learning. In what follows, I articulate the pedagogical implications of writing that privilege children's meaning-making and re/consider criticality in children's playful encounters.

Crafting a Point of View: The In/visibility of Children's Perspectives in Critical Pedagogies

Adult perspectives of children guide our aesthetics and facilitate values. At school, we attempt to pass down traditions and ways of being through a canon, an order, and assessments that struggle to define children's diverse and complex competencies. Templeton and Vellanki (2022) demonstrate how quickly we assign value and meaning to children's photographs and places. Taking up adult lenses, we struggle to see the complexity in work that steps outside of normative bounds. For example, photos of trash and other items of decay or blurry and non-legible photos were disregarded from sight in favor of aesthetically pleasing and curated pictures of childhood (Von Joo, 2024). Consequently, adults miss the network of care and intimacy attached to "unappealing" photographs (Templeton, 2018). In Wendy Luttrell's (2020) longitudinal work on children's photographs of their lived experiences, she further argues that messy rooms, material collections, and cherished objects are symbols and signifiers of children's identity and agency. Our quick dismissals of children's perspectives communicate our presumptions that young people's lives are momentary, fleeting, and en route to adulthood.

What matters most to young people is different from what adults might deem meaningful, appropriate, or worth our attention. In the political landscape, we elevate specific versions of criticality (e.g., giving speeches, involvement in political movements, taking on pressing social issues). We push young people to a future citizenship at the cost of amplifying the things concerning them in the moment, from bodily functions and control (Templeton & Harvey, 2024) to sexuality (Dyer, 2019) to experimenting with shifting identities, and navigating power struggles in a classroom of their peers. Our own uncertainty with children's capacities creates tensions in the classroom, especially when their play is unrecognizable to us and incongruent with our worldview. Regardless, they are crafting a point of view in playful moments; while these moments do little to "change the world", they are integral to how children situate and position themselves with others.

Similarly, writing is about composing a point of view and voice. This seems obvious, yet it rarely happens in school. While authors are constantly trying to develop these aspects in their writing, we reduce school writing to rudimentary, mechanical, and standardized skills that attempt to diminish children's voices. Beginning with how writing gets displayed at school, it is evident that we value writing that is neat, clean, orderly, with minimal mistakes, and ultimately complete. Children's writing populating school walls communicates what we value and expect from children's compositions. Rather than communicating children's point of view, they communicate a curricular point of view, laden with institutional and pedagogical intentions that sit outside of children's perspectives. This curation perpetuates hegemonic and normative ways of being and storying. Therefore, when we take children seriously, we acknowledge viewpoints engaging with the frivolous, grotesque, humorous, inappropriate, and distasteful (Jenkins, 2006). It is in these dismissals that children learn that their play is cursory and marginal to the real work at hand.

Play as Embodied, Multimodal Activity: Written Texts as Acts of Inclusion

Play scholar Vivian Paley described an interaction between two kindergarteners Derek and Georgina. Meticulously and carefully drawing a rainbow with her name signed at the bottom, Georgina walked over to hand Derek the "gift" with a simple, "I drew you this" (2011, p. 745). We would later learn that Derek frequently visited the "time out" area, struggling to figure out how to succeed with school-related tasks. The day he received the textual gift from Georgina was no exception. Yet, Georgina's simple act of inclusion would shift Derek's position in the classroom as well as his own sense of self. He involved himself in the storytelling, dictation, and play activity after Georgina offered her friendship and care to Derek. Their momentary interaction around writing was far more intimate than we could ever imagine from the phonetic, alphabetic demands we put on children. Letters on paper are important to stories, but the meaning and purpose linger and reverberate far beyond what remains on the paper. The text showcased children stretching and transforming the relational and structural boundaries of the classroom community.

In the classroom featured here, Lucas (an avid Star Wars fan) used his hand-drawn sheets of paper to demonstrate intergalactic battles (see Figure 7.2). His drawings of TIE (twin ion engine) fighters served as a backdrop to his storytelling. He drew in dotted lines and reflection points during his epic TIE fighter battle to show the movements in battle. He described, "Look, another TIE fighter is shooting at it ... but it still hit the shield. Look it still hits the shield ... another one shoots ... and they are not getting through." While the paper flattens the multimodal storytelling displayed by Lucas, with jumping out of his seat to drawing battle lines, it does not even begin to tell the larger story of play and meaning placed on a sheet of paper. Not unlike Georgina, Lucas used his text to initiate play with others, using the paper to continue the battle unfolding on paper. Clearly, "the writing that remains on a page is in some ways, a lingering shadow of the thicker, multimodal transactions in face-to-face human

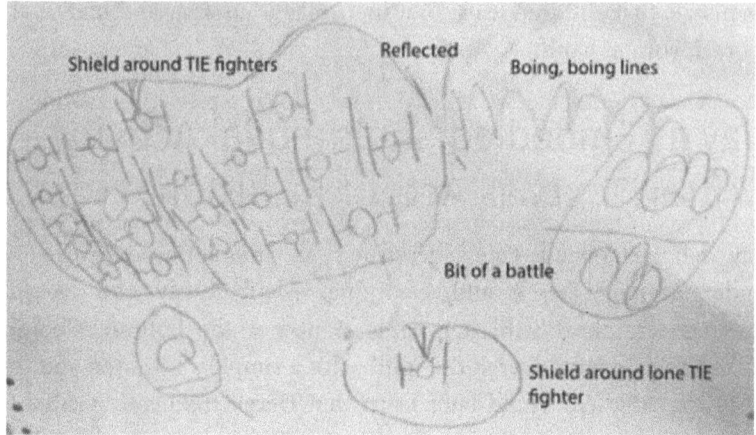

Figure 7.2 TIE fighter battle drawn by Lucas. The dotted lines and "boing, boings" as described by him are shots fired. The shots are reflected off the shields that cover the TIE fighters.

By Lucas.

mutuality" (Bomer & Laman, 2004, p. 424). Writing literally "moves" us and facilitates purposeful connections. bell hooks writes,

> Writing is my passion. It is a way to experience the ecstatic … I am still transported, carried away by the writing and reading … performing the words to both hear and feel them, I want to be certain I am grappling with language in a manner where my words live and breathe, where they surface from a passionate place inside me. (2000, p. 1)

For children like Lucas, writing and play were an embodied experience, "spontaneous, unscripted, undirected, and often unpredictable … with modal resources and materials" (Vasudevan, 2015, p. 3). He was *transporting* and *carried away* by his writing, traveling to another galaxy, amid an ensuing battle for the universe. He performed these words with gestures and movements, indicating that play and writing were inseparable. His mother once described his writing as a

> hashing out of elaborate play schemes … [with] explanations, sound effects, and a lot of 'look Mommy'! His body is physically engaged, jumping during especially exciting parts of the story. He walks his fingers into the heart of battle, and his body reverberates when the Death Star's explosion rattles the galaxy. (Yoon et al., 2016)

This is passion, ecstasy, and magic. Marks on a page serve a greater purpose when knowledge and identity (Street, 2003) are entangled with play and writing. Therefore, what conditions do our classrooms offer for writing to become embodied and living?

Setting Up the Context

The examples in this chapter draw from a yearlong ethnography on play and literacy in an inclusive kindergarten classroom in New York City. Designed to support children with Autism Spectrum Disorder (ASD) in an integrated classroom with "neurotypical" children, the classroom was co-taught and smaller in size to maintain space for related therapies and more responsive, differentiated instruction. The teachers here made an intentional choice to leave space and room for children to engage in play for 30–45 minutes, multiple times throughout the week. However, the general vibe of the classroom was playful, demonstrating the "capacity to use play outside the context of play" (Sicart, 2014, p. 21). The vignettes featured here are written texts that were constructed by children drawing from their sociocultural interests as well as these scheduled play times. The narratives featured are from "play stories" with contributions that varied over the course of the year. All stories were constructed by children, individually and collectively. Images for the stories came from children's own drawings, from photographs taken during play, or from images on the internet—sometimes selected by me and other times selected by children.

I served as the editor of these stories, meaning I took the time to retype the stories and honor the fact that they were writing a "book". I placed the selected images in concert with the texts. After each play story was completed, we (authors and myself) performed a "reveal" every Friday where we read aloud the finished text with comments and reflections from the authors. Authors accepted questions and comments from classmates as well. Every week, the new story was placed in the classroom library, and eventually, we created an anthology of stories across the year (see Figure 7.3). Each vignette centers on one of these play stories. Accompanying each of the three sections are the title pages and sample pages of the completed books. After sharing these particular examples, I offer pedagogical practices for educators.

1. **Human Sandwiches, Spaghetti Dinners, and Other Kitchen Adventures**
   Ms. Haeny with E▓▓n, J▓▓▓, and X▓▓▓▓

2. **Working on the Railroad: All Aboard!**
   Ms. Haeny with Xi▓▓, A▓▓n, and ▓▓▓

3. **The Transforming Superheroes: Here We Come!**
   Ms. Haeny with Ja▓en, Au▓ and Oi▓

4. **The Princess of the Night, Knight Lightyear, and Dr. A▓▓▓▓ - Superheroes by Day, Healers by Night**
   Ms. Haeny with L▓a, A▓▓▓ and A▓▓

5. **Just Regular Superheroes**
   Ms. Haeny, ▓▓▓, F▓▓, T▓▓▓r

6. **The Food Explosion**
   Au▓, L▓la, and Ms. Haeny

7. **We are Family**
   Xi▓ and L▓a

8. **At the Train Center**
   E▓▓n, ▓▓▓, Ms. Haeny

9. **Superheroes in the Kitchen**
   ▓▓▓r and F▓▓

10. **Two Roads**
    E▓▓n, A▓▓▓, and Ms. Haeny

11. **Pool Party**
    Ja▓en and A▓▓▓▓

12. **Car Math**
    ▓▓▓r, J▓▓▓, and Ja▓en

Figure 7.3 A page of the table of contents created for the play stories anthology. Names are redacted for anonymity. Gradually, authorship was released to the children with less guidance and direction from me.

Compiled by Haeny Yoon.

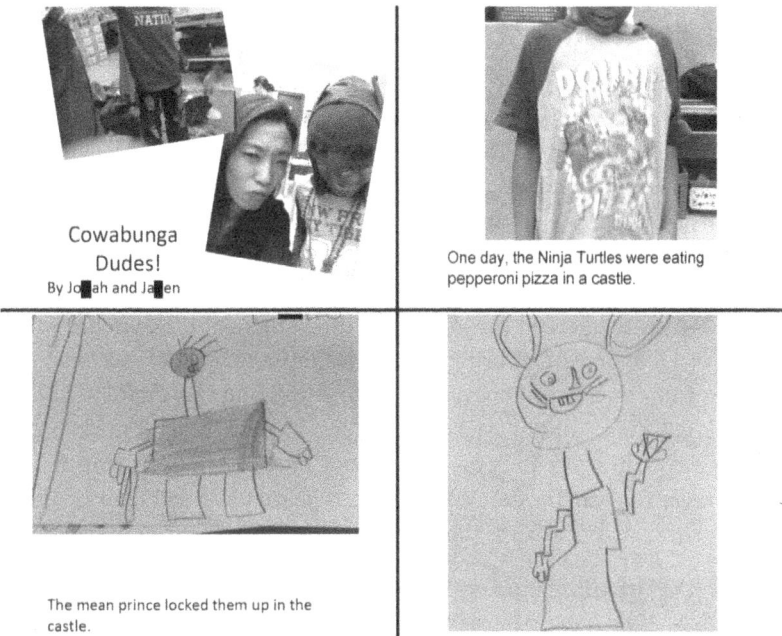

Figure 7.4 Cowabunga Dudes. From upper left, clockwise: (1) cover of the book; (2) Jalen's t-shirt of TMNT with accompanying text; (3) Lila's drawing of the "mean prince"; (4) drawing of Chuck E. Cheese.
Compiled by Haeny Yoon.

The Social Circulation of Ninja Turtles

"Cowabunga Dudes" was written by Jalen and Jonah (see Figure 7.4). It was no surprise that the Teenage Mutant Ninja Turtles were the inspiration for this story. Jalen embodied TMNT in his play and clothing, and one of those photographs made an appearance in the completed book. However, the story was a juxtaposition of both Jonah and Jalen's interests. These popular cultural artifacts mobilized their play while simultaneously providing elements for a story structure. Their written story drew from characters in their pop culture engagements, and their local contexts (e.g., Chuck E. Cheese) provided the landscape for the setting.

Cowabunga Dudes

One day, the Ninja Turtles were eating pepperoni pizza in a castle. The mean prince locked them up in the castle. But Ezra had a key to the castle and hid behind the gate. The entire Paw Patrol was there. Marshall blasted the gate with a water cannon, but the water cannon had apple juice in it. The mean prince was sitting on a bench, waiting and waiting. Donatello was mad that they were stuck in the cage. "I'm gonna get you when I get out this gate." Marshall sprayed apple juice on the mean prince. The Star Wars Rebels made mud snowballs and threw them at the man prince. A raven used his magic to bring the Turtles more pizza. He also freed the turtles from their cage. Raven gave them power and transported them to Chuck E. Cheese. They played games and had a party. They got tickets and won prizes. They got a lollipop. They loved Chuck E. Cheese's so much they slept there forever. They are never going to leave there and they ate pizza and made Chuck E. Cheese their cave. (text retyped)

Excited by the humor and outlandish turns in the story, several students offered drawings to contribute: Lila drew a mean prince, and Evan drew lollipops. Writing was entangled in their play; their textual construction was dialogic, demonstrating in real time how contributions and ideas reverberate through social participation and improvisation (Bakhtin, 1981; Wohlwend, 2009). The ninja turtles merged with Paw Patrol, meeting at Chuck E. Cheese's, an establishment near where many of the children lived. Pizza and parties flowed into Chuck E. Cheese's, a realistic outlet for the children's own celebrations. In this story, their beloved pop culture icons undoubtedly enjoyed this childhood space as well.

Embedded in this story is also a narrative of belonging and inclusion. TMNT was an obvious nod to Jalen, but Star Wars was also an interest circulating among many of the children. Lucas (neurodivergent, Autistic) often expressed his inclusion through Star Wars play and writing, as demonstrated earlier. Unsurprisingly, this story delighted Lucas, who found an obvious and explicit connection to the Star Wars characters. Finally, many discussions centered around Chuck E. Cheese, a shared affinity space and point of connection for the children in the classroom. It was a space they visited apart from school—a place of games and parties where children's social connection in and out of school was fostered and solidified. Whether it was the park, apartment complex, grocery store, or party places, life outside of school had great social importance to relationships.

Recirculation of Ninja Turtles Amid a Food Explosion

The next story was written by Lila, Aurelia, and myself (see Figure 7.5). The two girls had just finished playing at the kitchen center; not surprising, then, food was the material for their narrative. Across the year, it was common for children to craft stories around recent play events and personal stories from home. In this story, Lila and Aurelia used a combination of internet images, photographs of their own play, and photographs of me on my phone to construct the story. The girls' invitation to include me as a character in this co-constructed story was a significant gesture of inclusion. It meant something to me, and I imagine that these gestures are also important to children's belonging.

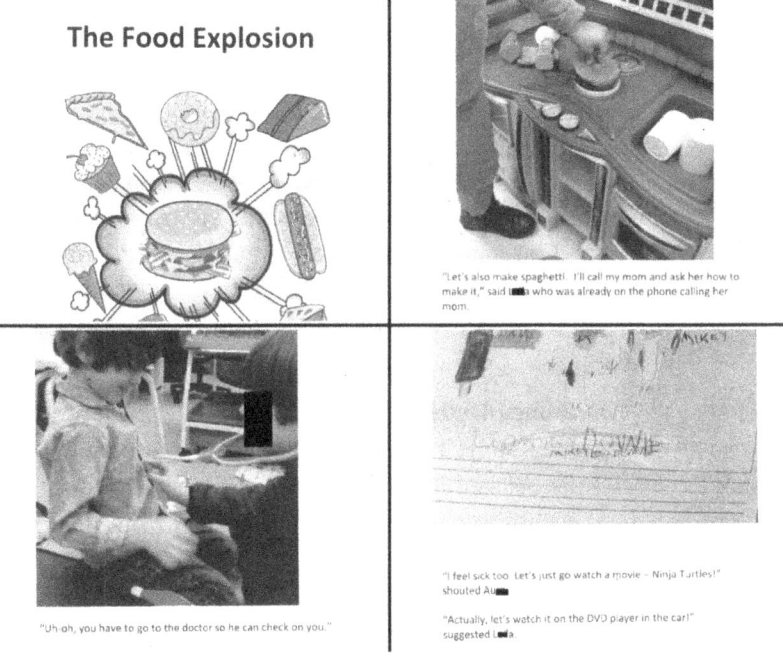

Figure 7.5 The food explosion. From upper left, clockwise: (1) cover of the book with a found, internet image; (2) photograph of Lila at play accompanied by the text; (3) a photograph of another instance of play with classmates accompanied by text; (4) Jalen's illustrated drawing accompanying the text reference to ninja turtles.

By Lila, Aurelia, and Haeny.

The Food Explosion

Once upon a time, there was Aurelia, Lila, and Haeny. They were joined by a talking banana and a sweet potato. The banana was telling them about their weekend when Aurelia and Lila got very hungry. "Let's eat the banana and the sweet potato," said Lila. Gulp, gulp. Gobble! Gobble!

"They were delicious," said Aurelia.

"Let's also make spaghetti. I'll call my mom and ask her how to make it," said Lila, who was already on the phone calling her mom. The spaghetti was on the stove. Lila started mixing things together. "A little bit of orange juice, a little bit of milk, and finally meatballs!"

"I'll make cupcakes," added Aurelia.

"Fine, I'd like 55 of them!"

After eating, Lila suggested, "Let's go to Chuck E. Cheese's. I will drive the car. We can eat pizza there. Let's also eat hot dogs in the car."

"And some ice cream," smiled Aurelia.

Haeny, who was silent up until this point, got in the car and muttered, "Ugh, I think I might be sick from eating a bunch of stuff that doesn't go together."

"Uh-oh, you have to go to the doctor so he can check on you."

"I'm just so sleepy. Let's buy a mattress to put in the car," said Lila.

"I feel sick too. Let's go watch a movie—Ninja Turtles!" shouted Aurelia.

"Actually, let's watch it on the DVD player in the car!" suggested Lila.

"I'm sleepy too. Can someone just get me a double coffee?" whispered Haeny from the back seat. All of a sudden.., POP! They exploded. Everyone learned an important lesson that day: Nobody should eat everything they want in one day.

Similar to "Cowabunga Dudes," the story piqued interests outside of the two girls themselves. Ninja Turtles also found their way into the story. Chuck E. Cheese, the beloved local institution, also served as a site for the setting. Some of these instances were directly lifted from their play (e.g., Lila actually pretended to call her mom for cooking tips), while other material served to add a layer of comedy. The image on the page showed a banana, split in half with personified terror on its face. At the end of the story, all three of us exploded, a rather gruesome end to a series of bad eating decisions. They also knew I loved coffee and managed to include their observations of my desires and tastes.

Children organize their ideas and try out new identities in these spaces of play—their imaginations free them from the expectations and confines that often organize their day. Both Aurelia and Lila tried hard to please the teachers. Lila, by all accounts, embodied a model student whose successful performance at school earned her credibility among the teachers and other children. Yet, play offered her a chance to be someone else—to play with ideas of destruction. It offered her a chance to lean into other sides of herself equally important to her identity, but hidden underneath boxed-in categories of schooling (Orellana, 2015; Yoon, 2015). The story documents the girls' desire to break free from rules governing who they could and should be as students, girls, and exemplars. The story was meant to shock and impress their peers. When the story was shared with the rest of the class, the uproarious laughter about gobbling up talking food, eating 55 cupcakes, and exploding humans accomplished meaningful social goals. In fact, humor was the driving force for all of the stories across the year—a writing genre that is overlooked and diminished in school. Their sense of audience and purpose was salient, and a successful "book" earned laughter and approval from others in the room, energized by the social circumstances (Dyson, 2013b).

The Ninjas Do Math? Reappropriating Turtle Identities

The final story was originally written by Trevor (see Figure 7.6). Trevor had specific and distinct interests: geography, history, and math. His interests were selective and deep, which meant he spent much of his time working on his own pursuits. While his peers were actively engaged in popular culture and media, he spent his play time making U.S. maps, recounting World War II events, and playing around with numeric configurations. At times, he was inflexible, given the particularity and uniqueness of play. Like Lucas, Trevor was Autistic, and like Lucas, Trevor thoughtfully used play and writing to make social connections. While inflexible in some areas, the story here represents Trevor's willingness to allow others to contribute to his work. As the sole author of the story, he willingly included Lucas and Jalen as co-authors because of their central role in the narrative content. Like "Cowabunga Dudes," he also accepted others' drawings as visual material, a practice children began in the latter half of the school year.

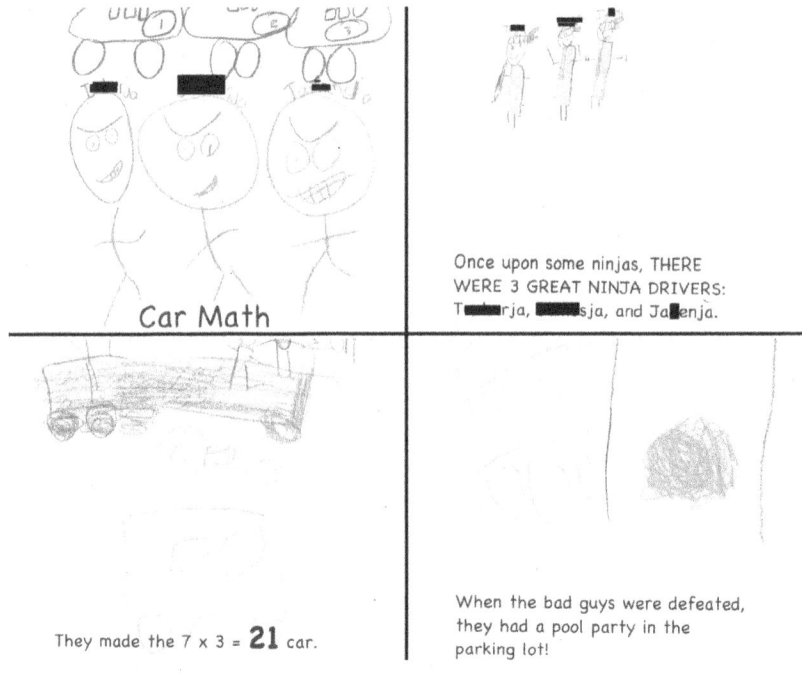

Figure 7.6 Car math. From upper left, clockwise: (1) cover of the story; (2) the beginning of the story introducing the ninja characters; (3) middle of the story where another child draws on top of the writing; (4) the story's conclusion that ends at a pool party, borrowed content from another story, previously written by Jalen and Aliyah.

By Trevor, Lucas, and Jalen.

Car Math

Once upon some ninjas, there were 3 great ninja drivers: Trevorja, Lucasja, and Jalenja. Then, there were other ones. 1,000,000 more ones! And then 5 operation cars came: +, −, ·, |, =. Trevorja drove 2. Jalenja drove 3, and Lucasja drove 1.

"What should we do with 7,5, and 12?" asked Lucasja.

"We should make the + and = to go in to form 7 + 5 = 12 car! What a surprise!" They made the 7 × 3 = 21 car. The 5 × 5= 25 car, and the 32 + 5 = 37 car. The 201 + 201 = 402 car. When they were finished, they shouted "HURR ... uh-oh!" The 1000 car was stuck in M100 bus! Bad guys came to save the M100. When the bad guys were defeated, they had a pool party in the parking lot! They went to planet ... THE END.

Trevor brought me the story and requested its addition to the growing book collection of play stories. Written on a single sheet of blank paper, I took up my role as publisher of children's stories. I typed up his story into distinct pages and left blank spaces for illustration. Trevor made the choice to accept others' solicitation to illustrate, a practice uncommon for Trevor to accept. Allowing others to contribute, shifting his original vision, and accepting words and images stumbling into and on top of each other represented a truly dialogic text that became new with every contribution. Certainly far from what Trevor had imagined, it was still something recognizable to his vision and a significant collaboration for him. His projects were often solo endeavors.

Of note is the foundation of the story—he wrote about his two friends and included a reference to Jalen's now-infamous affinity for Ninja Turtles. He added the "ja" after their names and started his story with "Once upon a ninja", a comical revision to how stories usually start. Knowing full well how meaningful Trevor's own affinities were, I imagine that including Jalen's interests was an intentional act of recognition of Jalen's being. He also allowed others to write on, with, and on top of his text. The collective text became a narrative of friendship and community. Trevor did not compromise the content; he loved math and symbols and found a way to showcase his knowledge and talent in a story that appealed to his classmates. Like many play scenarios throughout the year, there was a "bad guy" who was saved by the heroes, against the backdrop of the local context (i.e., M100 bus). In NYC, all the bus numbers started with an "M" and the M100 bus made stops close to their school. Chuck E. Cheese was not in this story because at one point, Trevor (who lived only a couple of blocks down from there) told me he hates it and wished he lived further away from it. Instead, he ended this story without the usual gathering at Chuck E. Cheese, but a pool party—an idea he got from a previous story written by Jalen and Aliyah.

Play Stories as Pedagogical Practice

Play stories serve to highlight children's voices, narratives, and the key elements of their play. These stories weren't random observations, but carefully documented patterns collected during both playtime and other activities. While teachers juggle countless roles and decisions, one of their most crucial responsibilities is to understand their students deeply—developing the skills to study and analyze young people's work. No pre-made curriculum can fully address the unique characteristics and needs of individual classrooms. Therefore, the most effective teaching approaches emerge when teachers ground their analytical and pedagogical decisions in their students' cultures, interests, and questions.

Teachers, much like ethnographic researchers, are uniquely positioned to understand and amplify how children make sense of their world through the materials and culture around them. Ethnography aims to understand a community from an insider's perspective, making the familiar strange (Geertz, 1973). Through detailed observations of how community members communicate, interact with cultural material, and engage in daily practices, ethnographic research challenges oversimplified assumptions about unfamiliar places—or places we think we know well. Schools fall into this latter category. Because everyone has attended school, we often assume we understand them completely. However, decades of research reveal that schools are intricate, uniquely constructed environments (Ladson-Billings, 2009). Each school's culture is shaped by its social actors—teachers, students, administrators, staff, and parents. Few people spend enough time in classrooms to truly understand how these distinct cultures develop. In what follows, I explain how teachers can adopt an ethnographer's perspective in their own classrooms.

Auditing, Teaching, and Learning

Vivian Vasquez (2014) describes audit trails as documentation of learning. Through systematic collection of artifacts, texts, evidence of learning, and children's conversations, she shows how teachers can physically record and keep track of learning experiences over time. Her audit trails included photographs, transcriptions of conversations, student work, notes from classroom lessons, questions, published texts, and any other artifact highlighting the connection to learning. The audit trail was meant to make visible classroom life for both teachers and children. Together, they co-constructed the process of learning that went beyond the final product. Perhaps, not all teachers have the capacity or the freedom to build curriculum from the ground up. There are many teachers (particularly in this social climate) whose ability to flexibly navigate curricular demands is limited. Yet, the spirit of the audit trail is useful in the way it centers documentation of classroom life.

The audit trail is about collecting moments of classroom life, drawing from multiple engagements throughout the day, and showing evidence of learning. But what happens when we are not sure if a moment is relevant to learning or connected to curricular goals? How do teachers make space for seemingly playful moments that may have little to do with learning objectives? Different from an audit trail, ethnographic documentation is less about proving learning is happening and more about collecting moments that resonate with classroom culture. These moments are not significant on their own, but cumulatively, they bring together ideas and narratives that tell a larger story of *becoming*. For example, TMNT, Star Wars, music icons, and local establishments were consistent sources for children's stories. Beyond its placement in children's texts, the relevance and importance of these artifacts became visible over time. What may seem small and insignificant became a larger part of classroom culture when examined together. Much of what matters to young people isn't always happening in official curricular activity. They appear on the edges of curricular activity, and we often ignore playful spaces as opportunities to study and engage with children's questions. In other words, children's play is not as random and inconsequential as it may seem—"threads knit together and dangle off of narrative lines" (Dyson, 2013a, p. 414), and our role is to tie these disparate threads together. Therefore, what if we expand the idea of an audit trail to include ideas, moments, and random bits that resist predetermined outcomes?

Artifactual Analysis as a Frame for Understanding Children's Play

Creating spaces to play is insufficient without a system that observes and documents what play *does* for young people. Taking young people seriously means taking our documentation of their practice seriously— as a pedagogical and curricular commitment worth noting just as much as those moments that directly account for learning. Now, what do we do with all these curricular moments collected across time? Sorting through the randomness is not a simple task, it requires time, energy, and practice.

I write this idea, acknowledging that the work of teacher as ethnographer is never straightforward or easy—if teaching were easy, anyone could do it. After a rich practice of documentation comes analysis.

Teachers are well accustomed to the demands of "collecting data" in the form of benchmarks, tests, and uniform assignments. This data is often seen as the end goal, yet in ethnographic research, collecting data is only the starting point—the beginning of a process that yields considerable insight into children's cultural lives. Therefore, what we do with the data collected is critical to repositioning children's identity (Yoon, 2015). Currently, data is often used to dis/able children's literate identity into hierarchies of competence. Schools measure children's reading levels, word recall, and writing abilities to determine their worth against one another. They are leveled and sorted until everyone demonstrates the same abilities through data. Once children reach milestones, this data is forgotten and set aside, unimportant for illustrating a holistic portrait of literacy competence.

Kate Pahl and Jennifer Rowsell introduce "artifactual literacies" (2013) as a way to think about the objects and material culture holding significance in children's identity work. Based on research of young children's "commercial, technological, and hand-made artifacts" (p. 265), they argue that early childhood literacies are materially situated in objects that travel with them from home to school, to their neighborhoods and peer groups. As illustrated in this chapter, children draw from these artifacts to play out plotlines and narratives; they gather around popular culture media and materials to connect and relate to one another; they engage with the resources of material culture as the foundation for their own storytelling. Inevitably, documentation that only relies on and elevates school learning shows a partial picture of children's work. Instead, children's play and (pop) culture expand how meaning is made and infused onto the texts children produce and circulate. The examples in this chapter reveal how prevalent these artifacts are to children's writing practice.

These artifacts, then, can also be viewed alongside one another, as they detail an intimate and distinct story of individual and collective meaning-making. What Pahl and Rowsell (2013) offer alongside other literacy scholars is that learning is not limited to the official times where young people demonstrate knowledge (Dyson, 1993; Wohlwend, 2011). Rather, young people reveal these parts of themselves at points that look and feel less explicit and directly correlated. We do well if we take seriously the artifacts of children's culture that have less importance to school constructions of success. Returning to the story of Jalen, juxtaposed with a "Leonardo" identity, I turn to "how" to think about children's artifacts and culture. Decades of research have shown us the importance of pop culture in the identity formation of young people. Along with these identity texts are belonging and community, interlaced with knowledge, participation, and capital of the pop culture phenomenon. Taking children's engagement seriously in these popular culture artifacts means we take time to engage with these artifacts ourselves: Watch the media, engage with printed texts, get educated about what the media artifacts mean, and listen to how young people are interpreting these experiences for themselves. In the case of TMNT, I spent time with the original comic strips, watched several episodes from the early nineties as well as the more recent renderings, and looked at fan sites devoted to the franchise. While not all material was relevant, a deeper and thorough examination of the material artifacts allowed for a deeper and thorough examination of Jalen's inter/intra-actions with TMNT.

Additionally, official times designated as play are not the only times children demonstrate cultural knowledge. Moments where children circulate social, cultural knowledge happen in playful encounters with one another across academic disciplines—during informal conversations of their writing, through meaningful dialog exchanged during curricular activities, embedded in the questions and approaches they take to deal with school materials. Therefore, play is everywhere, as long as we pay attention to the things that really matter.

Visibility and Value in a Textual Landscape

Reframing value by raising the visibility of children's spontaneous, incomplete, and playful enactments expands our social imagination and makes room for diverse stories. Rather than posting student work that is standardized and cleaned-up, I suggest displaying our walls with work that matters to children—their ninja turtle illustrations, their stories of Chuck E. Cheese and pool parties, and their creative renditions of talking bananas and food explosions. While these stories are not always cohesive and uniform, they tell a more complete and accurate account of children's meaning-making.

Museums carefully audit and curate their space to communicate ideologies. In the same way, schools also curate ideologies through images and photographs as well as displays of student work. Oftentimes, what lives outside of the classroom on carefully crafted walls are far from the emotional, messy, and joyful affairs that constitute children's sociocultural identities. We have long talked about the importance of texts—who gets represented, what gets represented, and how texts amplify as well as marginalize communities (Bishop, 1990; Gardner, 2023). These play stories are an example of how children contribute to classroom texts. The stories are written by them; they include them as characters; they take place in shared contextual spaces; they are featured with photographs, images, and illustrations by and of them. The stories do not follow neatly bounded genres or stories that outsiders looking in would readily recognize. Instead, they are displayed for children's benefit—to connote the value of their narratives, displayed in prominent places.

When we speak of "mirrors and windows" (Bishop, 1990), could we imagine books and curated work where the reflection is more literal and explicit? The decision to type these stories, curate their images, assign authorship, print in color across multiple pages, bind into books, and create an anthology was made to elevate the importance of play and story-making. The books were part of the classroom library so children could return to them often. The stories became an integral part of the weekly classroom practice. I worked just as hard to publish these stories as children did in telling them. Children deserved this level of mutuality and reciprocity from me.

Conclusion

> Moments slip by us and can seem difficult to grasp, even if we recognize their accumulating importance, so teachers need tools to slow down and linger in the acceleration of days, weeks, and years with children
>
> (Cartun & Dutro, 2020, p. 588)

The best pedagogical strategy for classrooms has less to do with a specific practice. Over the years, I have witnessed various ways teachers set up conditions for children's agency. Contrary to what we might assume, these practices range from structured to unstructured, guided to free, emergent to teacher-led, and tightly scheduled to flexible. Many might assume that play can only be free and unstructured. This limits the playful ways that children engage with one another, the teacher, and the curriculum. If we expand our vision of play, we might notice playful moments in the corners of rooms that "slip by us". In our hurried states, we inadvertently ignore significant moments and relationships that deepen our understanding of childhood culture and identities. Play is not a monolithic practice—what one person considers playful may be work to another. Some of us thrive under structure, preferring it, while others are constricted by it.

This same idea relates to notions of criticality. Critical Humanizing Writing Pedagogy highlights critical literacy—the ways that children speak back to and with the sociopolitical issues surrounding their communities (Kline & Kang, 2022; Land, 2022). Critical pedagogies assume young people are active contributors to social justice movements and capable of inciting change (Schutz et al., 2019). A writing curriculum that mobilizes young people's sense of agency alongside the issues that matter most to them situates writing as a political and revolutionary act. Embedded in critical pedagogies are culturally sustaining practices (Alim et al., 2020), centering the layered, overlapping, and distinct cultural communities where children participate and learn (Moll & González, 1994).

However, the children in this classroom cared about their relationships and connections with each other. Their writing hardly reflected the issues that we also want children to care about: climate change, racism, sexism, and other issues of civic engagement. Yet, children showed alternative ways of criticality. Their story contents reflected a depth of knowledge about one another that was studied and cultivated through repeated engagement. They knew one another well and intentionally brought in each other's interests as textual tools. Those who could easily be dismissed and excluded because of race and disability found a place in this classroom. Their identities were amplified in play and in the text. Of significance are the ways that children contributed to the conditions and practices that fostered belonging, community, and inclusion.

Play is elusive and expansive in its definition. Consequently, holding space for play as well as identifying its many forms are both challenging tasks in a scripted and tightly controlled curricular space. In this social context, I offer three questions for further consideration:

1. What popular culture phenomenon resonates in your classroom these days? How can you research and study these forms outside of the classroom?
2. What are the spaces of playful encounters in your classroom currently? For example, where do the children seem to be having the most fun and enjoyment (e.g., during math centers; in writing workshops). What are the conditions that are creating these joyful and playful spaces?
3. How can I document children's writing process more flexibly and authentically?
4. What is critical to children?, Whose ideas are elevated and whose ideas are marginal?, What is considered worth classroom space and time?, and How do we decide what stories are "appropriate" to tell?

References

Adger, C. T., Wolfram, W., & Christian, D. (2014). *Dialects in schools and communities*. Routledge.

Alim, H. S., Paris, D., & Wong, C. P. (2020). Culturally sustaining pedagogy: A critical framework for centering communities. In N. S. Nasir., C. D. Lee., R. Pea., & M. M. D. Royston (Eds.), *Handbook of the cultural foundations of learning* (pp. 261–276). Routledge.

Alim, H. S., Rickford, J. R., & Ball, A. F. (2016). *Raciolinguistics: How language shapes our ideas about race*. Oxford University Press.

Bakhtin, M. (1981). *The dialogic imagination: Four essays*. University of Texas Press.

Bishop, R. S. (1990, March 5). Windows and mirrors: Children's books and parallel cultures. In *California State University reading conference: 14th annual conference proceedings* (pp. 3–12).

Bomer, R., & Laman, T. (2004). Positioning in a primary writing workshop: Joint action in the discursive production of writing subjects. *Research in the Teaching of English*, 38(4), 420–466.

Cartun, A., & Dutro, E. (2020). The humanizing potential of risky writing: Tracing children's and teacher candidates' critical-affective literacy practices. *Reading Psychology*, 41(6), 583–604.

Collins, J., & Blot, R. K. (2003). *Literacy and literacies: Texts, power, and identity.* Cambridge University Press.

Dyer, H. (2019). *The Queer Aesthetics of Childhood: Asymmetries of innocence and the cultural politics of child development.* Rutgers University Press.

Dyson, A. H. (1993). *Social worlds of children learning to write in an urban primary school.* Teachers College Press.

Dyson, A. H. (2013a). The case of the missing childhoods. *Written Communication,* 30(4), 399–427.

Dyson, A. H. (2013b). *Rewriting the basics: Literacy learning in children's cultures.* Teachers College Press.

Flores, N., & Rosa, J. (2015). Undoing appropriateness: Raciolinguistic ideologies and language diversity in education. *Harvard Educational Review,* 85(2), 149–171.

García, O., & Kleifgen, J. A. (2019). Translanguaging and literacies. *Reading Research Quarterly,* 55(4), 553–571.

Gardner, R. P. (2023). Examining the aesthetics of black working-class childhoods in literature for children. In H. S. Yoon, A. L. Goodwin, & G. Celia (Eds.), *Reimagining diversity, equity, and justice in early childhood* (pp. 57–68). Routledge.

Geertz, C. (1973). *The interpretation of cultures.* New York: Basic Books.

Heath, S. B. (1983). *Ways with words: Language, life and work in communities and classrooms.* Cambridge University Press.

hooks, b. (2000). Remembered rapture: Dancing with words. *JAC,* 20(1), 1–8.

hooks, b. (2006). *Outlaw culture: Resisting representations.* Routledge.

Jenkins, H. (2006). 7 "Going Bonkers!" Children, Play, and Pee-Wee. In H. Jenkins (Ed.), *The Wow Climax* (pp. 159–184). New York University Press.

Johnson, L. P., & Sullivan, H. (2020). Revealing the human and the writer: The promise of a humanizing writing pedagogy for Black students. *Research in the Teaching of English,* 54(4), 418–438.

Kline, S., & Kang, G. (2022). Reflect, reimagine, revisit: A framework for centering critical writing pedagogy. *Language Arts,* 99(5), 300–311.

Kwon, J. (2021). Mobilizing historical knowledge through transcultural play: A multi-sited ethnographic case study of an immigrant child. *Early Child Development and Care,* 191(4), 624–639.

Ladson-Billings, G. (2021). Three decades of culturally relevant, responsive, & sustaining pedagogy: What lies ahead? *The Educational Forum,* 85(4), 351–354. https://doi.org/10.1080/00131725.2021.1957632

Land, C. L. (2022). Recentering purpose and audience as part of a critical, humanizing approach to writing instruction. *Reading Research Quarterly*, 57(1), 37–58.

Luke, A. (2018). *Critical literacy, schooling, and social justice: The Selected Works of Allan Luke*. Routledge.

Luttrell, W. (2020). *Children framing childhoods: Working-class kids' visions of care*. Policy Press.

Moll, L. C., & González, N. (1994). Lessons from research with language-minority children. *Journal of Reading Behavior*, 26(4), 439–456.

Orellana, M. F. (2001). The Work Kids Do: Mexican and Central American immigrant children's contributions to households and schools in California. *Harvard Educational Review*, 71(3), 366–390.

Orellana, M. F. (2015). *Immigrant Children in Transcultural spaces: Language learning and love*. Routledge.

Pahl, K., & Rowsell, J. (2013). Artifactual Literacies. In P. Albers, T. Holbrook, & A. S. Flint (Eds.), *New Methods of Literacy Research* (pp. 163–176). Routledge.

Paley, V. G. (2011). Voices inside schools: Getting to know Derek. *Harvard Educational Review*, 81(4), 745–750.

Prendergast, C. (2003). *Literacy and racial justice: The politics of learning after Brown v. Board of Education*. Southern Illinois University Press.

Schutz, K. M., Woodard, R., Diaz, A. R., & Peek, W. L. (2019). The disruptive potential of humanizing literacy pedagogies in elementary teacher education. *The Sojo Journal*, 5(1), 43–60.

Sicart, M. (2014). *Play matters*. MIT Press.

Street, B. (2003). What's "new" in new literacy studies? Critical approaches to literacy in theory and practice. *Current Issues in Comparative Education*, 5(2), 77–91.

Templeton, T. N. (2018). "That street is taking us to home": Young children's photographs of public spaces. *Children's Geographies*, 18(1), 1–15.

Templeton, T. N., & Harvey, M. (2024). Scatological matters and a politics of care in early childhood. *Teachers College Record: The Voice of Scholarship in Education*, 126(10), 57–87. https://doi.org/10.1177/01614681241307096

Templeton, T. N., & Vellanki, V. (2022). Decentering the adult gaze: Young children's photographs as provocations for place-making. *Language Arts*, 99(4), 227–239.

Thiel, J. J. (2020). Red circles, embodied literacies, and neoliberalism: The art of noticing an unruly placemaking event. *Journal of Early Childhood Literacy*, 20(1), 69–89.

Thorne, B. (1987). Re-visioning women and social change: Where are the children? *Gender & Society*, 1(1), 85–109.

Trammell, A. (2023). *Repairing play: A Black phenomenology*. MIT Press.

Vasquez, V. M. (2014). *Negotiating Critical Literacies with Young Children* (10th Anniversary Edition). Routledge.

Vasudevan, L. (2011). Re-imagining pedagogies for multimodal selves. *Teachers College Record: The Voice of Scholarship in Education*, 113(13), 88–108. https://doi.org/10.1177/016146811111301304

Vasudevan, L. (2015). Multimodal play and adolescents: Notes on noticing laughter. *Journal of Language and Literacy Education*, 11(1), 1–12.

Von Joo, L. (2024). *The Boundaries of Adventure Playgrounds* [Doctoral dissertation, Teachers College, Columbia University].

Wargo, J. M. (2015). "Every selfie tells a story … ": LGBTQ youth lifestreams and new media narratives as connective identity texts. *New Media & Society*, 19(4), 560–578.

Wohlwend, K. E. (2009). Damsels in discourse: Girls consuming and producing identity texts through Disney Princess play. *Reading Research Quarterly*, 44(1), 57–83.

Wohlwend, K. E. (2011). *Playing their way into literacies: Reading, writing, and belonging in the early childhood classroom*. Teachers College Press.

Wohlwend, K. E. (2020). *Literacies that move and matter: Nexus Analysis for contemporary childhoods*. Routledge.

Yoon, H. S. (2015). Assessing children in kindergarten: The narrowing of language, culture and identity in the testing era. *Journal of Early Childhood Literacy*, 15(3), 364–393.

Yoon, H. S. (2020). Critically literate citizenship: Moments and movements in second grade. *Journal of Literacy Research*, 52(3), 293–315. https://doi.org/10.1177/1086296x20939557

Yoon, H. S. (2021). Stars, rainbows, and Michael Myers: The carnivalesque intersection of play and horror in kindergarteners' (trade) marking and (copy) writing. *Teachers College Record: The Voice of Scholarship in Education*, 123(3), 1–22.

Yoon, H. S., Llerena, C., & Brooks, E. (2016). The unfolding of Lucas's story in an inclusive classroom: Living, playing, and becoming in the social world of kindergarten. *Occasional Paper Series*, 2016(36), 1–19.

8

Activism
Environmental Artivism as a Critical Multimodal Writing Pedagogy

Rebecca Woodard and Kristine Schutz

Climate change is being driven by human actions that are rapidly heating the planet (Intergovernmental Panel on Climate Change, 2022). Effects of climate change include a swift decline in biodiversity, more severe extreme weather, risks to food availability, and forced relocation. It also enhances existing vulnerabilities and inequalities (Johnson & Wilkinson, 2020, p. xviii). Individuals residing in areas with high poverty rates, weak governance, and limited access to resources face the greatest risks. Due to its complexity, climate change is seen as a "wicked problem" of our time (Lazarus, 2009). While concern about the environment has historically been positioned in the media as a luxury afforded primarily to affluent White folks, recent surveys in the U.S. suggest that Black and Latino communities express the most concerns about climate change (Ballew et al., 2020). Despite often being excluded from environmental leadership, there is a rich history of Black (Penniman, 2023), Indigenous (Gilio-Whitaker, 2019; Wildcat, 2009), feminist (Johnson & Wilkinson, 2020), and youth (Diavolo & Wagner, 2021) environmental thought that offers insights into diverse and interdisciplinary solutions to climate change (see Johnson & Wilkinson, 2020). All that is to say: climate change impacts everyone, exacerbates inequalities, and will be best addressed by harnessing a wide variety of perspectives and viewpoints, making it a worthy and timely topic for exploration in classrooms.

We have spent the past five years as literacy teacher educators engaging with children and teachers to learn about climate change and intersecting issues of justice (Woodard & Schutz, 2024) as part of what we call *urgent literacy pedagogies* that "support youth to read, write, inquire into, and collaborate about meaningful topics that are responsive to the social times" (Woodard & Schutz, 2022, p. 272). Urgent literacy pedagogies don't have to focus on climate change and the environment; they can orient to any worthwhile topic. Urgent literacy pedagogies support writing for activism to challenge power and change in communities. They are also an opportunity for educators to act as activists by intentionally resisting narrow literacy curriculum.

In this piece, we'll focus on one aspect of urgent writing pedagogies and how it supports activism: the use of art and multimodal composing. We'll refer to art that is oriented to activism as *artivism*, which is "a convergence, a hybrid of artistic production and activism that embraces their symbiotic relationship for transformational purposes" (Rhoades, 2012, p. 319). While we'll explore environmental artivism in this piece, artivism—and activism, more generally—can be fostered as part of any critical multimodal writing pedagogy about any meaningful topic.

Background

We connect our exploration of artivism as part of urgent literacy pedagogies to two major concepts—critical multimodal composing and interdisciplinary inquiry. Then, we briefly situate this work in literature on children's multimodal composing about the environment. We introduce each of these concepts as a concern or question that teachers often pose to us.

Critical Multimodal Composing

Teachers often ask us how art "counts" as writing. We think about writing more expansively than is typical in schools. Rather than privileging linguistic/alphabetic modes, we also encourage attention to ensembles of visual, aural, gestural, and/or spatial modes (see Woodard et al., 2024, p. 2). From the perspective that meaning is made through the use of a variety of meaning systems (see The New London Group, 1996), both writing and art can be seen as forms of *multimodal composing*. Children generally find multimodal composition enjoyable, and it supports their identity development as writers (Dalton & Jocious, 2013). Multimodal composition provides a space in which children can draw from their full literate, linguistic, and cultural resources (Rowe & Miller, 2016), communicate in meaningful ways to authentic audiences about topics that matter to them (Vasudevan et al., 2010), and joyfully engage their imaginations to craft (counter)narratives of refusal and hope (Johnson, 2024).

Embracing multimodal composing in the writing classroom is not a neutral choice. By expanding what "counts" as writing in school, teachers act to resist "monolithic school-based notions of literacy" and to incorporate and value "the varied literacy practices" of all students, and especially youth of Color, which can mean that "creativity and innovation are allowed to flourish" (Griffin & Turner, 2021, p. 440). This is a necessary corrective to a legacy of English Language Arts instruction that "can be, at its worst, an enforcement of Whiteness" in which learners are often required to "comply ... to a culture not their own" (Bomer, 2017, p. 12). Of course, multimodality is not inherently liberatory; it can "reproduce ... [Eurocentric norms] ... [and] re-inscribe schooling as usual" (Campano et al., 2020, p. 137). To be truly critical, multimodal composing pedagogies must do things like "critique power and create new educational communities" (Campano et al., 2020, p. 138), "create new possibilities for the future" (Toliver, 2021, p. 133), or serve as "sites of possibility and disruption that protect and advance ... [youth's] goals and aspirations" (Turner & Griffin, 2021, p. 51).

While art and other forms of multimodal composing should not replace text-based writing instruction, it can offer children additional tools to communicate effectively, an engaging way to think about rhetoric, and opportunities for disruption and possibility. Ultimately, it can cultivate more inclusive writing classrooms where more children see themselves as writers, composers, and creators who can make a difference.

Interdisciplinary Inquiry

Another concern we often hear from literacy teachers is that climate change is a "science topic" (Panos & Damico, 2021). We believe that climate change—and other urgent topics—are well suited to interdisciplinary inquiry in/through English Language Arts (ELA) instruction. Consider the unique and complementary lenses that different disciplines can bring to learning about climate change. Science can help children understand the scientific phenomena and causes, social studies can allow them to examine policies and sociopolitical structures, and the English Language Arts can foster their empathy and imaginations (NCTE, 2019). While we typically situate our explorations primarily in the ELA discipline (Woodard & Schutz, 2024), together, these perspectives can contribute to a more robust understanding of climate change. As literacy teachers, it is important to not identify any interesting topic as "off limits" or belonging to another discipline. Instead, consider what an ELA-oriented exploration can bring to an inquiry of any compelling topic.

Furthermore, although science and social studies instruction are often short shrifted in elementary contexts in favor of intensive instruction in the highly-tested ELA and math domains, these "fundamental academic domains ... provide rich content on which to build ... learning experiences" (Sarama et al., 2017, p. 1). Often framed as interdisciplinary inquiry or project-based learning, there are numerous examples of literacy instruction that meaningfully integrate with science and social studies (Hertzog, 2007; Muhammad, 2020). Embracing interdisciplinary inquiry can be a key aspect of critical multimodal writing pedagogies by orienting children's learning and thinking and doing toward topics that matter, regardless of what discipline(s) it might typically be associated with in school. We often find ourselves returning to the words of our science education colleagues to remind ourselves that, "Anyone who has spent meaningful time with young children can observe how artistic, scientific, literary, mathematical and ethical questions and ideas animate their engagement with the natural and social world. Yet our current system often teaches children to compartmentalize these ways of knowing—to the detriment of the deeper learning we could be cultivating" (Morales-Doyle et al., 2020, n.p). Much like embracing expansive conceptualizations of writing, resisting this false compartmentalization of disciplines can be considered a form of teacher activism.

Children's Multimodal Composing and Artivism About the Environment and Climate Change

Finally, teachers ask us for concrete examples of children's multimodal composing about climate change. Much of the research focused on climate change, specifically, has been conducted with adolescents. For example, the edited collection *Youth Created Media on the Climate Crisis* (Beach & Smith, 2024) includes chapters about youth creating documentary videos about environmental justice and the impacts of climate change (Goodman, 2020), making multimodal art (Jordan, Lockmiller, & Zuiker, 2023), and music about solar energy.

Research with young children tends to focus more broadly on the environment and sustainability. For example, Davis (2018) documents how observation and drawing helped children to understand the interconnectedness of trees, and Song (2008) describes how the creation of ecological public art afforded children opportunities to connect and take action. Other researchers have demonstrated how artforms like dance and dramatization expand children's views of environmental issues (McNaughton, 2004; Pollitt et al., 2021). In the Coastal Climate Kid Collective Project, children take curiosity walks with their families where they notice and wonder about their ecological communities, and then craft multimodal responses (Schenkel et al., 2024). Other research shares children's poetry about the environment and climate change (Makwanya & Dick, 2014), and their place-based writing about local lands, waters, and communities (Hamilton et al., 2021).

Collectively, research on children's multimodal composing and artivism about the environment supports a range of writing genres and forms, and can foster empathy, agency, critique, and hope—thus making it a site of criticality and possibility. Artivism, as we've described it here, has the potential to address multiple tenets of critical humanizing writing pedagogy including agency, collaboration, equity, and antiracism. In the next section, we introduce and unpack critical concepts for elementary educators looking to cultivate artivism in writing classrooms.

Pedagogical Implications

Three critical concepts to support artivism in writing classrooms are to: (1) design toward urgent literacy pedagogies; (2) incorporate the arts in literacy classrooms as a form of multimodal composing; and (3) center justice and action in writing instruction.

Big Idea 1: Design Toward Urgent Literacy Pedagogies

As we design learning opportunities that position young people to become artivists, we also encourage teachers to use curriculum design to engage as activists themselves—activists who care about contemporary social issues, who forward expansive understandings of writing and writers, and who see the importance of engaging children in meaningful, interdisciplinary work.

When working with educators to design toward *urgent literacy pedagogies*, we draw from Muhammad's (2020) Historically Responsive Literacy Framework, and the ways she prompts teachers in their curricular design to ask themselves, "What is *worthwhile* [emphasis added] for learning in my content area?" (p. 145). This, we think, should be at the heart of our curricular designs as we reimagine writing. We pay attention to how worthwhile content related to our curricula can be framed in engaging ways that are responsive to our learners and this moment in history. We consider the topics and issues that are relevant to today's children, families, and communities and how these position young people to act with agency. Worthwhile topics also have the potential to teach children something about their identities or those of others and to foster joy (Muhammad, 2020).

In our work, we recognize that not all children come to our classes with an interest in climate change in the environment. We can forge connections for children by being responsive to the places where they live and contemporary issues that arise. For example, we have found that when studying water protection, children where we live in Chicago are eager to learn more about how these issues impact Lake Michigan. We also have leaned into teachable moments of inquiry about contemporary, pressing issues as they appear in the news and impact learners' daily lives. For example, heat waves, air quality warnings, and extreme weather all provide a space for learners to come to understand the very real impact of climate change. Finally, within larger topics of study, we can identify subtopics for exploration that allow children choices to inquire into what they are most interested in.

Some teachers, particularly those who teach young children, worry about the complexity and heaviness of topics like climate change. We believe that young children have both the capacity and desire to engage with complex topics, albeit in different ways than older youth. For example, when we start talking about the environment with young learners, we don't jump straight to climate change. Instead, we center *literacy-based climate pedagogy* around core principles of interconnectivity (i.e., understanding how the social and natural worlds are intertwined, and how everything matters), relationality (i.e., recognizing our responsibility to live in relationship to and care for both fellow humans and the natural world), and action (i.e., working together to create change, solve complex problems, and impact systems; see Woodard & Schutz, 2024). Children and teachers read books, write stories and poems and arguments and multimodal texts, and investigate compelling questions as they study trees, soil, and bees. Through this kind of work, we engage children through textual inquiry; encourage standards-aligned reading, writing, and languaging practices; and foster their ecological identities, or their sense of self in relation to the natural world (Thomashow, 1996). Activism—and its focus on bettering the world and positive transformation—can centrally undergird urgent topics of study in literacy pedagogies. While argumentative writing is often at the top of the mind in supporting activism, artistic and literary forms of writing are also important ways to draw attention to problems, foster empathy, and to elicit calls to action.

In our book, *Teaching Climate Change to Children: Literacy Pedagogy That Cultivates Sustainable Futures* (Woodard & Schutz, 2024), we recommend five principles for literacy-based climate pedagogy unit design. We share them here with slight modifications to support more generalized urgent literacy pedagogy unit design (see Table 8.1).

Table 8.1 Principles for unit design of urgent literacy pedagogies

Principle 1	Explores meaningful and compelling topics or questions.
Principle 2	Fosters both conceptual understandings *and* identity development.
Principle 3	Orients to a consequential task.
Principle 4	Engages students in textual inquiry.
Principle 5	Intentionally supports literacy learning necessary for reading, writing, languaging, and doing.

Source: Adapted from Woodard & Schutz, 2024.

We elaborate more on the idea of consequential tasks (principle 3) and literacy learning oriented to doing (principle 5) at the end of this section.

Big Idea 2: Incorporate the Arts in Literacy Classrooms as a Form of Multimodal Composing

Considering art-making as a form of composing is consistent with perspectives that conceptualize literacy broadly as a way of making and communicating meaning multimodally (The New London Group, 1996). We regularly prompt teachers to consider, "*What would happen if we took [children's] artistic skills and multiliteracies seriously in schools? How might we see children in new ways that honor and validate the diverse and rich ways they consume and compose all kinds of texts? How might it help us to be in better relation with children, to know and love them for their whole selves?*" (Woodard & Schutz, 2024, p. 169).

We incorporate the arts as a central aspect of literacy-based climate pedagogy because we know they expand possibilities for constructing and communicating knowledge (Caughlan, 2005), offer opportunities to deliberate on feelings (Pikhkala, 2020) and cultivate empathy (Curtis, 2009), support children to make connections with people and nature (Walshe et al., 2023), and can foster motivation toward action (Song, 2008). Multimodal composing through the arts also supports intentionality when selecting different modes of communication, and considerations of purpose and audience. And, importantly, children enjoy the arts and find joy in them. Particularly given dwindling support for the arts in schools, making them central to the literacy curriculum can represent a personal form of activism for teachers.

In the next section, we share examples of how we have encouraged environmental artivism in our literacy pedagogies with children and pre- and in-service teachers. From collaborative multimedia poetry writing to disintegration art modeled on mentor texts to AI-assisted comic writing, we'll demonstrate how art is a form of critical multimodal composing that can support activism and foster engagement.

Big Idea 3: Center Justice and Action in Writing Instruction

Finally, justice and action are central to activist writing. In our work, we argue that "climate change is inseparable from issues of justice" (Woodard & Schutz, 2024, p. 28). Our instruction does not focus primarily on technical understandings of climate change (although we know how important this is). Instead, we use a humanizing critical lens to explore systemic causes; the role of overconsumption, money-making, and power; and differential and inequitable impacts. Furthermore, the core principles of interconnectivity and relationality inherently focus our work on considerations of justice and equity. Even if your focus is not on the environment or climate change, urgent literacies pedagogies, with their support of consequential and worthwhile reading and writing, offer opportunities to engage with issues of justice. Questions to guide a justice-oriented focus in writing pedagogies include: *What systems are involved in this topic or issue? Who benefits, how, and why? Who is most negatively impacted, how, and why? Who holds the power, how, and why? Which perspectives are centered (and not) in conversations about this topic? How can I support learning about this topic that draws from a "mosaic of voices" (Johnson & Wilkinson, 2020, p. xvi), and especially ones that have been marginalized and/or align with the identities of my students?*

Action should also be central to activist writing pedagogies. In Table 8.1, we talked about designing consequential tasks as part of urgent literacy pedagogy; these tasks provide "compelling reasons for children to engage as readers, writers, and thinkers, and to recognize that learning is a social endeavor" (Schutz & Woodard, 2024, p. 104). They have a *purpose* beyond being evaluated by the teacher, and often *audiences* beyond the teacher, too. We love the way Trott, Even, and Frame (2020) talk about reframing school learning endeavors from questions of "what is" toward questions of "what if". "What if" questions, we think, support consequential tasks and inquiries, as well as agency, collaboration, and action-oriented writing. Questions to guide an action-oriented focus in writing pedagogies include: *What will this writing help children do in the world? Who will see this writing? How will this writing help children to imagine a more joyful, humane, and just future? How will it support them to act agentively and collaboratively?*

Environmental Artivism in Action

We have explored how artivism and multimodal composition that is grounded in the three big ideas above can support children and adults as they engage in textual inquiry about topics related to climate change and environmental sustainability. Here, we provide a glimpse of this work in three different contexts: a teacher inquiry group; a pre-service teacher education literacy methods course; and a nature art camp for children in the intermediate grades. We unpack three artforms these artivists used to take action, including: collaborative poetry with mixed-media art, disintegration-style art, and sculpture. As you read, we invite you to consider how you might imagine applying the ideas from each different context with your own set of unique learners.

Cultivating a Climate Community of Educators: Collaborative Poetry with Mixed-Media Art

After our own reading of the anthology *All We Can Save: Truth, Courage, and the Solutions for the Climate Crisis* (Johnson & Wilkinson, 2020), we invited elementary educators to gather for a virtual inquiry group where we would read the book together and explore the topic of climate change, considering how to bring literacy-rich climate pedagogy to elementary classrooms. In our monthly Zoom sessions, we unpacked the section of the book we had just read, read and discussed children's literature about related topics, and composed responses to process and share our understandings (see Schutz et al., 2022; Woodard & Schutz, 2024 for session details).

While we had intended to use our time together to begin to develop, implement, and refine unit plans focused on climate change and environmental sustainability, we quickly realized that this collective needed to provide a space for processing not only the climate knowledge we were acquiring but also our feelings about the climate crisis and our work as educators during the pandemic. Therefore, we pivoted, and began to incorporate opportunities for art-making into our sessions. This included artforms like illustrated blackout poetry with mixed media art, as well as blackout poetry where we photocopied individual pages of our shared text, blacked out words to create poems, and illustrated them to enhance meaning (see Schutz et al., 2022 for examples). As we processed our own complicated feelings about the climate crisis, we found ourselves leaning into the way in which Johnson and Wilkinson's editing of *All We Can Save* not only educated us, but also helped us experience a broad range of emotions and the feeling of *needing to do something*.

Over the course of several meetings, we decided to collaboratively write a poem in the style of one poem we had read in the anthology. One participant, Ashley, a seventh-grade teacher at the time, suggested that we look to "Did It Ever Occur to You That Maybe You're Falling in Love" by Ailish Hopper (2020, pp. 203–204). She explained that the repetition and mood really stood out to her and that as a teacher, she could imagine using it as a mentor text that students could study to better understand the poet's craft, so they could try applying similar moves in their poetry-writing.

Across the next two sessions, we collaboratively authored a poem in this style while writing together in a Google Doc. We examined individual lines in Hopper's poem to notice and name the writer's move and we considered how poetic elements like rhythm, imagery, tone, and repetition convey meaning. We finished with a six-stanza poem entitled *We Will Refuse the Problem* (see Figure 8.1). Yet, our collaborative poem did not seem complete. We knew the use of images and color could help further enhance the meaning. So, we each chose one stanza to illustrate using oil pastels and then affixed the words. Finally, we combined the tagboard in a quilt-like, mixed media arrangement.

In many ways, this poem was a representation of our learning over time and ideas from our reading of *All We Can Save* and many children's books about the environment, our conversations about texts, concepts, and systems, our unanswered questions and feelings about the climate crisis. For example, the fourth stanza conveys our frustration with how the climate crisis has been addressed over time. It reads:

We reduce, reuse, recycle
the problem.
We calculate the carbon footprint of
the problem.
We watch sad animal videos about
the problem.
We Earth Day
the problem.
We recycle the problem.
We recycle the problem.
We recycle the problem.

We conclude the poem with a call to action in the form of questions to draw attention to the need for everyone to take some sort of action to address the climate crisis and convey a feeling of hope through the image in the background, a large question mark with beautiful color shining outward (see Figure 8.1).

Collaborative poetry can be a non-intimidating way to compose poetry, a type of writing that many people—both children and adults—have convinced themselves that they simply cannot do or do well. In fact, when

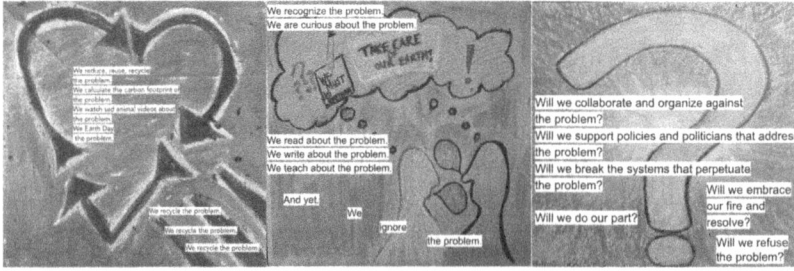

Figure 8.1 Part of our collaborative poetry with mixed-media art, "We Will Refuse The Problem."

By Tiffini, Rebecca, Ashley, Kristine, Jasmine, and Eva.

we began writing poetry, one participant, Eva, expressed her trepidation, yet as we engaged as a group, and our purpose of taking action became clear, she found that poetry writing was something that she could do and actually enjoyed.

We love the way in which this form of artivism offers entry points for learners of all ages, and we offer it as one idea to help learners collaboratively compose. While we can see how a form like this might easily get split into individual responsibilities (e.g., you find a mentor poem; you write our poem; you do the illustrations), we think it is important to help learners see that they always have something to offer, even if they feel like it's outside of their perceived expertise. When we have used this artform with children, we have collaboratively studied mentor texts, then as a class composed the initial stanzas collaboratively on a screen before splitting children into groups and sending them off to each write stanzas in our class-shared Google Doc. When each group's stanza is complete, we return to the group to revise and edit the poem to ensure that our message is clear and consistent throughout. Following that, children self-select groups that will illustrate each stanza. We discuss elements to consider when designing the illustration, but leave groups to make individual decisions. Finally, we stitch together individual stanzas to convey a form of artivism to display.

Immersing Young Learners in Nature and Art: Disintegration Style Art

Last summer, we designed and facilitated a nature art camp for local first through fifth graders on our university campus. As researchers, we were interested in understanding how to harness the power of the humanities and hands-on exploration as an on-ramp to learning about sustainable living.

The children's exploration of sustainability was focused on two questions: (1) *What do we notice when we look for nature in the city?* (2) *How does this help us to live sustainably?* Each camp day contained three core activities: a read aloud of a children's book, hands-on exploration of a garden on campus while interacting with an expert, and multiple opportunities to make art. These three components were key to building children's knowledge about what it means to live sustainably, art as a form of activism, and the appreciation of urban nature. Together we read and discussed picture books, explored many different gardens, and the children made various forms of art, including sketches, photographs from pinhole cameras, nature collages, and disintegration-style art (Beretta, n.d).

While the main focus of the camp was intended to be sustainable living, multiple teachable moments surfaced as we responded to the week's dangerous air quality due to wildfires. As good teachers do, we responded to the time, place, and feelings that children were experiencing to help them make sense of why our trips around campus had suddenly been rescheduled, having conversations about wildfires (what they are and what can cause them), air quality, and the need to care for our Earth and one another. We found excerpts of children's books about climate change that provided information to help the children process and understand the environmental crisis.

One artform that children took to and used to convey their concern about the Earth was disintegration-style art. We studied the artwork and website of French artist Sabrina Beretta (https://artetbe.com/about/) and were struck by the artform she created where one half of a representation of a living thing is represented whole and the other half appears scattered, as if it has exploded. She explains disintegration style art as "the association and/or the opposition of two sides, two perceptions, while suggesting a symmetry that does not exist" (Beretta, n.d). To begin, graduate student Evelyn Pollins gathered the children to look closely at some of Beretta's artwork. The group focused on a disintegration style representation of a butterfly in which one side of the butterfly is whole, and the other is shattered. They talked together about why Beretta might have intentionally decided to shatter the one side of the butterfly and discussed a quote on Beretta's website that says, "one small incident can have a big impact, and with one flap of the wings anything can shatter." Some students suggested that climate change is impacting living things, others related the shattering to natural disasters like the wildfires, while others considered the human impact on the Earth and its creatures. We discussed how Beretta makes a statement about how delicate our Earth and its inhabitants are and how many factors impact their health and well-being. One student suggested that Beretta is an *artivist*, a word we had discussed after seeing it in a mural on our trip to a heritage garden.

Students brainstormed ideas for what they could create in the disintegration style. For some, their ideas related to their growing understanding of climate change and the importance of sustainable living. For example, Mia chose a leaf. For others, like Noah and Hazel, their ideas related to their new understandings of wildfires and their concerns for living things that mattered to them. After creating their artwork, the children wrote a gallery card displaying the piece's title and a short explanation.

Figure 8.2 shows three masterpieces created by campers, each demonstrating how the children naturally took on the role of activists through their artwork—whether it was advocating for animals whose voices couldn't be heard during the wildfires and air quality advisories, or alerting others to the damage that climate change is doing to our Earth. Mia's artwork entitled *Shattered Lost Soul* shows a vibrant leaf filled with life on the left side, and then the shattered version to the right. On her gallery card, she wrote, "Climate change and deforestation hurt nature in unimaginable sizes. As this image shows, slowly the leaf turns black and shatters. This oil pastel drawing represents what humans do to nature and hope that in the future humans won't be so selfish." Through this explanation, Mia understands that climate change has been a problem for a long period of time, but that slow incremental change has accumulated into a now very urgent crisis.

In second-graders Noah and Hazel's artwork, we see how they focused their artivist efforts on how wildfire smoke that was currently impacting them might also harm animals they cared about. Throughout the camp,

Figure 8.2 Disintegration-style artwork: "Shattered Lost Soul" by Mia, "Smoke Hurts Pets" by Noah, and "Save the Foxes!" by Hazel

By Mia, Noah, and Hazel.

Noah talked a lot about dogs and was thrilled to look at pictures of a graduate student's dog. His art, entitled "Smoke Hurts Pets" featured the face of a dog. Likewise, Hazel related much of what she was learning to her love of foxes. She spoke about how wildfires and the associated smoke make trees and foxes "feel like they are choking." When Hazel shared her collection of artwork, including this disintegration-style art, at our art gallery opening, she explained how animals are being harmed by climate change and how she uses her artwork to help others understand it. She emphasized how humans are "destroying nature", and how the black pieces in her disintegration-style art are like "ashes" and "death to nature".

It is clear that the style of art inspired by Baretta served as an appropriate artform for campers to convey their understandings of the impact of climate change and natural disaster and make meaningful connections to things they care about. It also served as a space in which children were processing their understandings about wildfires and the climate crisis while making their art. In this book's companion website, we have provided a resource that lists professional *artivists* whose artwork amplifies issues related to climate change. We could imagine educators engaging in a similar process to that described above with a focal unit, first selecting an artist of interest from the resource and studying not just their artform but the purpose and meaning behind their work, and then inviting learners to create and communicate in the style of that artist. There are *artivists* around the world who create to communicate about issues that are meaningful to them. For example, Bisa Butler's quilts that represent Black life, and Thomas Dambo's recycled troll art that he designs and builds in and with communities could each serve as highly engaging mentors for young artivists.

Exploring Water Protection with Pre-Service Teachers: Sculptures

As teacher educators, we have brought the idea of artivism to our pre-service, intermediate grade literacy methods course. Most recently, we incorporated learning about literacy teaching and learning into a unit we call *Literacies through Troubled Waters*. Guided by the question, "Why is it important to protect water, and how can water be protected," we incorporate the principles articulated in the previous section to support candidates in understanding that the water crisis is *an urgent topic* that needs to be understood as a social issue with attention to justice..

In our seven-week inquiry, candidates engage with many different kinds of texts—including picturebooks, novels, informational texts, articles, documentaries, and art. Throughout the inquiry, we focus on what candidates are learning about water protection, but also what they are learning about literacy-rich climate pedagogy. They learn about topics like Indigenous perspectives on water protection, water scarcity, and biodiversity, while also deepening their knowledge about how to support children to navigate informational texts using text structures and features. (For more detailed descriptions of the inquiry unit and texts, see: Schutz & Woodard, 2024; Schutz & Woodard, 2022; www.teachingforsustainablefutures.com).

One of our goals as teacher educators is to expand pre-service teachers' conceptualization of what counts as writing/composition. Within the water inquiry, we help candidates see the benefits and potential of writing multimodal texts by offering invitations across the unit to make art and compose multimodally. Candidates compose many different kinds of texts including sketchnotes, black-out poems, and make art like quadramas, and sculptures (see Woodard & Schutz, 2024). Some forms are integrated into class activities, for example, creating sketchnotes as we read and process *We Are Water Protectors* by Carole Lindstrom, while others are offered as choices to communicate their learning. Year after year, they report that this type of composition enables them to communicate their understandings in ways that are much more fun, compelling, and interesting than traditional papers or reports.

One artform that has supported candidates' synthesis of their learning about self-selected topics like water scarcity, water governance, and water and renewable energy is sculpture. After candidates explored topics by reading numerous texts, listening to podcasts, and watching videos and documentaries, each group constructed a sculpture to represent a big idea about the topic. We provided many materials, including fabric, clay, pipe cleaners, tinfoil, and other items from the recycling bin. After 10–15 minutes, groups had assembled their sculptures and were prepared to present them to their peers.

While presenting their sculpture entitled *Divided* (see Figure 8.3), one group explained how their sculpture represented "uneven access to

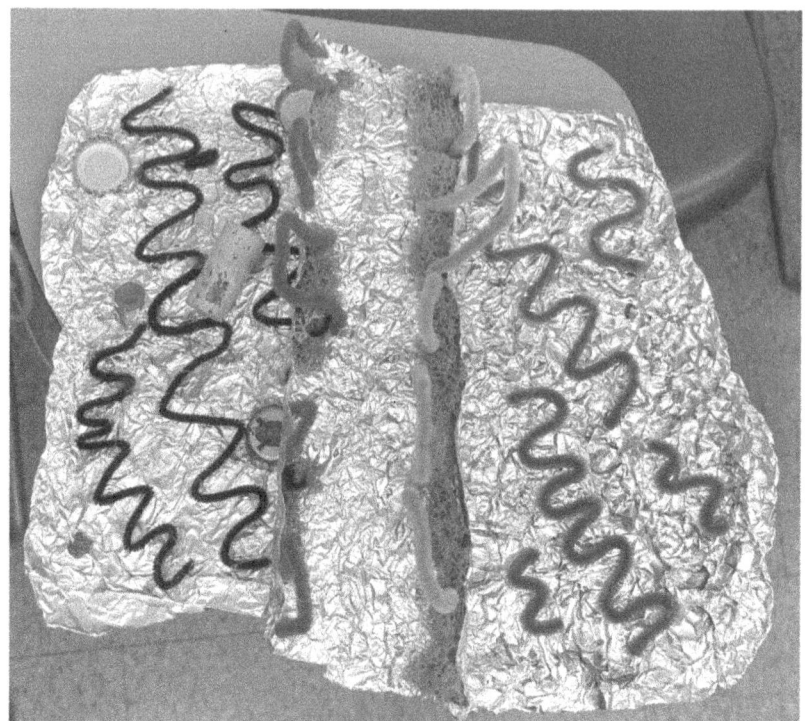

Figure 8.3 Pre-service teachers' sculpture: "Divided."
By Ana, Denise, Jessica, Sara.

clean water" by showing how one area of a city has access to clean water (depicted by blue pipe cleaners) while another area does not (depicted by brown pipe cleaners and items representing pollution in the water). They made connections to a documentary about the Flint water crisis, as well as the whole class reading of the novel *Thirst* by Varsha Bajaj, a book that draws attention to water inequity and the relationship to social structures of power. One student, Denise, shared that this is often the result of "government officials trying to save money", while Sara commented that she initially thought water pollution only affected "third world countries", but that she now understands that "it can affect anyone and can even lead back to social status." Through this work of art, candidates not only synthesized their own understandings of the topic, but also were able to advocate for attention to the systems that impact access to clean water.

At the conclusion of the unit, we facilitate a discussion to help pre-service teachers articulate the benefits of multimodal composition and art-making and consider how they might incorporate what they have experienced and learned into their own work with children. One teacher candidate, Isabelle, reflected that she enjoyed "being able to create something to help others understand what [she] learned" and that she felt "proud" of what she had made. She also shared that when making the sculpture, her group "had to communicate with each other to make and implement a plan after we decided what we wanted to share."

Sculpture has long been an artform that we have implemented into our own work in elementary classrooms as a way to support children in both making and communicating meaning. For example, we have used sculpture to help children consider big ideas of environmentally focused picturebooks or excerpts of texts. After reading *Fungi Grow* written by Maria Gianferrari and illustrated by Diana Sudyka, we asked fourth graders to use pipe cleaners to create a sculpture conveying one idea that the author and illustrator wanted readers to understand. Children first created independently, then combined in small groups and enhanced their ideas and sculptures, and finally composed exhibit labels explaining the meaning behind their sculptures. This approach could be used with any text or text set that explores meaningful social topics. We have also offered sculpture as an option for learners to synthesize their learning at the conclusion of an inquiry cycle. For example, children have investigated the interconnection among trees and how to communicate and care for one another through the Wood Wide Web. Sculpture has also provided a way for learners to share their learnings and take action in their own communities.

Closing

In this chapter, we explored how art and multimodal composition can serve as a powerful vehicle for taking action as part of urgent literacy pedagogies, in this case around issues related to climate change and environmental sustainability. Combining literacy learning about urgent, social issues with opportunities to engage as multimodal composers through artivism allows learners to explore, make sense of, and communicate, critique, and advocate about pressing, meaningful issues. While we have focused on environmental artivism, artivism can focus on any critical issue and be an engaging part of urgent writing pedagogies.

As readers begin to imagine how to apply the ideas from this chapter in their own context, we offer three reflection questions to jumpstart planning:

1. In designing an urgent literacy curriculum, what topic should be our focus? Consider what matters to your learners, what is responsive to time or place, and what they want to learn to help them improve the world.
2. What artforms do I notice and am drawn to in the world around me? How can we study and engage these artforms and use them to take action in the world?
3. How can I center justice and equity as we prepare to take action as artivists?

In a time when support for the arts in schools has been reduced, incorporating a focus on artivism into the broader literacy curriculum offers opportunities for learners to experience the benefits of the arts. Artivism and other forms of critical multimodal composing, with their orientation to urgent interdisciplinary inquiry, an expansive view of what counts as writing and who counts as writers, and criticality and possibility, allow teachers, too, to act as activists and resistors to dominant, White-centered paradigms of writing instruction in schools. Amplifying the words of Nigerian-American writer and photographer Teju Cole, we believe that critical multimodal writing pedagogies can help us to support "Writing as writing. Writing as rioting. Writing as righting. On the best days, all three."

References

Ballew, M., Maibach, E., Kotcher, J., Bergquist, P., Rosenthal, S., Marlon, J., & Leiserowitz, A. (2020, April 16). *Which racial/ethnic groups care most about climate change?* Yale Program on Climate Change Communication. https://climatecommunication.yale.edu/publications/race-and-climate-change/

Beach, R., & Smith, B. (2024). *Youth created media on the climate crisis: Hear Our Voices*. Routledge.

Bomer, R. (2017), What would it mean for English language arts to become more culturally responsive and sustaining? *Voices from the Middle*, 24(3), 11–15.

Campano, G., Nichols, T. P., & Player, G. D. (2020). Multimodal critical inquiry: Nurturing decolonial imaginaries. In E. B. Moje, P. P. Afflerbach, P. Enciso, & N. K. Lesaux (Eds.), *Handbook of Reading Research, Volume V* (1st ed., pp. 3–13). Routledge.

Caughlan, S. (2005). Advocating for the arts in the age of multiliteracies. *Language Arts*, 86(2), 120–126.

Cope, B., & Kalantzis, M. (2009). "Multiliteracies": New literacies, new learning. *Pedagogies: An International Journal*, 4(3), 164–195. https://doi.org/10.1080/15544800903076044

Curtis, D. J. (2009). Creating inspiration: The role of the arts in creating empathy for ecological restoration. *Ecological Management & Restoration*, 10(3), 174–184. https://doi.org/10.1111/j.1442-8903.2009.00487.x

Dalton, B., & Jocius, R. (2013). From struggling reader to Digital Reader and Multimodal Composer. In Evan Ortlieb & Earl H. Cheek (Eds.), *School-based interventions for struggling readers, K-8, Volume 3* (pp. 79–97). Emerald Group Publishing Limited.

Davis, S. (2018). The engagement tree: Arts-based pedagogies for environmental learning. *International Journal of Education & the Arts*, 19(8), 1–24. https://doi.org/10.18113/P8ijea1908

Diavolo, L., & Wagner, L. P. (2021). *No planet B: The teen vogue guide to the climate crisis*. Haymarket Books.

Gilio-Whitaker, D. (2019). *As long as grass grows: The indigenous fight for environmental justice, from colonization to Standing Rock*. Beacon Press.

Goodman, S. (2020). Teaching for environmental justice at the educational video center. *The Journal of Sustainability Education*, 23.

Griffin, A. A., & Turner, J. D. (2021). Toward a pedagogy of black livingness: Black students' creative multimodal renderings of resistance to anti-blackness. *English Teaching: Practice & Critique*, 20(4), 440–453. https://doi.org/10.1108/etpc-09-2020-0123

Hamilton, E. R., Staal, J., & Vander Ark, J. (2021). "We can do this at our school!": Place based education, literacy, & learning. *Michigan Reading Journal*, 53(2), 48–56.

Hertzog, N. B. (2007). Transporting pedagogy: Implementing the project approach in two first-grade classrooms. *Journal of Advanced Academics*, 18(4), 530–564. https://doi.org/10.4219/jaa-2007-559

Hopper, A. (2020). Did it ever occur to you that maybe you're falling in love? In A. E. Johnson& K. K. Wilkinson (Eds.), *All we can save: Truth, courage, and solutions for the climate crisis* (pp. 203–204). Random House.

Intergovernmental Panel on Climate Change (IPCC). (2022). *IPCC red alert: Summary of the 1st part of the 6th assessment report*. https://eco-act.com/ipcc/ipcc-6th-assessment-report-summary/

Johnson, A. E., & Wilkinson, K. K. (2020). *All we can save: Truth, courage, and solutions for the climate crisis*. Random House.

Johnson, W. F. (2024). "Harriet Tubman is a superhero": Conceptualizing young African American children's sociopolitical awareness as imaginative praxis. *Urban Education*. https://doi.org/10.1177/00420859241227962

Jordan, M. E., Lockmiller, C., & Zuiker, S. J. (2023). Centering Utopia: Fostering youth climate change education by exploring and envisioning hopeful futures. In R. Beach & B. Smith (Eds.), *Youth Created Media on the Climate Crisis* (1st ed., pp. 37–59). Routledge.

Lazarus, R. J. (2009). Super wicked problems and climate change: Restraining the present to liberate the future. *Georgetown Law Faculty Publications and Other Works*, 94, 1153–1234.

Makwanya, P., & Dick, M. (2014). An analysis of children's poems in environment and climate change adaptation and mitigation: A participatory approach, catching them young. *The International Journal of Engineering and Science*, 3(7), 10–15.

McNaughton, M. J. (2004). Educational drama in the teaching of education for sustainability. *Environmental Education Research*, 10(2), 139–155. https://doi.org/10.1080/1350462042000198140

Morales-Doyle, D., Vossoughi, S., Vakil, S., & Bang, M. (2020, August 19). *In an era of pandemic and protest, STEM education can't pretend to be apolitical*. Truthout. https://truthout.org/articles/in-an-era-of-pandemic-and-protest-stem-education-cant-pretend-to-be-apolitical/

Muhammad, G. (2020). *Cultivating genius: An equity framework for culturally and historically responsive literacy*. Scholastic.

National Council of Teachers of English (NCTE). (2019, March 1). *Resolution on literacy teaching on climate change*. https://ncte.org/statement/resolution-literacy-teaching-climate-change/

The New London Group. (1996). A pedagogy of multiliteracies: Designing social futures. *Harvard Educational Review*, 66(1), 60–93. https://doi.org/10.17763/haer.66.1.17370n67v22j160u

Panos, A., & Damico, J. (2021). Less than one percent is not enough: How leading literacy organizations engaged with climate change from 2008 to 2019. *Journal of Language and Literacy Education*, 17(1), 1–21.

Penniman, L. (2023). *Black earth wisdom: Soulful conversations with black environmentalists*. HarperCollins.

Pihkala, P. (2020). Eco-anxiety and environmental education. *Sustainability*, 12(23), 10149. https://doi.org/10.3390/su122310149

Pollitt, J., Blaise, M., & Rooney, T. (2021). Weather bodies: Experimenting with dance improvisation in environmental education in the early years.

Environmental Education Research, 27(8), 1141–1151. https://doi.org/10.1080/13504622.2021.1926434

Rhoades, M. (2012). LGBTQ youth + video artivism: Arts-based critical civic praxis. *Studies in Art Education*, 53(4), 317–329.

Rowe, D. W., & Miller, M. E. (2016). Designing for diverse classrooms: Using iPads and digital cameras to compose ebooks with emergent bilingual/biliterate four-year-olds. *Journal of Early Childhood Literacy*, 16(4), 425–472. https://doi.org/10.1177/1468798415593622

Sarama, J., Brenneman, K., Clements, D. H., Duke, N. K., & Hemmeter, M. L. (2017). Interdisciplinary teaching across multiple domains: The C4L (Connect4Learning) curriculum. In L. Bailey (Ed.), *Implementing a standards-based curriculum in the early childhood classroom* (1st ed., pp. 1–53). Routledge.

Schenkel, K., Brownell, C. J., & Wargo, J. M. (2024). Children communicating care through curiosity walks: Using scientific practices to cultivate knowledge about climate justice. *Science and Children*, 61(2), 76–82. https://doi.org/10.1080/00368148.2024.2315670

Schutz, K. M., & Woodard, R. (2022). Climate justice now: Layering texts about the urgent topic of water justice. *Illinois Reading Council Journal*, 50(2), 59–65. https://doi.org/10.33600/ircj.50.2.2022.59

Schutz, K. M., & Woodard, R. (2024). Water protection: An inquiry unit with pre-service English language arts teachers. *Climate Literacy in Education*, 2(2), 25–32. https://doi.org/10.24926/cle.v2i2.6287

Schutz, K. M., Woodard, R., Compisi, E., Cooley, T., Grullon, J., & Stanley, A. (2022). Climate justice now: Reimagining teacher book clubs to support inquiry into urgent topics. *Illinois Reading Council Journal*, 50(4), 69–74. https://doi.org/10.33600/ircj.50.4.2022.69

Song, Y. I. (2008). Exploring connections between environmental education and ecological public art. *Childhood Education*, 85(1), 13–19. https://doi.org/10.1080/00094056.2008.10523051

Thomashow, M. (1996). *Ecological identity: Becoming a reflective environmentalist*. The MIT Press.

Tobias, E. S., Bartlett, K., Jordan, M. E., & Zuiker, S. J. (2023). Addressing climate change and sustainable energy futures through creative music engagement. In R. Beach & B. Smith (Eds.), *Youth Created Media on the Climate Crisis* (1st ed., pp. 146–165). Routledge.

Toliver, S. R. (2021). Afrocarnival: Celebrating black bodies and critiquing oppressive bodies in Afrofuturist literature. *Children's Literature in Education*, 52(1), 132–148.

Trott, C. D., Even, T. L., & Frame, S. M. (2020). Merging the arts and sciences for collaborative sustainability action: A methodological framework. *Sustainability Science*, 15(4), 1067–1085. https://doi.org/10.1007/s11625-020-00798-7

Turner, J. D., & Griffin, A. A. (2021). Dream a little [STEAM] of me: Exploring Black adolescent girls' STEAM career futures through digital multimodal compositions. In B. J. Guzzetti (Ed.), *Genders, Cultures, and Literacies* (pp. 49–61). Routledge.

Vasudevan, L., Schultz, K., & Bateman, J. (2010). Rethinking composing in a digital age: Authoring literate identities through multimodal storytelling. *Written Communication*, 27(4), 442–468. https://doi.org/10.1177/0741088310378217

Walshe, N., Bungay, H., & Dadswell, A. (2023). Sustainable outdoor education: Organisations connecting children and young people with nature through the arts. *Sustainability*, 15(5), 3941. https://doi.org/10.3390/su15053941

Wildcat, D. R. (2009). *Red alert!: Saving the planet with Indigenous knowledge*. Fulcrum Publishing.

Woodard, R., Diaz, A. R., Phillips, N. C., Varelas, M., Tsachor, R., Kotler, R., Rock, R., & Melchor, M. (2024). 'Be creative and have fun': Elementary-aged children's digital and embodied composing in science. *Literacy*, 58(2), 167–177. https://doi.org/10.1111/lit.12365

Woodard, R., & Schutz, K. M. (2022). Urgent writing pedagogies in teacher education: Portraits of practice for an inquiry into water justice. In T. S. Hodges (Ed.), *The handbook of research on writing instruction: Practices for equitable and effective teaching* (pp. 270–295). IGI Global Scientific Publishing.

Woodard, R., & Schutz, K. M. (2024). *Teaching climate change to children: Literacy pedagogy that cultivates sustainable futures*. Teachers College Press.

9

Resistance

Writing as Resistance: Poetic Inquiry as a Liberatory Practice in the Classroom

Darius Phelps

Writing has long been a powerful tool for resistance, especially for students who are marginalized in society. In my classroom, when I taught grades 4th and 5th in an urban community and Title 1 school, I saw firsthand how writing allows students—particularly those of color or from underserved communities—to reclaim their voices, pushing back against systems that often try to silence them. For many of my students, writing was and still is an opportunity for self-expression, a way to challenge the dominant narratives that have shaped their lives. One of the most transformative ways I've witnessed this resistance come to life is through poetic inquiry. Below is a piece of my students' work that captures poetic inquiry in action.

Broken Crayons Still Color

Imagine being that one person that helps everyone but themselves.
Imagine giving all your happiness to someone who isn't even truthful to you.
Imagine being patient for someone less fortunate than you.

> *but once there ahead they don't wait for you.*
> *Imagine, wanting to give up on everything but knowing there are*
> *people relying on you.*
> *Imagine having depression, anxiety, insecurities, etc.*
> *& still fight through every single day in life.*
> *Can you imagine being that one person?*
> *It's always possible to fake a smile.*
> *All I know is …*
> *"Broken crayons still color"*

This poem, like so many others, reveals the ways my students use poetry to connect their personal experiences to the world around them, expressing their identities, emotions, and responses to injustice. Poetic inquiry doesn't just allow students to express themselves—it offers them a space to disrupt traditional academic norms and amplify voices that are often silenced. In my classroom, poetic inquiry is more than just a creative writing tool; it is a liberatory practice. This form of inquiry allows them to critically engage with their realities in a way that challenges societal norms and injustices. Drawing on Paris and Alim's (2017) work on *Culturally Sustaining Pedagogies*, I've seen how honoring my students' identities and encouraging them to critically examine inequities is integral to empowering them both academically and personally. Through this chapter, I want to invite you into my classroom and share how poetic inquiry can serve as a form of resistance writing. I will explore the ways in which poetic inquiry functions as a liberatory tool and offer practical strategies for educators to incorporate into their pedagogy. Reflecting on my own teaching experiences, I will share what has worked and what I've learned through the process. This chapter is not just about giving you a set of instructions, but about fostering an intimate dialogue—a conversation about how we, as educators, can support our students in using poetry to resist, reclaim, and reimagine their world (see Figure 9.1).

Background

Poetic inquiry, as both a research method and pedagogical tool, is deeply rooted in the power of narrative and the emotional engagement of students and their worlds. Historically, writing has been used as both a mechanism of control and a form of resistance, particularly for

Figure 9.1 Poetry reading.
By Darius Phelps.

marginalized communities. Colonizers and dominant institutions have often dictated whose stories are told and how knowledge is constructed, using written language as a means of oppression. However, marginalized communities have long used poetry and storytelling to reclaim agency, challenge dominant narratives, and resist systems of power.

The use of poetry to express personal truths has been central to various resistance movements. Scholars such as Sarah Faulkner (2019) describe poetic inquiry as "an avenue to disrupt traditional power dynamics in the classroom" (p. 76), inviting students to challenge established forms of knowledge. This aligns with the long-standing tradition of poetry as a tool for activism and community empowerment, from the Harlem Renaissance to contemporary spoken word movements. In my own teaching, I have seen how poetic inquiry enables students to articulate their lived realities while critically interrogating the structures of oppression that shape their lives.

In *Writing Wounded* (2011), Elizabeth Dutro (author of Chapter 4) provides invaluable insight into how poetry functions as both a healing practice and a form of resistance, particularly for students who have experienced trauma. Dutro explains, "Writing is a way for students to reclaim their voices in the face of personal pain and trauma, transforming those experiences into acts of resistance" (p. 7). This concept aligns with critical humanizing pedagogy, which prioritizes the voices of marginalized students, encouraging them to engage in reflection, expression, and activism through their writing. Paris and Alim (2017) support this intersection of writing and social justice in *Culturally Sustaining Pedagogies*, which emphasizes the importance of honoring and sustaining the linguistic and cultural practices of marginalized youth.

Poetic inquiry is particularly relevant within the framework of critical humanizing pedagogy, which seeks to center the lived experiences of those traditionally excluded from academic discourse. It invites students to take ownership of their narratives, fostering a sense of empowerment and agency. As Dutro (2011) asserts, storytelling, particularly in the form of poetry, "turns pain into resistance, reclamation, and healing" (p. 4). This idea resonates deeply with the students I teach, many of whom navigate systemic injustices such as racism, poverty, and family struggles. The insights of bell hooks (1994) reinforce this perspective—education, she argues, must be a space of freedom and transformation. In *Teaching to Transgress*, hooks writes, "The classroom remains the most radical space of possibility in the academy" (p. 12). This philosophy has been foundational in shaping my approach to poetic inquiry, as I strive to create spaces where students feel affirmed and empowered to challenge oppressive norms.

Historical and contemporary poets of color provide crucial models for this work. Writers such as Audre Lorde, June Jordan, Claudia Rankine, Kyle Liang, Ocean Vuong, Ty Chapman, Mahogany Browne, and Warsan Shire demonstrate how poetry resists racial, gender, and class-based oppression. Rankine's *Citizen* (2014), for example, explores microaggressions and everyday violences inflicted on Black bodies, highlighting how language can serve both as an instrument of oppression and a tool of resistance. Similarly, Lorde's *The Black Unicorn* (1978) and Jordan's *Directed by Desire* (2005) foreground poetry as a radical act of self-definition and liberation. Introducing these works in the classroom helps students recognize poetry not just as a creative expression but as a critical intervention in struggles for justice.

The role of student-created texts in social justice movements further underscores the power of writing as resistance. Guzzett and Gamboa (2004) examine zines as an alternative medium through which students, particularly adolescent girls of color, can challenge mainstream narratives and assert their voices (also described in Chapter 5). Like poetry, zines disrupt traditional hierarchies of knowledge, offering students a means to document their realities and articulate counternarratives. This scholarship highlights the intersection of poetic inquiry, critical pedagogy, and activism, reinforcing the idea that writing is not just an academic exercise but a tool for social transformation. By engaging with poetry as a method of inquiry, educators can help students critically examine the structures of power that shape their world.

Teaching contemporary poets, especially those from historically marginalized backgrounds, ensures that students see themselves reflected in the texts they read. Incorporating the work of contemporary poets allows students to explore themes of identity, power, and justice in ways that are relevant to their own lives. This approach not only fosters critical thinking but also empowers students to envision and advocate for transformative futures.

Pedagogical Implications

The integration of poetic inquiry into elementary classrooms has profound pedagogical implications for pre-service teachers, K-6 writing teachers, and teacher educators. Historically, writing instruction has prioritized rigid structures and standardized expectations that often exclude and marginalize students from historically oppressed communities. Poetic inquiry disrupts these traditional approaches by centering lived experiences, fostering critical inquiry, and positioning writing as a tool for resistance and liberation. Below are key pedagogical implications of poetic inquiry, each framed as an actionable practice.

Honoring Students' Lived Experience

As educators, especially those working with students of color, we must prioritize practices that honor students' lived experiences. Traditional forms of academic writing often prioritize objectivity and neutrality, leaving little room for the nuanced and deeply personal narratives that students bring to the classroom. Critical humanizing pedagogy, as inspired by Freire (1970) and later expanded upon by scholars like Paris and Alim (2017), emphasizes the importance of centering students' voices and experiences as a means of fostering empowerment and resistance. This approach requires us to move beyond traditional, "objective" writing, focusing instead on students' subjective, lived realities and empowering their truths.

As Ladson-Billings (1995) suggests, Culturally Relevant Pedagogy connects students' cultural backgrounds to academic learning, providing a foundation for critical engagement. In my classroom, I have seen how poetic inquiry serves as a vital tool for this purpose. Poetry allows students to draw from their identities, histories, and emotions, positioning their lived experiences as valuable sources of knowledge. For instance, pairing poetic inquiry with the work of poets of color such as R. A. Villanueva, Nikki Grimes, and Kyle Liang enables students to see their own experiences reflected in powerful literary forms. These poets not only challenge dominant narratives but also create spaces for marginalized voices to thrive, offering students examples of how to articulate their truths boldly and creatively.

When students engage in poetry, both reading and writing, they are given the opportunity to express their unique perspectives in ways that challenge the erasure of their voices in dominant educational narratives. Writing poetry from a place of authenticity allows students to reclaim ownership over their stories, offering them a direct means to resist systems that often seek to marginalize or silence them. As students write about their lived realities and connect with the voices of poets who reflect their identities and struggles, they develop a sense of agency and empowerment. This process not only transforms their relationship with writing but also reinforces the idea that their voices matter, both within and beyond the classroom.

Additionally, this practice disrupts the traditional deficit-oriented lens through which many marginalized students are viewed. Instead of being framed as students who need remediation or correction, they are positioned as knowledge holders whose experiences contribute valuable perspectives to classroom discourse. This shift fosters an inclusive learning environment where students feel valued, seen, and heard. For pre-service teachers, teachers, and teacher educators, understanding how to facilitate this process is crucial in fostering a more just and equitable educational system.

Cultural and Emotional Literacy

Poetry helps students engage with their emotions, creating a pathway to emotional literacy. For students who may have experienced trauma, particularly those of color navigating systemic injustice, poetry offers a powerful way to name their experiences. As Dutro (2011) argues, the art of writing provides students with the opportunity to "make sense of their lives, to feel empowered to speak their truths, and to confront the injustices they face" (p. 13). This process of emotional exploration through poetry supports the development of both empathy and cultural literacy, enabling students to understand themselves and others on a deeper level.

Writing poetry allows students to explore complex emotions in a way that traditional prose often does not. Through metaphor, imagery, and rhythm, they can articulate feelings that might otherwise be difficult to express. This practice is particularly important for young writers, as it provides them with an emotional outlet that fosters self-awareness and resilience. When students learn to engage with their emotions through poetic inquiry, they develop a stronger sense of self and a greater capacity for navigating social and emotional challenges. For K-6 writing teachers, integrating poetic inquiry into the curriculum enhances students' ability to engage with culturally and emotionally rich texts. Poetic inquiry invites students to delve deeply into the layered meanings of poems, engaging with complex themes of identity, justice, love, and resilience. When students read poetry from diverse perspectives, they not only see their own experiences reflected but also gain insight into the lived realities of others, enriching their understanding of the world. This exposure to a wide range of voices fosters empathy and cross-cultural understanding, essential skills in today's diverse classrooms (Greene, 1995). It allows students to develop a nuanced appreciation of the experiences of others, which can challenge stereotypes, dismantle prejudices, and promote inclusivity.

Poetry's connection to oral traditions further deepens this engagement, as it invites students to experience language not only as a written form but as a living, spoken art. By participating in the oral delivery of poems, whether reading aloud or composing their own work, students tap into storytelling practices that honor their cultural backgrounds. Oral traditions are a powerful means of connecting students to their heritage and community, allowing them to see their own cultural expressions validated and celebrated (Smith, 2021). This practice creates a classroom environment where diverse voices are valued and heard, fostering a sense of belonging and cultural pride among students. Additionally, the rhythmic and often communal nature of poetry allows students to develop their listening, speaking, and performance skills, all of which are integral to building a strong sense of self and community.

For teacher educators, this highlights the critical need to prepare pre-service teachers to integrate poetry into literacy instruction in ways that emphasize emotional and cultural depth. Too often, poetry is relegated to an isolated, academic exercise, but when we treat poetry as a living practice, one that connects students to their inner lives and the world around them, it becomes a powerful tool for personal growth and social change. Teacher educators should be equipped with the knowledge and frameworks to guide future teachers in using poetry not only to teach literary techniques but also to foster empathy, critical thinking, and social awareness. Frameworks such as *Culturally Sustaining Pedagogies* (Paris & Alim, 2017) encourage educators to honor and sustain students' cultural identities while also encouraging them to critique and transform the inequities in their lives. Similarly, trauma-informed teaching (Hammond, 2014) provides teachers with the tools to recognize the emotional and psychological needs of students, ensuring that poetry becomes a means of healing and empowerment, rather than simply a means of academic achievement.

By equipping future educators with these tools, we foster classrooms where writing becomes an avenue for both personal transformation and collective understanding. Through poetry, students are invited to reflect on their own stories, explore the stories of others, and engage in a larger, ongoing dialogue about justice, identity, and community. This holistic approach to writing nurtures both the intellect and the spirit, creating classrooms where students not only develop the technical skills of writing but also grow as compassionate, culturally aware, and socially responsible individuals.

Critical Thinking and Reflection

Poetic inquiry is not just a creative exercise but a form of critical inquiry (Faulkner, 2019). Writing poetry requires students to reflect deeply on the power structures that affect their lives. It encourages them to think about their identity and place in the world, asking, "How do these systems of power affect me, and how can I resist them through my writing?" This process aligns with critical literacy frameworks (Freire & Macedo, 1987), which emphasize the role of literacy in unveiling and challenging oppressive structures. Traditional writing instruction often reinforces dominant narratives by emphasizing neutrality, objectivity, and formal conventions (Applebee, 1996). However, poetic inquiry disrupts these norms by centering students' lived experiences and emotions as valid forms of knowledge production.

Poetry offers a brave space where students can explore their identities while simultaneously interrogating larger societal issues, such as racism, poverty, grief, and gender inequality (Dutro, 2019). By analyzing poetry written by activists and marginalized voices, students develop a keen awareness of how literature can serve as a form of resistance. Engaging with works by poets such as Audre Lorde, Langston Hughes, and Aja Monet, students learn to question dominant narratives and recognize the ways in which storytelling shapes cultural perceptions. This aligns with Kinloch's (2011) argument that literacy practices, particularly those rooted in lived experience, offer powerful avenues for identity, community, and social justice.

For pre-service teachers, this means understanding how to guide students in analyzing and producing texts that challenge oppressive structures. Pedagogical approaches such as critical pedagogy (Morrell, 2008) can be leveraged to help students see poetry as both an expressive and analytical tool. Encouraging students to compose and deconstruct poetry within the framework of critical literacy prepares them to engage with the world as active, socially conscious participants.

Empowerment Through Voice

The act of writing poetry gives students a sense of empowerment. When students write about their struggles, their identities, and their dreams, they take back control over their stories. As Freire (1970) suggests in *Pedagogy of the Oppressed*, education must be an act of liberation, where students actively engage in the process of becoming agents of change. This notion of empowerment through literacy is echoed by hooks (1994) in *Teaching to Transgress*, where she argues that education should be a practice of freedom, encouraging students to voice their realities in ways that challenge hegemonic structures.

Traditional writing instruction often prioritizes rigid structures, standardized forms, and depersonalized perspectives, which can alienate students, particularly those from marginalized backgrounds (Delpit, 1988). Poetry, however, disrupts these conventional approaches by providing a medium where students can assert their identities and lived experiences. Muhammad (2020) highlights how literacy practices rooted in identity, criticality, and creativity not only enhance student engagement but also foster deeper intellectual and emotional investment in their writing. Poetry functions as a form of counternarrative (Solórzano & Yosso, 2002), enabling students to challenge dominant ideologies and assert their own epistemologies. For instance, students who engage in spoken word poetry often develop a heightened awareness of social injustices and a stronger commitment to civic engagement. By crafting poems that speak to issues such as racial identity, immigration, and gender equity, students transform writing into a site of resistance and activism.

For teacher educators, this emphasizes the importance of equipping pre-service teachers with strategies to foster student voice. Encouraging students to write and share their stories can have a profound impact on their confidence and willingness to engage in critical dialogue. Ladson-Billings (1995) stresses that Culturally Relevant Pedagogy requires teachers to validate and incorporate students' cultural knowledge into learning spaces. Pre-service teachers must therefore be trained in pedagogical approaches that center student narratives, such as multimodal composition and critical poetry pedagogy (Morrell, 2008). By incorporating these methodologies into teacher preparation programs, we ensure that future educators are equipped to create classrooms where writing is not merely an academic exercise but a transformative act of self-definition and social change.

Connection to Social Movements

Poetry isn't just some academic exercise, it's a tool, a weapon in the fight for justice, a way to flip the script on the world we live in. Guzzetti and Gamboa (2004) lay it out, showing how writing for social justice can be a collective movement. It's not just one voice, but a chorus of voices, young people stepping up and joining the larger cultural conversations about resistance. Poetry, along with zines and other self-published forms, gives students a way to connect their personal stories to the bigger picture—bridging the gap between their own experiences and the larger movements pushing for change. It's about taking what's personal and making it political.

Poetic inquiry isn't just about writing, it's about being vulnerable, opening up about who you are and what you've been through, and then using that vulnerability to make sense of a world full of injustice. Poetry gives students the chance to connect their personal narratives to the broader forces shaping society, understanding how their individual lives intersect with systemic oppression. Teachers can use poetic inquiry as a lens for students to explore how poets, both past and present, have fought back with their words and raised awareness. When we bring in writers like Langston Hughes, Audre Lorde, or Amanda Gorman, we're showing students how poetry can take on racism, gender inequality, and all the other injustices that still plague us today. These poets didn't just write for the sake of writing—they used their words to resist, to challenge, and to demand a better world. And students can do the same.

Poetry doesn't stop at the classroom door—it vibrantly spills out into real-life action. Students don't just write for the sake of writing. When given the opportunity, they perform, they publish, they speak their truths in zines or at open mics, using their words as a form of resistance. I've seen this firsthand in my own classroom. I guided students to write poems about gun violence and discrimination, and those poems ended up in front of school leaders at staff meetings, pushing for real conversations and change. Linking poetry to social movements isn't just about the words we write; it's about making sure those words lead to action, ensuring that students know their voices matter and can make a difference. When we tie poetic inquiry to social justice, we're telling our students their voices aren't just valid, they're *essential*. They've got the power to not just reflect on the world, but to shape it.

Pedagogical Practices

Incorporating poetic inquiry into elementary classrooms is both an art and a practice that requires careful planning, scaffolding, and an understanding of how to support students through their creative and reflective processes. From my experience, I can say that one of the most powerful ways to integrate poetic inquiry is by creating an environment where poetry feels accessible, meaningful, and empowering for all students. In my own classroom, I've witnessed tremendous growth in students as they learn to express themselves and reflect on their world through poetry. Below, I'll share some strategies that have worked well in my classroom, tying in my personal experiences to guide and inspire fellow educators.

Setting Up Poetic Inquiry in Elementary Classrooms

Incorporating poetic inquiry into elementary classrooms requires intentional planning and scaffolding to ensure that students are supported throughout the process. For teachers, pre-service teachers, and teacher educators, the goal is to create a writing workshop environment where poetry is not only accessible but also meaningful and empowering for students. Here are some steps to get started, followed by practical strategies and prompts.

Building a Foundation for Poetic Inquiry

For students, especially those new to the practice, it's crucial to first lay the groundwork for what poetic inquiry can be. In my classroom, I make sure to create a space where poetry isn't seen as an intimidating task but as a tool for students to explore their personal stories and emotions. This foundation for poetic inquiry includes:

- **Exploring What Poetry Is**: The idea of poetry can sometimes feel distant or inaccessible to students, so we begin by breaking down what poetry actually is. I make it clear that poetry doesn't have to follow rigid rules—it's an expression of the self, a way of channeling our thoughts and emotions onto paper. I encourage students to understand that poetry is a means of creative freedom, and it is there for them to shape as they see fit. We explore various forms, from free verse to haiku, spoken word to slam poetry. This openness encourages students to explore and find a form that resonates with them.
- **Creating a Brave Space**: A major part of poetic inquiry is ensuring that students feel safe to take creative risks. In my classroom, we co-construct classroom norms around respect and trust. We create a "Brave Space" rather than a "Safe Space", emphasizing that while we are supportive of one another's work, we also encourage each other to challenge ourselves and be vulnerable in our writing. I tell my students, "Poetry is a risk, but you're not alone. We're all in this together."

Structuring a Writing Workshop for Poetic Inquiry

To make poetic inquiry successful, I use a structured yet flexible writing workshop model. Each student in my classroom is encouraged to explore poetry in their own way, but with a balance of scaffolding and guidance, including:

- **Mini-Lessons**: Every writing session in my classroom starts with a mini-lesson focused on a specific poetic device. For example, we might look at how metaphor is used in a poem by R. A. Villanueva (2014) from *Reliquaria*. The students reflect on how metaphors can enhance the emotional impact of poetry. By using mentor texts from diverse poets, I show students that poetry isn't just about form, but about creating emotional resonance. For instance, after reading a poem that uses repetition, students can begin to experiment with repetition in their own work.
- **Shared Writing**: One of the first activities I do is collaborative writing. We often write a class poem together, selecting a theme that resonates with the students. Last spring, we wrote a poem about change, as several students were transitioning to middle school. By writing together, students learn how a poem evolves and how to support each other's ideas. This activity not only models the writing process but also builds confidence in those who might feel nervous about writing on their own.
- **Independent Writing Time**: After modeling and shared writing, I give students uninterrupted time to work on their own poems. This quiet time allows students to dig into their personal experiences and thoughts. Some students write about challenges they've faced, while others reflect on something joyful. I provide prompts like "Write a poem about a time you stood up for something important." These moments of independent writing give students the chance to develop their unique voice and story.
- **Revision and Feedback**: In my classroom, we emphasize that the writing process doesn't end with the first draft. I encourage students to revise their poems by focusing on clarity and emotional impact. During peer feedback sessions, students work in pairs to offer constructive feedback. I model this process by sharing my own writing, demonstrating how to make revisions that improve both meaning and flow. A peer review session might sound like, "I really like the line about the sunrise. Maybe you could make the metaphor stronger by describing the colors more vividly." This feedback helps students understand that writing is a craft, and it's okay to revisit and refine their ideas.
- **Sharing and Celebrating**: The final step in our writing workshops is sharing. We celebrate student work in a "Poetry Circle," where

students share their poems aloud with one another. We end every session with this activity, which fosters an atmosphere of support and mutual respect. It's incredible to see students who were once shy or uncertain about sharing their work proudly reading their poems in front of their peers. These poetry circles are always a moment of celebration, where students are affirmed for their voices and creativity.

Writing Prompts for Poetic Resistance

Once the groundwork is laid, I've found that introducing writing prompts that invite students to reflect on their experiences and challenge societal norms can be a powerful entry point for poetic inquiry. In my classroom, I've used prompts like these to help students tap into their own voices, reflect on their experiences, and begin to see poetry as a tool for resistance. These prompts serve not only as ways to practice poetic craft but also as a means for students to explore their identities, their place in the world, and the societal systems that affect them. Here are a few of the prompts I've used in my classroom that encourage poetic resistance:

- *"Write a poem about a time you felt silenced. What did you want to say, and how can you say it now?"*
- *"Write a poem about a moment when you felt out of place or unwelcome. How would you challenge that feeling through poetry?"*
- *"What does justice look like or mean to you? Write a poem that expresses your vision of a just world."*
- *"Think of a person, place, or object that gives you strength. Write a poem that celebrates this source of empowerment."*
- *"Imagine you are writing a letter to your future self. What advice or encouragement would you give?"*

These prompts aren't just exercises in creative writing; they are invitations for students to engage deeply and excavate all that lies within them. I've noticed that when students are asked to reflect on moments when they've felt silenced or unwelcome, they often tap into powerful emotions and truths. It's in these moments that their writing becomes a form of resistance. I remember one student who wrote about an experience of being marginalized because of their accent. Their poem was raw, full of emotion, and unapologetically honest. By creating space for students to reflect on these types of experiences, we give them permission to voice their pain, their frustrations, and their hopes. Poetry becomes an act of reclaiming power in those moments when they've felt powerless.

A key part of fostering poetic resistance is helping students see that their voices matter, that their words have weight. To support them in this, I model writing responses to these prompts myself. I share my own poems and discuss my thought process, showing students how to translate personal experiences into poetry. This process isn't just about showing them the mechanics of poetry; it's about letting them see how writing can be a way to process, heal, and resist. When I write a poem in response to a prompt, I'm not only demonstrating poetic form, I'm giving my students permission to explore their own identities through language, and I'm showing them that vulnerability and strength can coexist on the page.

One of the prompts I use, asking students to write about a source of empowerment, has always sparked some of the most moving responses. I recall a student who wrote a poem about their grandmother, who had been an immigrant and a survivor of hardship. The poem was filled with imagery of strength, love, and resilience. By asking students to explore what gives them strength, we allow them to access their inner resources, and in doing so, we foster a sense of agency. When students write about these sources of empowerment, it reminds them that they can draw upon their personal histories, their families, and their communities as sources of strength in the face of adversity.

Through these writing prompts, students not only refine their poetic craft but also begin to recognize poetry as a tool for social change. They learn to see poetry as a means of challenging the status quo, questioning authority, and expressing their hopes for a better future. I've seen students transform through this process—from feeling unsure of their voice to writing poems that demand to be heard. These writing prompts encourage students to find their voice, not just in the classroom, but in the world. The prompts serve as a starting point, but the real magic happens when students take those words and use them to navigate the complexities of their own lives.

Poetry Circles and Sharing

Creating poetry circles in the classroom allows students to engage deeply with their own writing and that of their peers in a safe, supportive, and brave space. These circles create a sense of community and foster trust, making the classroom an environment where students feel validated and empowered to share their authentic voices. Through sharing their poetry, students begin to see their individual narratives as part of a collective conversation about resistance, social justice, and change. In my experience, poetry circles have been transformative in helping students build confidence in their creative expression. They provide an opportunity for students to see the connections between their personal stories and those of their peers, fostering empathy and collective understanding (Figure 9.2).

Through implementing these poetry circles, I've learned the importance of starting with emotional honesty when introducing poetry. I often tell my students, "Your words are the heartbeat of your story; they don't need to rhyme, fit into stanzas, or follow any rules—just let them flow from within you." By creating this brave space where form and structure take a backseat to feeling and voice, I've witnessed profound transformations and evolution. Students who were once hesitant to write begin to uncover their truths, using poetry to process their experiences, name their pain, and celebrate their identities. I remember one particular student who, at first, resisted writing anything at all. When I shared R. A. Villanueva's (2014) work and the raw vulnerability in his poems, especially concerning his family history, it clicked for him. He realized that poetry could be messy and still hold power. His first poem, written after our discussion, was an unstructured reflection on struggles as an immigrant. It didn't rhyme or follow any poetic conventions, but it brought the class to silence because of its raw, heartfelt authenticity.

By engaging in open dialogue about their work, my students were exposed to diverse perspectives that deepen their awareness of systemic injustices and the power of solidarity. Poetry circles exemplify this potential by affirming students' experiences and helping them discover the liberatory power of their words. The poetry circle process reinforces the idea that each student's experience matters and that their voices are essential in challenging dominant narratives. Through structured peer

Figure 9.2 Poetry circles and sharing.
By Darius Phelps.

feedback and open discussion, students also develop critical thinking skills, honing their ability to articulate their messages with precision and impact. The supportive nature of poetry circles encourages risk-taking, allowing students to delve into challenging topics and confront personal and societal issues in their writing.

When it comes to connecting poetry to social justice, I often use the words of writers who have been on the frontlines of resistance. For instance,

I pair the works of Audre Lorde with discussions about intersectionality or Langston Hughes with explorations of systemic racism and how it affects our world. Then, I challenge my students to write their own poems about the issues that matter most to them, whether that's gun violence, climate change, or the inequities in their schools and classrooms. I've seen poetry become a tool for them to channel frustration into action, turning what they write into letters for local community leaders or spoken word performances at local events.

Using my student responses, I've even reimagined assessment in my poetry units to focus on growth and expression rather than rigid rubrics and strict structures. In my classroom, students are encouraged to reflect on what their poems mean to them and how they feel their voices have grown through the process. Poetic inquiry isn't about perfection; it's about liberation, a lesson I strive to impart every day: "Your words matter because YOU matter."

Mentor Texts and Model Poems

Mentor texts play a crucial role in showing students how poetry can serve as both art and activism. As an educator, I have witnessed the profound impact that carefully chosen mentor texts can have on my students' understanding of poetry's power to address societal inequities, confront personal and collective trauma, and inspire change. I've seen how texts like Amanda Gorman's (2021) *The Hill We Climb*, Claudia Rankine's (2014) *Citizen*, R. A. Villanueva's (2014) *Reliquaria*, and Jenny Xie's (2018) *Eye Level* spark deep conversations and reflections, both personal and political.

I've found that when students read works like Gorman's (2021) *The Hill We Climb*, they are not just learning to analyze literary form and structure—they are seeing how poetry can be a call to action. Gorman's (2021) inaugural poem is a prime example of how personal experience can merge with a collective vision for transformation. I've had students tell me how reading her words made them feel as though their own voices mattered, that they, too, could speak out against injustice with conviction. It's a powerful moment when students see poetry not just as an academic exercise but as something that can transform the world around them. Similarly, Claudia Rankine's (2014) *Citizen* challenges students to engage deeply with the experiences of racial microaggressions and systemic racism, which, in turn, opens up conversations about their own encounters with inequality. Through Rankine's work, students begin to see poetry as a tool for both personal catharsis and collective resistance.

R. A. Villanueva's (2014) *Reliquaria* and Jenny Xie's (2018) *Eye Level* are particularly effective for exploring how cultural heritage and identity intersect with poetic expression. I've used these texts in my classroom to help students reflect on themes like belonging, loss, and resilience. These are deeply personal topics for many of my students, who often come from diverse backgrounds, and reading poems that grapple with the same themes helps them feel seen and understood. When students read Villanueva, they often begin to ask questions about their own cultural identities, their family histories, and the ways those histories have shaped who they are today.

By analyzing these mentor texts, students are encouraged to ask reflective questions that guide their own writing journeys: *How do these poets use their voices to resist? What societal structures are they addressing? How can I draw on my own experiences to craft poems that speak to these themes?* These questions are more than prompts—they are invitations for students to connect with the text and with their own lived realities. I've seen how these moments of reflection and connection often lead to students producing poetry that challenges norms, asks hard questions, and envisions a better future.

But mentor texts aren't just about analysis, they are catalysts for creativity. I've seen how students become inspired by Gorman's (2021) *The Hill We Climb* to write their own inaugural poems addressing issues they care about, from climate change to racial justice to mental health. After reading Rankine's (2014) *Citizen*, students have written poems that reflect on their personal experiences with societal inequities, turning their frustrations and hopes into artistic statements of resistance. Villanueva's work has led to poems about ancestry and cultural memory, with students exploring their roots in ways they may never have considered before. These creative endeavors are a powerful way for students to take the skills they've learned from mentor texts and apply them to their own unique experiences.

Through mentor texts and poetry circles, I've been able to create spaces in my classroom where students feel empowered to raise their voices for advocacy and change. These practices are not just about teaching literary devices. They are about creating an environment where poetry becomes a tool for personal and collective transformation. In my classroom, poetry becomes more than just words on a page—it becomes a bridge to understanding, to resistance, and to the possibility of a more just world.

Conclusion

As an educator and researcher, I see poetic inquiry as a vital tool for empowering students and resisting systemic injustices. Through this practice, students not only find their voices but also connect them to a broader call for liberation. This work ties closely to my dissertation research on poetic inquiry and Culturally Responsive Pedagogy, particularly as it intersects with pre-service teacher education. By equipping future teachers with these tools, we ensure the next generation of educators can foster classrooms that humanize, empower, and liberate.

Poetic inquiry is not just a method of writing; it is a transformative act that helps students resist dominant narratives, reclaim their stories, and envision a more just world. By incorporating this practice into our classrooms, we do more than teach; we create spaces for healing, resistance, and change. As educators, let us continue to affirm our students' voices, helping them understand that their words have the power to challenge systems, create connections, and inspire liberation.

Reflective Questions

As you think about incorporating poetic inquiry into your own classroom, consider these reflective questions:

1. How can poetic inquiry help students explore their identities and resist dominant narratives in their writing?
2. What mentor texts can you use to help students see how poetry has been used for resistance and social change?
3. How can you reimagine assessment to honor the emotional and critical work involved in poetic inquiry, to allow your students to show their freedom of expression?

4. In what ways can you connect poetic inquiry to broader social justice movements, helping students see their writing as part of a larger fight for change?

References

Applebee, A. N. (1996). *Curriculum as conversation: Transforming traditions of teaching and learning*. University of Chicago Press.

Delpit, L. (1988). The silenced dialogue: Power and pedagogy in educating other people's children. *Harvard Educational Review*, 58(3), 280–299. https://doi.org/10.17763/haer.58.3.c43481778r528qw4

Dutro, E. (2011). Writing wounded: Trauma, testimony, and critical witness in literacy classrooms. *English Education*, 43(2), 193–211. www.jstor.org/stable/23017070

Dutro, E. (2013). Towards a pedagogy of the incomprehensible: Trauma and the imperative of critical witness in literacy classrooms. *Pedagogies: An International Journal*, 8(4), 301–315. https://doi.org/10.1080/1554480X.2013.829280

Dutro, E. (2017). Let's start with heartbreak: The perilous potential of trauma in literacy. *Language Arts*, 94(5), 326–337. www.jstor.org/stable/44809908

Dutro, E. (2019). *The vulnerable heart of literacy: Centering trauma as powerful pedagogy*. Teachers College Press.

Faulkner, S. L. (2019). *Poetic inquiry: Craft, method, and practice*. Routledge.

Freire, P. (1970). *Pedagogy of the oppressed* (M. B. Ramos, Trans.). Bloomsbury Academic.

Freire, P., & Macedo, D. (1987). *Literacy: Reading the word and the world*. Bergin & Garvey.

Gorman, A. (2021). *The Hill We Climb: An Inaugural Poem for the Country*. Viking.

Greene, M. (1995). *Releasing the imagination: Essays on education, the arts, and social change*. Jossey-Bass.

Guzzetti, B., & Gamboa, M. (2004). Writing for social justice. In R. L. Blake, A. S. B. McKinney, & B. K. Sutton (Eds.), *Teaching writing for social justice* (pp. 189–211). Heinemann.

Hammond, Z. L. (2014). *Culturally responsive teaching and the brain: Promoting authentic engagement and rigor among culturally and linguistically diverse students*. Corwin.

hooks, b. (1994). *Teaching to transgress: Education as the practice of freedom*. Routledge.

Jordan, J. (2005). *Directed by desire: The collected poems of June Jordan*. Copper Canyon Press.

Kinloch, V. F. (2005). Poetry, literacy, and creativity: Fostering effective learning strategies in an urban classroom. *English Education*, 37(2), 96–114. https://doi.org/10.58680/ee20054114

Ladson-Billings, G. (1995). Toward a theory of culturally relevant pedagogy. *American Educational Research Journal*, 32(3), 465–491. https://doi.org/10.3102/00028312032003465

Liang, K. (2024). *Good Son*. Sundress Publications.

Lorde, A. (1978). *The Black unicorn: Poems*. W. W. Norton & Company.

Morrell, E. (2008). *Critical literacy and urban youth: Pedagogies of access, dissent, and liberation*. New York: Routledge.

Muhammad, G. (2020). *Cultivating Genius: An Equity Framework for Culturally and Historically Responsive Literacy*. Scholastic.

Oliver, M. (1994). *A poetry handbook: A prose guide to understanding and writing poetry*. HarperCollins.

Paris, D., & Alim, H. S. (2017). *Culturally sustaining pedagogies: Teaching and learning for justice in a changing world*. Teachers College Press.

Phelps, D. (2024, November 25). *The power of teaching living poets: Embracing every hue*. National Council of Teachers of English. https://ncte.org/blog/2024/11/power-teaching-living-poets/

Rankine, C. (2014). *Citizen: An American lyric*. Graywolf Press.

Shire, W. (2011). *Teaching My Mother How to Give Birth*. Flipped Eye Publishing.

Smith, L. T. (2021). *Decolonizing methodologies: Research and indigenous peoples* (3rd ed.). Zed Books.

Solórzano, D. G., & Yosso, T. J. (2002). Critical race methodology: Counter-storytelling as an analytical framework for education research. *Qualitative Inquiry*, 8(1), 23–44. https://doi.org/10.1177/107780040200800103

Villanueva, R. A. (2014). *Reliquaria*. University of Nebraska Press.

Woodson, J. (2014). *Brown girl dreaming*. Nancy Paulsen Books.

Xie, J. (2018). *Eye level*. Graywolf Press.

10

Love

Revolutionary Love: A Critical Approach for Teaching Young Writers

Michele Myers

Love Made the Choice

By: Summer

Love made the choice.
When He chose to die on Calvary's cross.
It was the love that He has for you and me
That He chose to die on Calvary.
It wasn't the nails in His hands nor His feet that held Him there
No, it was His love that He so freely shared.

Love made the choice again this Valentine's
When He said, my child, I have a home prepared that is holy thine.
Sweetly, death came to bring you a new life in glory
And we live on to tell this story.

Yes, love made the choice when He came to set you free
Of a life of sickness and misery.

> Like He said He would, He came back for His bride.
> And you took His hand and stood by His side.
> In an instant you became whole.
> I can only imagine you walking down those streets of gold.
>
> Yes, love made the choice to give you immortality
> And I am confident that one day He will come and choose me.
> So rest in peace in your home above
> And know that you will be missed and dearly loved.

The above poem was written by Summer, my daughter and a former intern in a literacy methods course I taught as part of the Master of Arts in Teaching (MAT) program at a tier-one research university in the southeastern part of the U.S. The poem, written during our weekly writing workshop, was crafted during a unit titled, *The Stories of Our Lives*. I designed the unit to help my interns learn how writers craft stories reflecting their lived experiences. To internalize this important principle, my MAT students were authentically immersed as writers. This is aligned with several key principles upheld by the National Council of Teachers of English (NCTE) (https://ncte.org/statement/teaching-writing/), including the beliefs that writing grows out of many purposes, everyone has the capacity to write, writing can be taught, and teachers can help students become better writers. Adhering to these principles motivated me to cultivate invitational spaces that supported and affirmed the community of writers we were becoming. My interns could bring their full selves—their faith or lack thereof, their identities, sexuality, linguistic practices, or any aspect of who they are—and feel free to draw on them in their writing.

Summer was brought up in the church, and therefore, she drew on her faith to craft her poem. Her poem commemorates and honors her great-grandmother, Maebel, who died from Alzheimer's Disease. According to the National Institute on Aging, Alzheimer's Disease is a brain disorder that affects memory and destroys one's ability to function. It is the seventh leading cause of death in the U.S. among older adults. There are racial disparities in Alzheimer's diagnoses between Blacks and Whites. In fact, Black participants in Alzheimer's disease research studies were 35 percent less likely to be diagnosed with Alzheimer's and related dementias than White participants, despite national statistics showing that Black Americans are twice as likely as White Americans to develop dementia (Lennon et al.,

2022). Maebel died on Valentine's Day—a day of love. Summer's poem suggests that it was love that made the choice to die for the world, and it was love that took her great-grandmother to a place where she was free from suffering and disorientation, to a place of peace. Her poem was written to remember something that her great-grandmother could not do anymore, but that Summer would do through her writing. Engaging in this process became the catalyst that urged Summer to start a campaign to raise funds to support Alzheimer's research and awareness for early detection.

This chapter illuminates what happens when educators act, teach, and cultivate loving learning opportunities that honor students' full humanity, ethnic and racial identities, and linguistic practices—centering students in the writing curriculum built both for and with them. I use the **Believe-Know-Do Framework** (Wynter-Hoyte et al., 2022) to showcase the pedagogical implications that loving educators perform when they act, teach, and care for and about children in revolutionary ways. In this chapter, I also share strategies that educators can use to support students in authentically writing about topics that matter to them. I conclude the chapter with reflective questions to deepen understanding of the principles discussed.

Revolutionary Love as a Theoretical Framework and Call to Action

The grounding theoretical framework for this chapter is Revolutionary Love (Wynter-Hoyte et al., 2022). Revolutionary Love (RL) is an action-oriented form of critical literacy (Comber, 2003; Freire, 1972; Freire & Slover, 1983; Janks, 2010; New London Group, 1996; Pandya & Avila, 2014; Vasquez, 2005; 2014; 2015; 2017) and culturally sustaining pedagogies (Paris, 2021; Paris & Alim, 2014). It occurs when educators recognize the innate brilliance, potential, and cultural richness of their young writers and intentionally cultivate learning opportunities that center and honor their full humanity.

RL is not just a theory—it is, more importantly, a call to action. It is the transformative efforts that drive social change and activism. RL connects love to the broader struggle for freedom and equality, empowering communities to unite and fight against systemic injustices.

It is the courageous love that Paulo Freire (1970) describes when he posits that love is an act of bravery that fights for freedom. Freire, who viewed education as a means of liberation, emphasized the importance of "conscientização," or critical consciousness. This involves recognizing the social, political, and economic contradictions in society and taking action to eradicate those oppressive systems. RL is the kind of love that our dearly departed ancestor, bell hooks, referenced when she espoused that where there is no justice, there is no love (hooks, 2000). She avowed that to love children meant to uphold and respect their rights. And this can only be acknowledged through our actions. In education, RL is enacted through the intentional and critical pedagogical moves that educators perform to fight against racist and oppressive systems while honoring and affirming the humanity, intelligence, ethnic and racial identities, and linguistic practices of the young writers they teach.

Inspired by this call to action, my sister scholars and I developed the RL Believe-Know-Do Framework (see Table 10.1) and wrote about it in our book, *Revolutionary Love: Creating a Culturally Inclusive Literacy Classroom* (Wynter-Hoyte et al., 2022). Our work is influenced by the

Table 10.1 Revolutionary Love: Believe-Know-Do Framework

Believe	Know	Do
Teachers who embrace revolutionary love understand that what they believe is foundational to the ways they engage with students.	**Teachers who embrace revolutionary love understand the importance of knowing their students, their pedagogy, and the resources they use to teach their students.**	**Teachers who embrace revolutionary love understand that what they do—their practice—needs to be loving, liberatory, and affirming, and center their students' identities and cultural and linguistic heritages and practices.**
Teachers are committed to examining and disrupting any beliefs that are deficit oriented so that their practices are affirming of the students they teach.	They are knowledgeable about their students' cultural and linguistic identities and the systems that marginalize their students, as well as the practices that affirm the students they teach.	They intentionally create learning communities for and with students so that students can learn at their fullest potential and feel seen, heard, and valued.

traditions of loving and liberatory beliefs and practices of Black and Latine educators and scholars (Acosta, Foster, & Houchen, 2018; Foster, 1997; King & Swartz, 2016; Lesesne, 2020; Walker, 1996) who understood the moral, ethical, and intellectual importance of affirming the humanities of Black, Latine, and other minoritized children—too often absent in Eurocentric curricula. RL educators recognize that their **beliefs** form the foundation of how they engage with students; they understand the importance of **knowing** their students, their teaching methods, and the resources they use; and they are committed to **doing** work that is loving, liberatory, and affirming.

In short, RL educators actively challenge biases, understand their young writers' full identities, and engage in practices that resist harmful educational systems. As an educator, these principles grounded my work with my MAT interns with the hopes that they too would soon do this for the young writers that they would one day live alongside and teach. In the pedagogical implications section that follows, I will share details of our Believe-Know-Do Framework and how it can be applied when cultivating learning opportunities where young writers thrive.

Pedagogical Implications of Revolutionary Love

Believe: RL educators know that what they believe is foundational to the ways they engage with students. They know that beliefs, whether conscious or unconscious, affect how they educate young writers; therefore, they are critically self-aware and reflective of those beliefs and continuously interrogate their biases and practices to dismantle deficit-ridden notions that can limit the intellectual and academic brilliance of the young writers in their care.

Believe: RL educators believe that everyone holds knowledge. Educators who embrace RL recognize that knowledge is not limited to educators but is shared by everyone in the classroom. They understand that young writers are not blank slates; instead, they bring a wealth of experiences and "funds of knowledge" (Moll et al., 1992) that can be harnessed to create curricula. A skilled RL educator engages with their young writers, conferring with them, documenting insights, identifying patterns, and creating instructional opportunities that affirm their strengths, address areas for growth, and expand their worldviews. By viewing children as knowledgeable and capable, these educators provide ample opportunities for young writers to share their ideas with peers and the teacher, fostering a collaborative and empowering learning environment.

Know: RL educators know that writers compose the stories of their lives. Writers write for different purposes, different audiences, and in different genres (Calkins, 1994; Graves, 1983; Routman, 2005). Research documents that educators best cultivate a child's literacy development when they invite children to critically read and compose texts that have personal significance to them (Janks, 2014; Vasquez, 2017a). RL educators know that when writers compose, they are not simply engaging in autonomous skills and practices void of the social and cultural context in which those compositions are situated. No, they are crafting moments from their lives. And those moments are rich, individualized experiences. Some moments may be tragic, like the loss of a great-grandmother or pet. Other moments may be joyous, like remembering vacations in DisneyWorld or Sunday Suppers with that great-grandmother and other family members, or moments playing with friends at a sleepover. No matter what, when writers compose, they are capturing authentic, lived experiences that are meaningful to them. RL educators understand what Janks (2010) means when she posits that writers should be able to "produce texts that matter to them in different formats and for different audiences and purposes and [for educators to] allow them to draw on and extend their range of semiotic resources" (p. 156). As such, RL educators understand that young writers should have the autonomy to choose what they write about.

Know: RL educators know that it is more important to teach the writer and not a scripted program. Over the course of my career, I have had numerous opportunities to witness writing programs come and go. Most of these programs were focused on teaching and assessing writing as a product through formulaic methods. Writers might be given a graphic organizer with a topic in the center and four boxes around it to add a minimum of four details. Or writers might be taught traits of writing (conventions, sentence fluency, word choice, voice, ideas, and organization) to improve their work. These are not necessarily bad, but what is missing from those approaches is the importance of centering the needs of young writers. Writing instruction is often focused on editing and revising for grammar and conventions, constructing formulaic pieces such as the five-paragraph essay, or responding to prompts for standardized tests. These foci should be secondary to what matters most: the young writer. Yes, it is important to teach these skills, but RL educators teach them because young writers need them to convey an important message to their audience. RL educators do not teach them simply because they were listed on a checklist or pacing guide. Instead, they teach them because their goal is to tailor their instruction to cater to the needs of the young writers in their classrooms. This often results in young writers engaging in writing because it is doable and enjoyable.

Know: RL educators know which resources and materials to use to best meet the needs of their diverse learners. RL educators understand the importance of knowing their young writers, their pedagogy, and the resources they use to teach. These educators move beyond surface-level affirmations to genuinely see and value the diversity within their classrooms. In their literacy instruction, they strive to create inclusive, empowering learning environments, so they take meaningful actions toward liberation and justice to effect change one student at a time. This often results in deeper, more meaningful connections with their young writers, their families, and the community at large. This foundational principle of RL (Wynter-Hoyte et al., 2022) is aligned with critical literacy principles that require educators to use students' diverse cultural knowledge, multimodal, and multilingual practices (Lau, 2012) to build curricula. They understand that representation matters; therefore, they use resources that reflect and extend the knowledge of the young writers they teach. This is grounded in Sims Bishop's (1990) influential concept of "mirrors, windows, and sliding glass doors." These RL educators honor their young writers' uniqueness and celebrate the interconnectedness of our shared humanity.

Do: RL educators actively disrupt "White supremacist norms" in education. As mentioned throughout, RL connects loving actions to the broader struggle for freedom and equality as it empowers communities to unite and fight against systemic injustices. It is the transformative force that can drive social change and activism, aligning with critical literacy principles that aim to transform inequitable, problematic social practices. This is important because the ingrained hegemony of society has conditioned many educators to internalize the superiority of Whiteness and the inferiority of all other races, often resulting in deficit views about Black, Latine, and other minoritized individuals. RL educators maintain the goal of dismantling practices, beliefs, and systems that are inherently oppressive.

Do: RL educators teach writing using a workshop model that empowers children to participate without fear, hesitation, or shame, allowing them to embrace their identities as writers. Cultivating spaces for young writers to freely live their lives out loud on the pages of their writers' notebooks or journals without judgment is one of the many things RL educators **do.** They approach writing as an individualized process that can be taught and learned through a culturally sustaining workshop approach. They structure their writing workshops so that writers have extended opportunities to write daily in low-stakes environments from the fabric of their lives (Calkins, 1994; Graves, 1983; Ray, 1999). RL educators know that writing is a continuous process—it's never really "done." There is always room for revision, new ideas, or different perspectives; therefore, the work of young writers is celebrated and affirmed at every stage in the process. This encourages all writers to write without fear, hesitation, or shame—and to approach writing with confidence and a sense of possibility.

Reimagining Writing Workshop Through Revolutionary Love

Proponents of a process-oriented approach to writing (Atwell, 1987; Calkins, 1994; Graves, 1983; Ray, 1999) emphasize that writers write for real audiences about topics that matter to them. In this approach, the teacher takes on various roles: engaging in the writing process, modeling writing, providing feedback, and creating a collaborative, supportive environment where writers can thrive. Students are active participants who take ownership of their writing, reflect on their progress, and engage in peer collaboration. They are encouraged to view writing as a process that includes brainstorming, drafting, revising, editing, and sharing.

While these principles have positively shaped writing instruction, it is also important to approach the process model with a critical lens. Kang and Kline (2020) contend that the process approach to writing is rooted in positions of power and privilege—prioritizing certain texts, genres, and styles while marginalizing those of students from diverse cultural and linguistic backgrounds. Bomer (2017) urges writing teachers to break away from traditional writing workshops and adopt Culturally Sustaining Pedagogies. This shift requires a more deliberate and inclusive approach to selecting texts, supporting student-driven topic choices, honoring multilingual and multimodal composing, diversifying assessment methods, and embracing a broad range of genres connected to a vast array of social, cultural, and political purposes.

Our RL Writing Workshop expands on traditional process-oriented approaches to writing workshops by deliberately incorporating culturally sustaining pedagogical principles that honor and value the diverse and complex ways students, especially Black and Latine students, author the stories of their lives. In the sections that follow, I bring to life core principles and practices that RL educators use to liberate their writing workshop. I illustrate these ideas through the unit I created for my graduate interns, *The Stories of Our Lives*. The goal of this unit was to emphasize justice, humanity, and social transformation, while helping my interns understand the importance of empowering writers by centering their voices and experiences—alongside critically examining traditional power dynamics in educational settings.

Breaking Away from Prescribed Curriculum: The Stories of Our Lives Unit

To give my graduate interns context for why this is important, I shared that they may be hired by school districts with prescribed curricula and pacing guides that allocate a set number of weeks to teaching narrative writing—often on predetermined topics like *My First Day of School*, *The Camping Trip*, or *My Summer Vacation*. They may be directed to spend one week each focusing on elements of narrative writing—such as character, setting, plot, theme, resolution. I then shared that their initial attempts to comply with the prescribed curricular mandates may reveal that many students have difficulties writing authentically about such prescribed topics for a variety of reasons. I pose the question: "What will you do?"

I emphasize that RL educators understand the importance of following the lead of their young writers, despite the need to navigate restrictive curricular mandates. When planning, RL educators allow the needs and experiences of the children to guide their instructional discussions. They exert agency by inviting their young writers to craft meaningful narratives drawn from the adventures of their actual lives—not from predetermined topics that may not be personally relevant to them.

Too often, scripted curricula are not designed with diverse populations in mind. As a result, many assigned topics are not inclusive. For example, some children may NOT have gone on a camping trip or a summer vacation. Asking them to write stories rooted in their actual lives and experiences offers more accessible and affirming options. The *Stories of Our Lives* unit offers an example of a teaching pathway grounded in the perspective of RL.

Get to Know Your Writers: Identity Matters

The first step in creating the *Stories of Our Lives* unit begins with getting to know your writers and the topics that matter to them. RL educators **believe** that identity matters. Our identity matters because our identities shape how we understand ourselves, how we relate to others, and how we engage in the world around us. When writers feel and know that their identities are understood, respected, and honored, they are more likely to thrive academically, socially, and emotionally (Myers & Mayes, 2023). A strong sense of identity promotes security and confidence in one's abilities. RL educators **know** that it is crucial to affirm a writer's identity and to get to know them on multiple levels because it lays the foundation for a positive, effective learning environment. They also **know** this fosters trust, creating the conditions for children to feel comfortable, understood, and confident in taking risks without fear of judgment. RL educators **do** many of the following.

Writing Interest Survey 2.0

Personalizing your RL Writing Workshop begins with you **doing** things to intentionally get to know your writers—building on their strengths and planning instruction that is tailored to their needs and identities. One way to begin is with a writing interest survey. Sample questions might include: How is important information captured in your family? What type of writing do you do at home with your family members? How do you capture moments that you want to remember?

These questions suggest that meaningful moments can be captured in many forms: oral, visual, written, and more. They also recognize that writing is often a communal act, one that people engage in to remember, reflect, and share. Additionally, these questions emphasize that writers write for varied purposes, audiences, and in many different genres. In our book, *Revolutionary Love: Creating a Culturally Inclusive Literacy Classroom* (Wynter-Hoyte et al., 2022), we provide a comprehensive Writing Interest Survey 2.0 that helps you learn more about your writers' likes and dislikes and habits of writing. Additionally, in this book's companion website, there is a resource guide to explore more around RL's pedagogical practices.

Identity Webs

Another great way to get to know your writers is to have them create Identity Webs. Identity Webs encourage students to think deeply about who they are, what influences them, and how different aspects of their identities shape their experiences. Identity webs can serve as a brainstorming tool, helping writers identify key themes, topics, or stories to write about. When working with my interns, I shared my personal identity web (see Figure 10.1), and I had them create their own to share as well.

Figure 10.1 Dr. Myers' Identity Web.
by Michele Myers

My goal was twofold. First, I wanted them to see me beyond my role as professor. By humanizing myself, they could begin to understand that I have likes and dislikes, goals and aspirations—much like their own. My second goal was to spark curiosity and build empathy among my students so that we could form stronger bonds with each other and begin to dismantle the stereotypes and unconscious biases we all hold. All of this is necessary when creating learning environments for young writers to thrive. I wanted the interns to experience this process firsthand.

Family Storytelling

Another way that RL educators get to know their writers is by getting to know their families. Families are a key component of our identities, and are often steeped in rich oral traditions—particularly within Black and Latine communities, where storytelling is an integral part of cultural life. Family stories offer unique insights into culture, identities, and personal histories. I reminded my interns that some students may have families with complex histories or different cultural backgrounds, so it is essential to create open, non-judgmental spaces where all stories are honored and respected. This can help students feel more comfortable sharing their stories.

RL educators honor students' identities by honoring students' families in their writing workshops through oral storytelling. To model this for my interns, I asked each of them to bring in an artifact that was important to their family and share the story of that artifact with their classmates. Some of the students brought in their renditions of recipes that were passed down from one generation to the next. Others brought in family heirlooms such as photos, coins, bibles, jewelry—and told the stories they held. Yet others brought in clothes and memorabilia to share. What my interns discovered was that oral traditions are a great way to foster social interactions and idea sharing. Additionally, it helps children feel connected to their heritage, building a sense of pride and identity. My interns also discovered that oral storytelling can lead to vibrant, unique writing that is full of personality.

Connecting Writing to Their Communities

Connecting writing to the communities that students live in is another powerful way to make learning more relevant, engaging, and meaningful for students. When we connect literacy to a student's community, it affirms their identities and cultures. This validation helps students feel seen and revered, which is critical for building confidence and a positive relationship with learning. It also strengthens their sense of belonging in both the classroom and the community. To do so, start by reading any book that highlights the character's neighborhood.

To model this for my interns, I read *Last Stop on Market Street* by Matt de la Peña. In it, CJ and Nana take a bus ride through their neighborhood until they get to the last stop, which is a soup kitchen that they volunteer at. After reading the book, my interns and I created a list of places in the community that CJ and Nana passed by or visited, and then we discussed places my interns go to or pass in their own communities.

Next, I asked the interns to bring in pictures of people, places, and things that were significant in their communities. Some of the pictures included communal spaces such as churches or temples, restaurants, barber and beauty shops, and nail salons; others featured recreational spaces such as playgrounds, parks, and skating rinks. Still others included images of people such as the unhoused veteran, the grocer, the mail carrier, and the feral cat. These pictures reflected community people, places, and things they were knowledgeable about and provided authentic topics to write about.

We then discussed how these places can be the springboard for writing in different genres. For instance, for narrative writing, they could write about the time that they went to the barber shop or about a visit to the playground, making sure to include dialogue. They could write persuasively to try to convince their audience to order the buffalo wings or empanadas from their favorite restaurant. They could engage in descriptive writing when they created a lost pet sign for the feral cat. Or they could write letters and have the post carrier deliver them to members in the community.

As I shared with my interns, the possibilities are endless. Ultimately, they discovered that connecting writing to their communities is a powerful way to represent the unique histories, traditions, and values they hold. It also afforded them opportunities to see their own cultural backgrounds reflected and validated—fostering a sense of pride in who they are.

Use Culturally and Linguistically Diverse Texts as Models

Using culturally and linguistically diverse texts as models in writing is the last principle that I will share in this chapter, but it was not the last principle I shared with my interns. I drew on the wisdom of Rudine Sims Bishop, who writes, "Literature transforms human experience and reflects it back to us, and in that reflection we can see our own lives and experiences as a part of the larger human experience. Reading, then, becomes a means of self-affirmation, and readers often seek their mirrors in books" (1990, p. ix). I shared with my interns that our experiences are individual and unique but yet are woven into the larger tapestry of the global human experience. Because of this, representation matters. Bishop's (1990) concept of windows, mirrors, and sliding glass doors speaks to the importance of all students—regardless of gender, race, ethnicity, linguistic practice, family composition, physical and/or mental abilities, spiritual disposition, and more—can find themselves in the content they study while also learning about the lives and experiences of others.

This ultimately contributes to a more inclusive, empowering, and dynamic learning experience for everyone. When students see characters or stories that mirror their own experiences, cultures, and identities, it validates their existence and helps them develop a strong sense of self-worth. When students are exposed to texts that serve as windows, they understand the diversity of the world and build empathy because they are being exposed to perspectives they might not encounter in their own communities. This fosters a greater appreciation for differences and encourages inclusivity and open-mindedness. When texts serve as sliding glass doors, students have opportunities to mentally and emotionally step into someone else's shoes through reading or writing. They are not just passive observers but active participants who can gain a deeper

Table 10.2 Text Set for Name Stories

Title	Author	Year of Publication
Alma and How She Got Her Name	Juana Martinez-Neal	2018
The Name Jar	Yangsook Choi	2013
My Name is A Story	Ashanti	2022
Joyful Song: A Naming Story	Lesléa Newman	2024
Your Name is a Song	Jamilah Thompkins-Bigelow	2020
When Jo Louis Won the Title	Belinda Rochelle	1994
Quinnie Blue	Dinah Johnson	2000

understanding of others' lived experiences. To demonstrate this for my interns, we research how different ethnic and cultural groups name their children. We then created a text set of books about names (see Table 10.2).

This was followed by writing our name stories and sharing them with classmates. Through using culturally and linguistically diverse texts as a springboard for writing, my interns learned how these texts can create a more inclusive and dynamic writing workshop. This gives all students the opportunity to see themselves represented while also gaining a broader understanding of others. In turn, this fosters a more engaging, supportive, and enriching learning environment.

Concluding Thoughts

This chapter celebrates the bold, brilliant writers—like Summer—who thrive when we center their cultural and linguistic identities in our writing curricula. It also highlights the **Believe-Know-Do Framework** outlined by Wynter-Hoyte et al. (2022) in *Revolutionary Love: Creating a Culturally Inclusive Literacy Classroom*. Through the *Stories of Our Lives* writing unit we see the possibilities of liberating principles and RL's pedagogical practices. The goal was to demonstrate how they—future RL educators—can deepen their understanding of their writers' strengths and needs while designing writing curricula that are both engaging and relevant to their students' lives. Children are brilliant and have meaningful stories to tell about their cultural, linguistic, and racial identities and histories. RL educators can empower students to center their voices and lived experiences to fight for justice, transformation, and advocacy. Teaching writing is more than simply words on a page; we have the opportunity to encourage, grow, and support writers toward a more just, joyful, and loving world. As you consider how to apply the ideas and practices from this chapter in your own context, I offer several guiding questions to help you begin:

Reflective Questions

1. What do you believe, know, and do that reflects critical humanizing practices for educating writers?
2. What are the impacts of mandated curricula and decontextualized learning on your ability to teach writing in a revolutionary loving, and empowering way?
3. What strategies do you currently employ for connecting your students' families and communities as cultural resources to aid them in their writing? What more can you do?
4. Do all students, regardless of gender, ethnicity, race, socioeconomic status, spiritual affiliation, physical and mental abilities, linguistic practices, and so on, see themselves reflected in the material you use to teach them? Who's missing? How will you secure these resources?

References

Acosta, M. M., Foster, M., & Houchen, D. F. (2018). "Why seek the living among the dead?" African American pedagogical excellence: Exemplar practice for teacher education. *Journal of Teacher Education*, 69, 341–353.

Alim, H. S., Paris, D., & Wong, C. P. (2020). Culturally sustaining pedagogy: A critical framework for centering communities. In N. S. Nasir, C. D. Lee, R. Pea, & M. McKinney de Royston (Eds.), *Handbook of the cultural foundations of learning* (pp. 261–276). Routledge.

Anzaldúa, G. (1987). How to tame a wild tongue. In Gloria Anzaldúa (Eds.), *Borderlands/La Frontera: The New Mestiza* (pp. 53–64). Aunt Lute Books.

Atwell, N. (1987). *In the middle: Writing, reading and learning with adolescents.* Heinemann.

Aukerman, M., & Chambers Schuldt, L. (2021). What matters most? Toward a robust and socially just science of reading. *Reading Research Quarterly*, 56, S85–S103.

Baines, J., Tisdale, C., & Long, S. (2018). *"We've Been Doing It Your Way Long Enough": Choosing the Culturally Relevant Classroom*. Teachers College Press.

Baker-Bell, A., Paris, D., & Jackson, D. (2017). Learning Black language matters: Humanizing research as culturally sustaining pedagogy. *International Review of Qualitative Research*, 10(4), 360–377.

Baugh, J. (1999). Considerations in preparing teachers for linguistic diversity. *Language and Reading*, 92, 81–97.

Bishop, R. S. (1990). Windows and mirrors: Children's books and parallel cultures. California State University reading conference: 14th annual conference proceedings.

Bomer, R. (2017). What would it mean for English Language Arts to become more culturally responsive and sustaining? *Voices from the Middle*, 23(3), 11–15.

Boutte, G. S. (2007). Teaching students who speak the African American language: Expanding educators' and students' linguistic repertoires. In M. E. Brisk (Ed.), *Language, Culture, and Community in Teacher Education* (pp. 47–70. Routledge.

Boutte, G. S., King, J. E., Johnson, G. L., & King, L. J. (Eds.). (2021). *We be lovin' Black children: Learning to be literate about the African diaspora*. Myers Education Press.

Braden, E., Boutte, G., Wynter-Hoyte, K., Long, S., Aitken, C., Collins, S., Frazier, J., Gamble, E., Hall, L., Hodge, S., McDonald, C., Merritt, A., Mosso-Taylor, S., Samuel, K., Stout, C., Tafel, J., Warren, T., & Witherspoon, J. (2022). Emancipating early childhood literacy curricula: Pro-Black teaching in K-3 classrooms. *Journal of Early Childhood Literacy*, 22(4), 500–539.

Braden, E., Long, S., Wynter-Hoyte, K., Boutte, G., Frazier, J., Mosso-Taylor, S., & Volk, D. (2024). Curricular violence and the education of Black children: Working toward positive peace through pro-Black practices. *International Journal of Early Childhood*, 55(3), 347–367.

Brown, A. L., Dilworth, M. E., & Brown, K. D. (2018). Understanding the Black teacher through metaphor. *Urban Review*, 50, 284–299. https://doi.org/10.1007/s11256-018-0451-3

Calkins, L. M. (1994). *The art of teaching writing*. Portsmouth, NH: Heinemann.

Cambourne, B. (1995). Toward an educationally relevant theory of literacy learning: Twenty years of inquiry. *The Reading Teacher*, 49(3), 182–190.

Comber, B. (2003). Critical literacy: What does it look like in the early years? In N. Hall, J. Larson, & J. Marsh (Eds.), *Handbook of early childhood literacy* (pp. 355–368). Sage.

Costello, M., & Costello, D. (2016). The struggle for teacher professionalism in a mandated literacy curriculum. *McGill Journal of Education*, 51(2), 833–856.

Foster, M. (1997). *Black teachers on teaching*. New Press.

Freire, P. (1970). *Pedagogy of the oppressed*. Seabury Press.

Freire, P. (1972). Education domestication or liberation? *Prospects*, 2(2), 173–181.

Freire, P., & Slover, L. (1983). The importance of the act of reading. *The Journal of Education*, 165(1), 5–11.

Gee, J. P. (2015). The new literacy studies. In J. Rowsell & K. Pahl (Eds.), *The Routledge handbook of literacy studies* (pp. 35–48). Routledge.

Givens, J. R. (2021). *Fugitive pedagogy: Carter G. Woodson and the art of Black teaching*. Harvard University Press.

González, N., Moll, L. C., & Amanti, C. (Eds.). (2006). *Funds of knowledge: Theorizing practices in households, communities, and classrooms*. Routledge.

Goodman, K. S. (2014). Reading: A psycholinguistic guessing game. In K. Goodman & Y. Goodman (Eds.), *Making sense of learners making sense of written language* (pp. 103–112). Routledge.

Goodman, K., & Goodman, Y. (2012). Learning to read: A comprehensive model. In R. J. Meyer & K. Whitmore (Eds.), *Reclaiming reading* (pp. 19–41). Routledge.

Graves, D. H. (1983). *Writing: Teachers and children at work*. Portsmouth, NH: Heinemann.

Gutiérrez, K. D., & Johnson, P. (2017). Understanding identity sampling and cultural repertoires: Advancing a historicizing and syncretic system of teaching and learning in justice pedagogies. In D. Paris & H. S. Alim (Eds.), *Culturally sustaining pedagogies: Teaching and learning for justice in a changing world* (pp. 247–261). Teachers College Press.

Halliday, M. (2004 [1980]). Three aspects of children's language development: Learning language, learning through language, learning about language. In M. A. K. Halliday (Ed.), *The Language of Early Childhood: Vol. 4 The Collected Works of M.A.K. Halliday*. London: Continuum.

hooks, b. (2000). *All about love: New visions*. William Morrow.

Irvine, J. J., & Fraser, J. W. (1998). 'Warm demanders'. *Education Week*, 17(35), 56.

Janks, H. (2010). *Literacy and power*. Routledge.

Janks, H. (2014). Critical literacy's ongoing importance for education. *Journal of Adolescent & Adult Literacy*, 57, 349–356.

Kang, G., & Kline, S. (2020). Critical literacy as a tool for social change: Negotiating tensions in a pre-service teacher education writing course. *Journal of Language and Literacy Education*, 16(2), 1–16.

Kelly, L. B., & Taylor, L. (2024). What do so-called critical race theory bans mean for elementary literacy instruction? *Reading Research Quarterly*, 59(2), 173–192.

King, J., & Swartz, E. (2016). *The Afrocentric Praxis of Teaching for Freedom*. Taylor and Francis.

King, J. E., & Swartz, E. E. (2018). *Heritage knowledge in the curriculum: Retrieving an African episteme*. Routledge.

Kline, S., & Kang, G. (2022). Reflect, reimagine, revisit: A framework for centering critical writing pedagogy. *Language Arts*, 99(5), 300–311.

Ladson-Billings, G. (1994). What we can learn from multicultural education research. *Educational Leadership*, 51(8), 22–26.

Lau, S. M. C. (2012). Reconceptualizing critical literacy teaching in ESL classrooms. *The Reading Teacher*, 65(5), 325–329.

Lennon, J. C., Aita, S. L., Bene, V. A. D., Rhoads, T., Resch, Z. J., Eloi, J. M., & Walker, K. A. (2022). Black and White individuals differ in dementia prevalence, risk factors, and symptomatic presentation. *Alzheimer's & Dementia*, 18(8), 1461–1471.

Lesesne, P. J. (2020). A sistah circle of seven: Black women's self-perceptions of their teach for America (TFA) experiences in the U.S. Mid-Atlantic Region (147) [Doctoral dissertation, University of Pennsylvania].

Moll, L. C., Amanti, C., Neff, D., & Gonzalez, N. (1992). Funds of knowledge for teaching: Using a qualitative approach to connect homes and classrooms. *Theory Into Practice*, 31(2), 132–141.

Muhammad, G. (2023). *Unearthing joy: A guide to culturally and historically responsive curriculum and instruction*. Scholastic Inc.

Myers, M., & Mayes, L. (2023). *An educator's guide to child and family resilience*. Scholastic Incorporated.

National Council of Teachers of English, (2015). *Resolution on the Need for Diverse Children's and Young Adult Books*. https://ncte.org/statement/diverse-books

New London Group (1996). A pedagogy of multiliteracies: Designing social futures. *Harvard Educational Review*, 66, 60–92.

Pandya, J. D., & Avila, J. (2014). *Moving critical literacies forward: A look at praxis across contexts*. Routledge.

Paris, D. (2021). Culturally sustaining pedagogies and our futures. *The Educational Forum*, 85(4), 364–376. https://doi.org/10.1080/00131725.2021.1957634

Paris, D., & Alim, H. S. (2014). What are we seeking to sustain through culturally sustaining pedagogy? A loving critique forward. *Harvard Educational Review*, 84(1), 85–100.

Ray, K. W. (1999). *Wondrous words: Writers and writing in the elementary classroom*. National Council of Teachers of English.

Routman, R. (2005). *Writing essential: Raising expectations and results while simplifying teaching*. Portsmouth, NH: Heinemann.

Vasquez, V. (2005). Creating spaces for critical literacy with young children: Using everyday issues and everyday text. In J. Evans (Ed.), *Literacy moves on* (pp. 78–97). David Fulton Publishers.

Vasquez, V. (2014). Re-designing critical literacies. In J. Zacher Pandya & J. Ávila (Eds.), *Moving critical literacies forward: A new look at praxis across contexts* (pp. 174–186). Routledge.

Vasquez, V. (2015). Podcasting as transformative work. *Theory into Practice*, 54(2), 1–7.

Vasquez, V. M. (2017a) Critical literacy. *Oxford Research Encyclopedia of Education.* https://doi.org/10.1093/acrefore/9780190264093.013.20

Vasquez, V. (2017b). *Critical literacy across the curriculum in K-6 settings*. Routledge.

Walker, V. (1996). *Their highest potential: An African American school community in the segregated south*. University of North Carolina Press.

Wynter-Hoyte, K., Braden, E. G., Myers, M., Rodriguez, S., & Thornton, N. (2022). *Revolutionary love: Creating a culturally inclusive literacy classroom*. Scholastic Incorporated.

Closing Thoughts: Reimagining, Together

This book began with a call to reimagine writing instruction. Across these chapters, we've seen the transformative possibilities that emerge when educators take up that call through approaches that are both critical and humanizing.

Critical Humanizing Writing Pedagogy (CHWP) is a stance, a set of commitments, a framework, a way of being with young writers. It asks us to disrupt systems of power while embracing joy. To nurture creativity alongside criticality. To view writing as a tool for both personal and collective transformation.

At its heart, this is the intricate work of bridging. These bridges take many forms, as evidenced throughout this book.

- **Theory and Practice:** Forging a true partnership where critical theories come alive in classrooms, and letting practice refine and expand our understanding.
- **Criticality and Humanity:** Enacting the weight of justice alongside the warmth of care.
- **Identity and Instruction:** Teaching in ways that honor children's full selves.
- **Student Voice and Teacher Wisdom:** Trusting both the brilliance of students and the deep expertise of educators.
- **Imagination and Action:** Refusing the binary between dreaming and doing. We need a balance of both.
- **Classroom and Community:** Connecting students' in-school learning to the out-of-school realities and the worlds they are helping to shape.

These bridges are not easy to build. They ask much of us—reflection, resistance, vulnerability, and love. But they are how we center children's full humanity and move toward classrooms that are more just and humanizing.

Closing Thoughts

We close with heartfelt thanks to the contributors to this volume. It has been a profound privilege to learn with and from you. This collaboration is what reimagining looks like.

To our readers—thank you for being part of this journey. We hope the ideas in this book support and challenge you to reflect, adapt, and grow alongside your students and colleagues. *Writing Reimagined* is not a solo endeavor—it lives in community, in practice, and in the everyday choices we make together.

We'd love to stay connected. Share your classroom stories using the hashtags #writingreimagined and #CHWP or reach out through the companion website (www.writingreimagined.org). This work is collective, iterative, and filled with possibilities.

Let's keep writing.
Let's keep bridging.
Let's keep reimagining, together.
With gratitude,
Grace Kang and Sonia Kline

Index

3 Rs (realms of fantasy, fairness, and friendship) 162

ablism 27
Abolitionist Teaching 8
activism 12, 17, 195–214
African Diaspora Participatory Literacy Communities (ADPLCs) 138–139
agency
    and linguistic and cultural identities 28–29
    and voice 29, 30–31, 40, 42
agentive texts, trauma stories as 109
agentive writing 29, 31, 56
AI-assisted comic writing 203
All We Can Save 204–206
amateur press movement 125
American Dream 126
antiracism 82, 200
    approach to trauma 105
    joy in 112
    language ideologies 70
appropriation 151–152, 155, 158
art as writing 196
art for activism *see* artivism
artifactual literacies 186–187
artivism 18, 196, 200, 210–214
    environmental 18, 195
assessment
    culturally relevant 95
    multimodality 140–143
    self-assessment 141
    strengths-based 59, 62–63, 68–70
    teacher 141

translingual writing 68–70
    in writing, defined 94–95
audit trails 184–185
aural text 137, 138
authenticity
    language 96
    in writing 32–33
Authors Theater activity 152
Autism Spectrum Disorder (ASD) 175

Bajaj, Varsha: *Thirst* 212
Bakhtin, M. 150, 161, 178
    dialogic theory 158
Banks, Adam J. 132
Barnes, Derrick: *I Am Every Good Thing* 81, 89
Believe-Know-Do Framework 19, 245, 257
Beretta, Sabrina 208, 210
Bishop, Rudine Sims 249, 256
Black Language 4, 56, 79, 83
    authenticity and 96
    as resistance 80–82
Black Livingness 132
Black students in segregated schools, denial of literacy to 4
book bans 5
Brave Space 231
Bridges, Ruby: 'I Am Ruby Bridges' 90–91
Brothers and Sisters Learn to Write, The (project) 155
Brown v. Board of Education (1954) 4
Browne, Mahogany 222
Butler, Bisa 210

Canva 134
Chapman, Ty 222
City University of New York, New York State Initiative on Emergent Bilinguals 67
Clap Clap (Traditional children's song) 147–148
classism 27
Cleveland, President Grover 126
climate change 134, 189, 195–196, 201
  activist writing 203, 208–210
  multimodal composing and artivism about 199–200, 204–205
  as "science topic" 198
Coastal Climate Kid Collective Project 199
code-meshing across languages and dialects 56
code-switching as problem-solving strategy 61
collaborative multimedia poetry writing 203
  with Mixed-Media Art 204–207
collaborative writing 31, 133, 232–233
collective writing activities 43–44
comics 126, 127, 140
Common Core State Standards 61
communities 32–33
  collective writing activities 43–44
  community sharing and celebration 45
  connecting writing to 255–256
  establishing community norms 42
  of writers 42–45
"conscientizacao" 246
"corriente" 58
counternarratives 29, 30
  definition 30
  forms of 30
critical consciousness 245–246
Critical Cultural Language 78–85

Critical Humanizing Writing Pedagogy (CHWP) 6, 189
  "critical" and "humanizing" 7–8
  "critical", defined 8
  definition of 7–12
  "humanizing", defined 8–9
  as lens 7
  as practice 7
  teachers, commitments and practices of 11–12
  as theoretical framework 7
critical linguistic awareness 79
critical literacy, dimensions of 28
Critical Mentor Text Sets 33–36
Critical Multimodal Composing 196–197
critical pedagogy 7
  in activism 223, 227
  trauma and 153, 155
Critical Race Theory 5
critical witness 110, 113–115
cultural knowledge 170
Culturally and Historical Responsive Literacy 8
Culturally Relevant Pedagogy 8, 224, 228–229
Culturally Responsive Pedagogy 8
Culturally Sustaining Pedagogies 8, 226, 245
Culturally Sustaining Writing Pedagogy (CSWP) 54
curriculum restrictions 5

Dalton, A.: *Show the World!* 93
Dambo, Thomas 210
data collection 186
dedications, writing 92–94
design thinking 56
dialogue journals 39
digital compositions 34
digital literacy 132–133
  tools 133–135

digital technology 133–135
digital tools 135
digital videos, respository of 138–139
disabilities, individuals with, denial of literacy to 4
disintegration art 203
disintegration style art 207–210
Disney characters 151
divisive concepts, laws of 5
DJing 132
Dyson, Anne Haas 16–17, 154–7, 160, 162, 185

Ebonics Resolution (1996) 4
ecological public art 199
embodied actions, play as 170, 173–175
empathy 28, 34, 56
    and cultural literacy 225
empowerment through literacy 228
English Language Arts (ELA) 198
environmental artivism 18, 195–214
environmental justice 199
environmental sustainability 199, 204, 205, 207, 213
expected responses in scripted curricula 116
expository writing 114

faithful witnessing 110
family storytelling 254
Freire, Paolo 152, 224, 228, 245–246
funds of identity 61, 70
funds of knowledge 54, 70

generative artificial intelligence (Gen AI) 6
Gianferrari, Maria: *Fungi Grow* 213
Gorman, Amanda 229
    Hill We Climb, The 237, 238
Grant, Shauntay: *Up Home* 88, 93
Gray, Gary E.: *I Am From* 83–84, 87, 89

Greenfield, E.: *She Come Bringing that Little Baby Girl* 96
Grimes, Nikki 224

healing justice 110
hooks, bell 174, 222, 228, 246
Hopper, Ailish: "Did It Ever Occur to You That Maybe You're Falling in Love" 205
Hughes, Langston 227, 229, 237
humor, use of 181

I Too Am America 87
identity 13, 25–26, 39, 252
    Black language and Black identity 80–81
    defining 27
    "funds of identity" 61, 62, 70, 71
    intersectionality and 29
    metaphors for 27
    play and 167–169, 170–171, 186–187
    stereotypes 153
    translanguaging and 51–3, 61–62, 70
    transparent 40–42
    visual and written language and 83–85, 87, 90
Identity Webs 253–254
idiolect 61, 62, 63, 66, 67, 70
in/visibility of children's perspectives 171–173
Independent Writing Time 232
indigenous children 4
infographics 136–138
informational sentence stems 91–92
informational writing, using sentence stems 91–92
injustice, responses to 220
intentional testimony 113
intentionality 202
interconnectivity and relationality 203

interdisciplinary inquiry 198–199
intersectionality 27, 29, 237

Johnson, Dinah:*Indigo Dreaming* 96
Jordan, June 222
  Directed by Desire 223
journaling 39–42
joy in antiracist literacy pedagogies 112
justice and action in writing instruction 203–204

Kingston, Maxine Hong 103

language
  awareness 63–64
  cultural and racialized, books including 96–97
  as cultural tool for expression 85–86
  ideologies 63–65
LGBTQ+ communities 6
Liang, Kyle 222, 224
Lin, Jiemei 77
Lindstrom, Carole: *We Are Water Protectors* 211
Literacies through Troubled Waters (unit) 210
literacy
  definitions of 170
  school-based notions of 197
literacy-and-identity studies 28
literacy-based climate pedagogy 201, 202
literacy curricula 128–129
literary lens approach to children's writing 117
literacy-rich climate pedagogy 201, 202, 204, 211
Literacy Squared project 52, 68
little magazine 125
Liu, Zamora 113
lived experience, honoring 224
Lorde, Audre 222, 227, 229, 237

Black Unicorn, The 223
love *see* revolutionary love
Lyon, George Ella: *Where I'm From* 83

Maillard, Kevin Noble 93
Martinez, Claudia Guadalupe: *Still Dreaming/Seguimos Soñando* 85, 89, 93
Martinez-Neal, Juana: *Fry Bread* 92–93
Meallem, Avril 43
Mendez v. Westminster case 85
Menon, U.: *My mother's tongue: A weaving of languages* 89
mentor text 14, 33–36, 56, 98, 113–115, 205
  and model poems 232, 237–239
  teacher writing as 113
  trauma-sensitive 113
metaphor 225, 232
Mini-Lessons 232
"mirrors, windows, and sliding glass doors" 34, 249
Monet, Aja 227
monolingual ideologies 4, 53, 54, 67, 129–130
monolingual texts 129
monomodal writing practices 127
Mora, Oge 83, 84
Morrison, Toni 103
Muhammad, Gholdy 132, 200, 228
multicultural education 8
multicultural identities and voices 59, 60–61
multicultural practice 57–58
multilingual and dialectical language 14
multilingual identities and voices 59, 60–61
multilingual learning environment 59–60
multilingual practice 57–58
multilingual student writers, learning from 66–68

multilingualism 54
multimedia constructions 173–175
multimodal composition 197
    about environment and climate change 199–200
    power and promise of 125–127
multimodal constructions 173–175
multimodal practice 57–58
multimodal scholarship, critical stance toward 131
multimodal texts 34, 211
multimodal writing 57
multimodality 125–144
    arts as form of 202–203
    assessment 140–143
    power and promise of 127–130
multiple identities, honoring 31–32
murals 87
music 17, 34
    icons 185
    about solar energy 199

National Council of Teachers of English (NCTE) 244
"Nature Is Speaking" series 138

open mics 139, 230
oral language 86
oral tradition 226, 254
    African American oral tradition and multimedia creation 132
    poetry and 226
    story telling 86
Outcault, Richard: *Hogan's Alley* 126

Padlet 139
parallel bilingualism 68
peer feedback sessions 232
peer review session 232
peer-to-peer feedback 141
Pena, Matt de la: *Last Stop on Market Street* 255

Peoples, Daria 93
Personal Language Inventory 65
personal narratives 30, 98, 127, 169, 224, 229
    trauma and 111, 114, 119
phonemic awareness 5
phonics 5
photographs and places 171–172
picture books, writing instruction through 87–98
place-based writing 36–39
play 17, 167–190
    artifactual analysis 185–187
    visibility and value in textual landscape 187–188
    and writing demarcation 171
    written texts as acts of inclusion 173–175
play stories 17, 175
podcasts 34
poetic inquiry 18–19
    building a foundation for poetic inquiry 231
    connection to social movements 229–230
    creating a brave space 231
    critical thinking and reflection 227–228
    and culturally responsive pedagogy 239
    empowerment through voice 228–229
    exploring what poetry is 231
    in elementary classrooms 230
    as liberatory practice 219–223
    structuring a writing workshop for 231–233
poetic resistance, writing prompts for 233–234
poetry
    emotional exploration through 225
    as method of inquiry 223

oral traditions and 226
Poetry Circles 232–233, 235–237
Pollins, Evelyn 208
popular culture in childhood 16–17
  in childhood composing 147–149
  in childhood cultures 149–152
  definition 149
  in identity formation 187
  response to children's participation 160–163
popular music 155–160
print texts, dominance of 127–128
process-oriented approach to writing 250
public art 87

racialized bilingual students, denial of literacy to 4
raciolinguistics 8, 13, 14, 64, 77–98
racism 27
  systemic 237
Rankine, Claudia: *Citizen* 222–223, 237–238
reader response theory 90–91
Reading Rainbow 134
reciprocity 109
recontextualization 150–153, 155, 158, 159
Reflect, Reimagine, and Revisit Framework 30, 130, 132, 144
relationality 201
resistance 219–240
Revolutionary Love 14, 19, 82–83, 245
  Believe-Know-Do Framework 246–247
  culturally and linguistically diverse texts as models 256–257
  pedagogical implications 247–250
  reimagining writing workshop 250–252

Safe Space 231
Scarborough's *Reading Rope* 86

school shootings 106
Science of Reading (SOR) 86
  overemphasis on 5
Science of Writing (SOW) 86
sculptures 210–213
self-assessment or reflections 141
self-concept 28
self-reflective language use 64–65
self-reflective writing 28
sentence stems 91–92
sexism 27, 162, 189
Shakespeare, William 149
shared writing *see* collaborative writing
Shire, Warsan 222
show-and-tell writing 37
skills-based instruction 5
slams 139
slavery, denial of literacy 3–4
sliding glass doors, texts as 34, 249
Smith, Nikkolas 90
social affiliations 151
social justice movements 223
Standard English 65
Star Wars 178, 185
Stories of Our Lives, The (writing workshop) 244, 251–252
storytelling
  cultural perceptions 227
  in form of poetry, 222
Sudyka, Diana 213
superhero media 17, 149, 151, 152–155

Tapestry Poetry 43–44
Teenage Mutant Ninja Turtles (TMNT) 152, 167–169, 177, 179–183, 185, 187
testimonio 109, 132–133
textual toys 151
TikTok 134
Tonatiuh, Duncan
  Dear primo: A letter to my cousin 88

Separate is Never Equal: Sylvia Mendez and Her Family's Fight for Desegregation 85
traditional banking model of education 30
translanguaging 13, 14, 32, 51–71, 173–175
translingual writing, assessment of 62, 68–70
transparent journaling 40–42
trauma 15–16, 103–121
   assumptions about 114
   as children's knowledge, not damaged children 107
   children's testimony to 117–119
   critical witness 109–110, 113
   disruption of binary categories of children's emotion 114
   innovation within curriculum-required writing instruction 115–116
   investment and connection to writing 115
   joy, care, and connection in pedagogies 112
   language/terms used 107
   model vulnerability 113
   reciprocity 115
   responsiveness in writing classrooms 107–108
   as systemic and multifaceted 106
   teacher commitments and actionable practices 110–112
   testimony 109–110
Trump, Donald 6

urgent literacy pedagogies 18, 196, 200–202

Veggie Dance 155
video essay 136–138
videos 34
Villanueva, R.A. 224, 235
   Reliquaria 237, 238
visual social semiotics 78
visual symbolism 15
Vuong, Ocean 222

Wadia, Shernaz 43
"White supremacist norms" in education 249
White Supremacy Culture 129
Williams' "Happy" song 147, 148, 150
windows, mirrors, and sliding glass doors concept 256
windows, texts as 34, 249
witnessing
   as "active ethical stance" 110
   children's testimony 109–110
   defined 109
Woodson, Jacqueline: *Visiting Day* 111
worship of the written word 129
worthy witnessing 110
writing as resistance 18–19
writing assessment 69
writing community creed or agreement 42, 43
writing identities 10
Writing Interest Survey 2.0 252–253
writing processes 10
writing products 10
writing purposes 11

Xie, Jenny: *Eye Level* 237, 238
X-Men superheroes 152, 153, 161

Yang, Kao Kalia
   Rock in My Throat, The 77–78
   Yes We Will: Asian Americans Who Shaped this Country 92

zines 125, 140, 223, 230

About the Editors

Grace Kang is a professor of Literacy at Illinois State University. She teaches literacy methods courses and mentors pre-service teachers in a PDS in the Chicago suburbs—where she attended elementary school, and a school-university partnership in Champaign—where she resides and serves on the school board. Her research explores Critical Humanizing Writing Pedagogy and social justice-oriented teacher education, specifically in writing. Her research has been published in *Written Communication, JOLLE, Language Arts, and The Reading Teacher*. She enjoys traveling with her husband and four children and considers herself a true foodie (and even writes for a local food blog).

Sonia Kline is a professor at Illinois State University. She teaches literacy methods courses and researches Critical Humanizing Writing Pedagogy in teacher education and elementary classrooms. Her work appears in journals such as *Language Arts* and *The Reading Teacher*, and she is lead co-editor of *Literacy Research: Theory, Method, and Practice*. Originally from England, Sonia brings her full self to her work as a former elementary teacher, advocate for equity and belonging in education, and mother of a brilliant young adult, Emma, with dis/abilities. She finds joy and balance in cycling, yoga, and a good book with tea.

As co-editors, we—Grace and Sonia—bring over 50 years of combined experience teaching writing and literacy, and learning alongside educators, scholars, and students who have deeply shaped our thinking. We first met as doctoral students at the University of Illinois, Urbana-Champaign, in 2010 and have been long-term collaborators, friends, and work sisters ever since.

We approach our work with gratitude, humility, and a shared belief that we are all learning together to improve our students' learning and lives.

All educators and writers need great collaborators, and we're deeply grateful to have found each other—and to be in community with the brilliant authors in this book.

About the Authors

Crystal Chen Lee was an associate professor of English Education at North Carolina State University. Her research lay at the nexus of teacher education, literacy, community engagement, and marginalized youth. Crystal founded and directed The Literacy and Community Initiative, a university-community partnership that amplifies student voices through student publication, advocacy, and leadership. She was the co-author of *Amplifying Youth Voices through Critical Literacy and Positive Youth Development: The Potential of University-Community Partnerships*. She received her Ed.D. from Teachers College, Columbia University. Crystal passed away on June 14, 2025. She will be deeply missed. We are beyond grateful for her contribution to this book.

Shawna Coppola has been an educator for over two decades, teaching at the K-12, undergraduate, and graduate levels. Certified as a literacy specialist in the state of New Hampshire, Shawna is a sought-after speaker and consultant to a variety of schools and organizations across the U.S. She currently works as an adjunct professor of writing at a local community college, and centers her pedagogy around curiosity, care, and critical thinking. Shawna has written three books about teaching student writers in grades K-8 and is currently working on her doctoral research exploring the intersections of autism, gender, and composition studies.

About the Authors

Elizabeth Dutro is a professor of literacy studies. She collaborates with K-12 teachers and children to study justice-focused framings of trauma and how difficult life experiences can inform humanizing literacy instruction that centers students' knowledge; and works with research practice partnerships that include opportunities for teachers to learn together in the context of their daily work and relationships with students. Her research appears in numerous journals and she is the author of *The Vulnerable Heart of Literacy: Centering Trauma as Powerful Pedagogy* (2019, Teachers College Press) and co-editor of *Trauma-Informed Teaching: Toward Responsive, Humanizing Classrooms* (2022, National Council of Teachers of English).

Roberta Price Gardner is associate professor of Literacy and Reading Education at Kennesaw State University. Her research critically examines children's literature through the lenses of race, place, class, gender, and language. Her work has been published in leading journals, including *Urban Education, Theory into Practice, Journal of Children's Literature, Research in the Teaching of English, Children's Literature in Education, Literacy Today,* and *Language Arts*. She is the co-editor of *Reading & Teaching with Diverse Nonfiction Children's Books*, and serves as co-editor of the International Literacy Association's journal *The Reading Teacher*.

Margarita Gómez, professor of Literacy Education at Loyola University Maryland, is a former bilingual teacher, educator, and researcher focusing on teacher preparation to serve multilingual students. Through collaborative inquiry, her research highlights equitable writing instruction and assessment for multilingual learners.

About the Authors

Anne Haas Dyson, professor emerita of the University of Illinois at Urbana-Champaign, is a former teacher of young children and a fellow of AERA. Among her previous appointments was as a longtime professor at the University of California, Berkeley, where she received the Distinguished Teaching Award. She has spent over 45 years studying the childhood cultures and literacy learning of young schoolchildren, for which she has received numerous awards. Among her book publications are *Child Cultures, Schooling, and Literacy: Global Perspectives on Children Composing their Lives* and *Writing the School House Blues: Literacy, Equity, and Belonging in a Child's Early Schooling.*

Cornelius Minor is a Brooklyn-based educator and part-time Pokémon trainer. He works with teachers, school leaders, and leaders of community-based organizations to support powerful literacy practices in cities (and sometimes villages) across the globe. Cornelius has been featured in *Education Week, Brooklyn Magazine,* and *Learning for Justice Magazine.* His book *We Got This* is studied widely, and he has been a featured speaker at conferences all over the world. He is a dedicated hip hop fan, and, on some evenings, you can find him online saving the universe with his PlayStation or on paper saving the realm in Dungeons & Dragons.

About the Authors

Michele Myers is a holistic, social justice educator dedicated to ensuring ALL children receive a humanizing education that values their histories, languages, cultures, and communities as learning assets. Her passion for change drives her work beyond the university into schools and communities. She creates curriculum grounded in children's rich knowledge to support literacy development. Her research focuses on culturally sustaining pedagogy and family networks in literacy. Dr. Myers is co-author of *Revolutionary Love: Creating a Culturally Inclusive Literacy Classroom* (2022) and *The Educator's Guide to Building Child & Family Resilience* (2023), both published by Scholastic.

Katie B. Peachey is a doctoral candidate in the Literacy and English Language Arts program at North Carolina State University. She previously taught middle school and high school English in central Pennsylvania. Her dissertation study focuses on humanizing writing communities in out-of-school spaces. Peachey is also a preservice teacher educator and an alternative licensure program facilitator. Her current research interests include critical literacy, writing instruction/feedback, and writing communities.

Darius Phelps (he/him) is a poet, writer, and scholar whose work centers the liberatory possibilities of poetic inquiry, culturally responsive pedagogy, and critical literacy. A former elementary school teacher and now professor, he mentors pre-service educators in reimagining classrooms as spaces of resistance, restoration, and radical love. His scholarship amplifies the voices of historically marginalized students, exploring how poetry can serve as both pedagogy and prophecy.

About the Authors

Sanjuana C. Rodriguez is an associate professor of Literacy Education and co-director of the Academy for Language and Literacy at Kennesaw State University. She is one of the current co-editors of *The Reading Teacher*. Dr. Rodriguez is a former elementary grades teacher and literacy coach. Her research interests include early literacy development of culturally and linguistically diverse students, diverse children's literature, and the experiences of Latinx pre- and in-service teachers. She has published in various journals, including the *Journal of Children's Literature, Teachers and Teaching*, and *Race, Ethnicity and Education*. She is the co-author of the book *Revolutionary Love: Creating a Culturally Inclusive Literacy Classroom*.

Kristine Schutz is an associate professor and program coordinator of Language, Literacies, and Learning at the University of Illinois-Chicago where she also directs the Collaboratory for Literacies and Learning. Her research and teaching aim to support educators in envisioning, designing, and enacting literacy instruction that honors children's humanity and cultivates a more just world. In 2024, she co-authored the book *Teaching Climate Change to Children: Literacy Pedagogy that Cultivates Sustainable Futures* with long-time collaborator, Rebecca Woodard.

About the Authors

Rebecca Woodard is an associate professor of Curriculum and Instruction at the University of Illinois-Chicago. She is a co-editor of the elementary-section journal for the National Council for Teachers of English, *Language Arts*, and the faculty director of the Chicago Area Writing Project. Her co-authored 2024 book from Teachers College Press, *Teaching Climate Change to Children: Literacy Pedagogy that Cultivates Sustainable Futures*, includes a chapter on arts-based composing. Becca researches teaching and learning for sustainable futures, with an emphasis on multimodal composing, consequential and interdisciplinary learning, and literacy-based climate change education. Connect with her at rwoodard@uic.edu.

Joanna W. Wong is a professor in the College of Education at California State University, Monterey Bay. She is a second-generation, multilingual Chinese American. Her teaching and research address equity issues related to the language and literacy education of racialized, multilingual K-12 students and teacher preparation to serve multilingual learners.

Haeny Yoon is an associate professor and program director of Early Childhood at Teachers College, Columbia University. Her work explores the ways teachers and children negotiate spaces of play as pedagogical, curricular, and intellectual practice. She is the co-host of a Digital Futures produced podcast, *Pop and Play*, holding serious and playful conversations with researchers, educators, designers, children, and media-makers about the role of play and creativity in their personal and professional lives.